PHILIP'S

LOCAL STREET ATLAS

SCALE
2.7 inches to 1 mile
1:24 000

ISLE OF WIGHT

www.philips-maps.co.uk
First published in 2004 by Philip's,
a division of Octopus Publishing Group Ltd
www.octopusbooks.co.uk
Carmelite House, 50 Victoria Embankment
London EC4Y 0DZ
An Hachette UK Company
www.hachette.co.uk

Third edition 2022
First impression 2022
IOWCA

ISBN 978-1-84907-610-4

© Philip's 2022

Map data

This product includes mapping data licensed from Ordnance Survey® with the permission of the Controller of Her Majesty's Stationery Office. © Crown copyright 2022. All rights reserved. Licence number 100011710.

Photographic acknowledgements:
Alamy Stock Photo: /Robin Weaver XII bottom left; /Available Light Photography XII bottom right; /SJ Images XIII top; /Edward Dyer XV top. *Dreamstime.com:* /Hartmut Albert front cover; /Alexey Fedorenko XII top & XV bottom right; /Gordon Bell XIV bottom left; /Petemasty XIV bottom right; /Paula Joyce XV bottom left.

Printed in China

CONTENTS

II	**Key to map pages**
IV	**Route planning**
XII	**Best places to visit**
XVI	Major administrative and Postcode boundaries
1	**Key to map symbols**
2	**Street maps** at 2²/₃ inches to 1 mile
54	**Street map of Portsmouth** at 5¹/₃ inches to 1 mile
55	**Index** of towns, villages, streets, hospitals, industrial estates, railway stations, schools, shopping centres, universities and places of interest

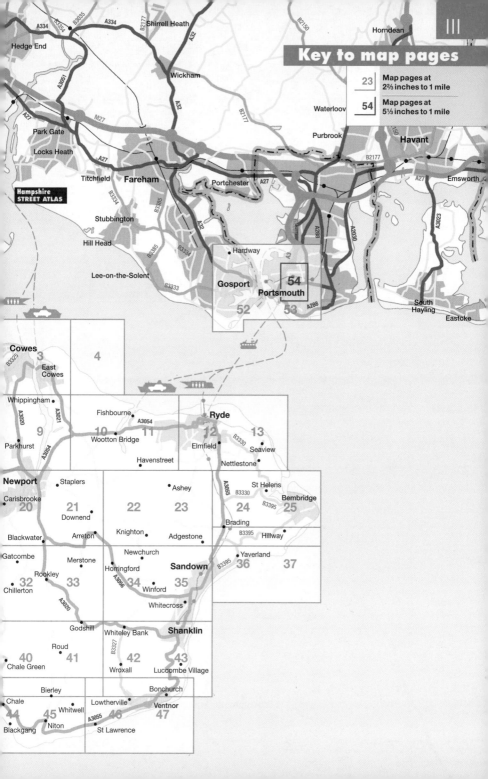

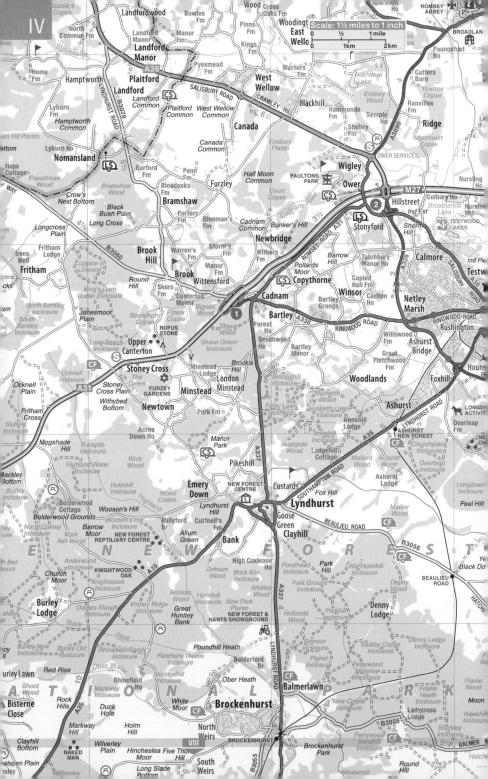

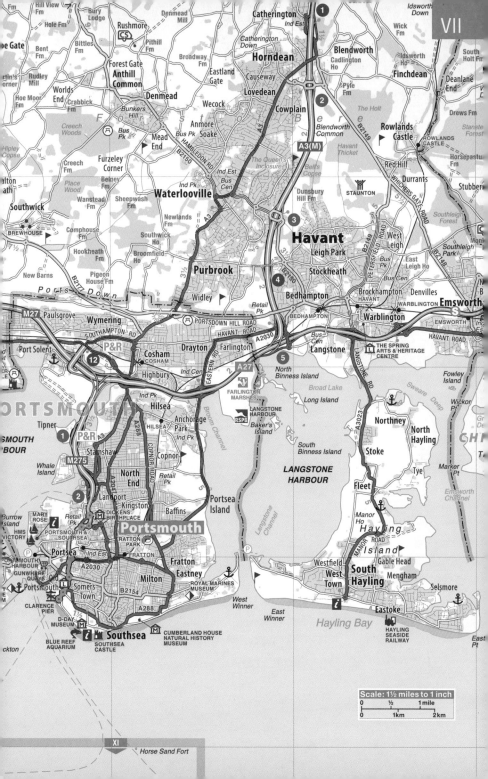

No Mans Land Fort

s Quay

Fishbourne

QUARR
ABBEY

Pelhamfield

RYDE PIER
HEAD

RYDE
ESPLANADE

Ryde

Appley   Puckpool Pt

St John's
Park

Wootton
Creek

Wootton

Kite
Hill

Quarr
Hill

Puck
Ho

Binstead

Weeks

RYDE ST
JOHNS ROAD

A3054

Seagrove Bay

ide

ridge
TON

Firestone
Copse

Haylands

Swanmore

Oakfield

Elmfield

Pondwell

Seaview

The Priory
Priory Bay

ROSEMARY
VINEYARD

B3330

Woodhouse

HAVENSTREET
ill

Havenstreet

Upton

SMALLBROOK
JUNCTION

Bartlett's
Green Fm

Whitefield Wood

Park
Fm

Nettlestone

St Helen's Fort

rn
mbley
reat
ood

Guildford
Fm

ISLE OF WIGHT
STEAM RAILWAY

Ashey

Whitefield
Fm

BEAPER SHUTE

A3055

Bullen
Ho

St Helen's

Bembridge
Harbour

Bembridge Pt

Ethel Pt

Chillingwood

Duxmore
Fm

ASHEY
WEST ASHEY

Hardingshute
Fm

B3330

Marsh
Ho

B3395

Steyne
Cross

Bembridge

Lane
End

N HILL
TRY PARK

Rowlands
Fm

Ashey Down

Nunwell
Fm

RSPB

BRADING
MARSHES

BEMBRIDGE
WINDMILL

Foreland

Arreton Mersley Down
Down

NUNWELL
HO

Brading

BRADING

Bembridge

B3395

Foreland
Fields

The Run

ETON DOWN

WIGHT
ME MUSEUM

Brading
Down
VINEYARD

Yarbridge

SANDOWN

Bembridge
Down

Hillway

Long Ledge

Arreton

H   T

Haseley
Manor

River Yar

Hill
Fm

Alverstone

Adgestone

ROMAN
VILLA

Morton

BROADWAY

SANDOWN ROAD

5½

Bembridge
Down

Culver Down

Whitecliff
Bay

Newchurch

Yar

Yaverland

BEMBRIDGE
FORT

Culver
Cliff

Hale
Manor
Fm

Queen's
Bower

SANDOWN

Ind Est

B3395

ISLE OF
WIGHT ZOO

GUERNSEY
JERSEY

A3056

AMAZON
WORLD

Winford

Branstone

WIGHT
AVIATION
MUS

NEWPORT ROAD

SANDOWN

Isle Of Wight
(Sandown)

DINOSAUR
ISLE

Sandown

Merrie
Gardens

Lake

LAKE

SANDOWN

Sandford

Apse
Heath

Ind Est
Bus
Cen

Landguard
Manor

Shanklin

BAY

Bobberstone
Fm

Whiteley
Bank

Upper
Hyde

SHANKLIN

A3020

ROAD

French
Mill

Winstone
Fm

Yard
Fm

A3055

SHANKLIN
CHINE

DONKEY
TUARY

B3327

Shanklin Down
235

Horse Ledge

Span
Fm

Wroxall

Luccombe
Village

Luccombe Bay

Rew
Fm

Wroxall
Manor Fm

235

Lowtherville

Upper
Bonchurch

Dunnose

CHURCH ROAD

Steephill

Bonchurch

Ventnor

Horseshoe Bay

rence

BOTANIC
GDNS

Ventnor
Bay

COASTAL
VISITOR CENTRE

Best places to visit

Historic Buildings and Monuments

Afton Down Obelisk A cliff-edge monument to a 15-year-old who fell to his death here in 1846, built as a warning to visitors. *Afton Down* **27 E6**

Appuldurcombe House A partially restored Baroque house built in the 18th century, with 11-acre grounds, including gardens designed by Capability Brown, a nature trail, and an Owl and Falconry Centre with daily flying displays. Special events include plays and military re-enactments. *Wroxall, near Ventnor* ☎01983 852484 🖥www.appuldurcombe.co.uk **42 A4**

Ashey Sea Mark A solid white sea-mark constructed for sailors in 1735. *Ashey Down Summit* **23 A4**

Bembridge Fort An abandoned 1860s land fort. Guided tours only. *Between*

Culver Cliff and Brading 🖥www.nationaltrust.org.uk **24 E1**

Bembridge Windmill The only surviving windmill on the island, built c.1700 and retaining its original wooden machinery. *Mill Road, Bembridge* 🖥www.nationaltrust.org.uk ☎01983 873945 **25 B3**

Brading Roman Villa A 1st-century AD Roman villa excavated in the 1880s, with important 4th-century mosaics. Visitor centre and exhibition. *Morton Old Road, Brading* 🖥www.bradingromanvilla.org.uk ☎01983 406223 **23 F1**

Carisbrooke Castle An imposing castle on a ridge, with a museum, a Donkey Centre, an 800-year-old Great Hall, a well-house with a treadwheel, and excellent views. *Carisbrooke, Newport* ☎0370 3331181 🖥www.english-heritage.org.uk **20 B4**

▶ *Bembridge Windmill*

▼ *Osborne House*

◀ *Carisbrooke Castle*

Grays Monument A memorial to a 9-year-old chimney sweep killed by his employer in 1822. *Church Litten, Newport* **20 E6**

Hoy Monument A tall stone column topped by a large finial sphere, erected in 1814 by local merchant Michael Hoy to commemorate a visit to Britain by Tsar Alexander I. *St Catherine's Down (near Blackgang)* 🖥www.nationaltrust.org.uk **44 F8**

Long Stone Neolithic barrow (large grave) marker situated on tumuli and dated 3000–2000BC. *Mottistone Down, near Brighstone* 🖥www.nationaltrust.org.uk **29 D5**

Needles Old Battery A dramatically sited 1862 coastal fort built to prevent invasion by the French, with an exhibition, the original gun barrels, a restored laboratory, searchlight position and position-finding cells, children's information boards and activity packs, and a 65m tunnel leading to a splendid viewpoint over the Needles (famous chalk pinnacles) and a tearoom. *West High Down, Alum Bay* ☎01983 754772 🖥www.nationaltrust.org.uk **26 B4**

Newport Roman Villa The remains of a Roman farmhouse built c. AD280, with part of a bath and a hypocaust system,

recreations of everyday scenes (and re-enactment days), and a Roman herb garden. *Cypress Road, Newport* ☎01983 529720 🖥www.iow.gov.uk **20 E6**

Nunwell House and Gardens A handsome family residence built in 1522, with the Parlour Chamber where Sir John Oglander played host to Charles I on his last night of freedom. There are displays on the family's military connections, an Old Kitchen exhibition, and 5 acres of grounds, including a walled garden with views across the Solent. *Coach Lane, Brading* ☎01983 407240 www.nunwellhouse.co.uk **23 F3**

Old Town Hall, Newtown A 17th-century hall, on the edge of the island's only National Nature Reserve contains an exhibition on local history, including 'Ferguson's Gang' of anonymous benefactors. See also **Newton National Nature Reserve** *Newtown* ☎01983 531785 🖥www.nationaltrust.org.uk **6 E2**

Osborne House Queen Victoria's imposing three-storey seaside retreat and the place where she died, built in 1848, given to the nation by Edward VII and managed by English Heritage. Interior highlights include the Indian Room, Victoria's bedroom and closet, and the royal nursery. The grounds include a late 18th-century walled kitchen garden and pleasure grounds that survived from the previous estate on the site, and the parterre gardens and terraces have been restored to their Victorian layout. *East Cowes* ☎0370 333 1181 🖥www.english-heritage.org.uk **3 F2**

Quarr Abbey Benedictine monastery situated within an Area of Outstanding Natural Beauty, with woodland walks, wildflower meadow, art gallery and a visitors centre explaining the day-to-day life of the monks. It is possible to attend services in the Abbey Church. *Ryde.* ☎01983 882420 www.quarrabbey.org **11 C6**

St Catherine's Oratory (Pepper Pot) An octagonal tower, built in 1328 as a penance

for stealing property from a wreck. It is said to have been used as a lighthouse. *St Catherine's Down, Chale* 🖳www.english-heritage.org.uk **44 E5**

Tennyson Monument
A marble Maltese cross erected in memory of Alfred Lord Tennyson after his death in 1892; the poet had settled at Farringford in 1853. *Tennyson Down, Freshwater Bay* 🖳www. isleofwightattractions.co.uk ☎01983 280111 **26 H5**

Yarmouth Castle A Tudor castle, Henry VIII's last fortress, with exhibitions on the history of the castle and shipwrecks, fine views over the Solent from its battlements and good picnic spots on its rampart lawns. *Yarmouth* 🖳www.english-heritage.org.uk ☎0370 333 1181 **15 C6**

Gardens & Parks

See also Appuldurcombe House, Nunwell House and Gardens (Historic Buildings)

Ever Garden 18th-century cottage and sculpture garden, in which sculptures form an integral part of the design. The garden is split into zones, with both traditional and contemporary planting, and the cottage contains information on its previous occupants. *Warnes Lane, Brighstone.* 🖳www.evergarden.co.uk **30 B2**

Mottistone Manor Garden
A terraced garden with borders and a kitchen garden surrounding a medieval/ Elizabethan manor house in a wooded valley with views of the Channel. *Hoxall Lane, Mottistone* ☎01983 741302 🖳www.national-trust.org.uk **29 D4**

Old Smithy Gardens
Landscaped gardens set around a former blacksmith's forge (now a retail complex). *High Street, Godshill* ☎01983 840364 🖳www.theoldsmithy. com **41 D8**

Ventnor Botanic Garden
A 22-acre botanic garden founded in 1970, with plants from around the world, a Visitor Centre with exhibitions

and library, a coastal path, a picnic area and a playground. *Undercliff Drive, Ventnor* ☎01983 855397 🖳www.botanic.co.uk **46 D4**

Wayside Herbs and Flowers
A small herb and wildflower garden with herb shop, children's trail and small museum of the Stone Age. *Bamfurlong Chine Lane, Yafford* ☎07879 613389 **38 H8**

Places of Worship

All Saints (Church of the Lily Cross) A church on a 950-year-old site of Christian worship; the present (4th) church was built in the early 14th century, with two naves separated by a wooden screen, one for parishioners, the other for manorial workers. The 'Lily Cross' wallpainting was uncovered in the 19th century. *Godshill* **41 D8**

Church of the Holy Cross
Originally a Norman church retaining its old doorway with a sculpted grotesque, a 13th-century chancel, and a 15th-century bell thought to have come from nearby Quarr Abbey, now housed in a 1925 bellcote. The churchyard contains the tomb of Samuel Giant, said to have been the biggest man in the world, who died in 1844. *Binstead* **11 F6**

St Andrew An isolated ancient church overlooking a treacherous stretch of coast, built in the 12th century but altered and enlarged several times, with a 15th-century tower. *Chale* **44 C6**

St Boniface The island's second-smallest church, on a place of worship dating back as far as the Saxon occupation and dedicated to a Saxon saint. *Bonchurch* **47 D7**

St George A church on the site of a private chapel of the lords of the manor of Arreton, first recorded in AD901; the present building is mainly 11th century, with some late Saxon or early Norman elements and a 13th-century tower. The churchyard contains the tomb of Elizabeth Wallbridge, heroine of bestselling story 'The Dairyman's Daughter'. *Arreton* **21 E2**

St Mary the Virgin A church with a Norman nave containing a simple Jacobean table serving as an altar, beneath which Saxon remains were discovered, and a memorial to Reverend Leigh Richmond, author of 'Annals of the Poor'. *Brading* **24 B3**

St Mildred Built in the 1850s, this fanciful Gothic-inspired church was used by Queen Victoria when at Osborne House. As well as royal memorials and the queen's pew, it contains a beautiful bronze screen by Alfred Gilbert in the chancel arcade. *Beatrice Avenue, Whippingham* **9 E8**

St Peter Originally a Norman building, the current grade-1 Perpendicular church mostly dates from the 15th-century. It has an unusual layout, a pulpit that is entered through one of the piers, Jacobean benches and a 15th-century mural of St Christopher. *Shorwell* **31 B2**

Museums & Galleries

See also Carisbrooke Castle

Bembridge Heritage Centre An exhibition of village life past and present, in a former Victorian school building. *Lane End Road, Bembridge* 🖳www.bembridgeheritage. org.uk **25 C5**

Brighstone Village Museum A small museum on Victorian life. *North Street, Brighstone* 🖳www.bembridge heritage.org.uk **30 B2**

Calbourne Water Mill and Rural Museum A working water mill first mentioned in the Domesday Book, with various small museums (including an old fire station and bakery), displays on renewable energy, punts and children's activities,

▲ *Mottistone Manor Garden*

and surrounded by ancient oak woodland providing a habitat for badgers, red squirrels and more. *Newport Rd, Calbourne* 🖳www.calbournewatermill. co.uk ☎01983 531227 **17 E2**

Classic Boat Museum
A collection of restored sailing and motor boats displayed in the Boat Shed (West Cowes) with boating memorabilia and artefacts in the Gallery (East Cowes). 🖳www.classicboatmuseum.com ☎01983 280723 (Boat Shed) **3 B3** ☎01983 244101 (Gallery) **3 C4**

Cowes Maritime Museum
A small exhibition tracing local maritime history through models and paintings. *Library, Beckford Road, Cowes* ☎01983 823433 🖳www.iwight.com **3 B4**

Dimbola Lodge
A photography museum and gallery in the one-time home of 19th-century photographer Julia Margeret Cameron, with displays of antique cameras and exhibitions of Cameron's and others' images, including contemporary work. *Terrace Lane, Freshwater Bay* ☎01983 756814 🖳www.dimbola.co.uk **27 C6**

East Cowes Heritage Centre
Small museum on the history of East Cowes in permanent and temporary exhibits. *8 Clarence Road, East Cowes* ☎01983 280310 🖳www.eastcoweleheritage. co.uk **3 C3**

Godshill Model Village
A detailed model village, reproducing 1930s Godshill and Shanklin, complete with thatched cottages, pubs and churches, set within a landscaped tree-filled garden. *High Street, Godshill.* ☎01983 840270 🖳www. modelvillagegodshill.co.uk **41 D8**

Island Planetarium An astronomy centre and planetarium theatre hosting multimedia shows, stargazing evenings and lectures. *Fort Victoria Country Park, near Yarmouth* 🖥www.islandastronomy.co.uk ☎01983 761555 **14 F6**

Isle of Wight Bus Museum A collection of island buses and coaches, plus exhibition of transport memorabilia and photographs, in a former bus depot. *Park Road, Ryde. 01983 567796* 🖥www.iwbusmuseum.org.uk **12 D5**

Isle of Wight Military Museum A good selection of World War 2 and postwar armoured vehicles and other equipment, guided tours. Regular displays in summer include rides round the tank course. *490 Newport Road, Cowes* 🖥www.wmahm.org.uk ☎01983 632039 **9 A4**

Lilliput Antique Doll and Toy Museum More than 2000 dolls and playthings dating from c.2000BC to 1945. *High Street, Brading* 🖥www.lilliputmuseum.net ☎01983 407231 **24 B3**

Museum of Island History A museum charting the island's history from prehistoric times, with interactive exhibits, quizzes, games and more. *Guildhall, High Street, Newport* 🖥www.iwight.com ☎01983 823433 **20 E7**

Quay Arts Centre An art gallery and live events venue in a 19th-century brewery warehouse. *Sea Street, Newport Harbour* ☎01983 822490 🖥www.quayarts.org **20 E7**

Shipwreck Centre and Maritime Museum Local maritime heritage displays, including items recovered from shipwrecks, diving equipment, ships' models, and exhibits about the lifeboat services. *Arreton Barns Craft Village, Arreton* ☎01983 533079 🖥https://museum.maritimearchaeologytrust.org **21 E2**

Nature & Animals

See also Appuldurcombe House and Carisbrooke Castle

Amazon World A simulated rainforest with a large Jurassic-themed adventure park, exotic animals, falconry displays and talks by the keepers. *Watery Lane, Newchurch, near Arreton* 🖥www.amazonworld.co.uk ☎01983 867122 **34 C5**

Butterfly World Indoor landscaped gardens (a Japanese garden with koi carp, a tropical garden and an Italian garden) with freeflying butterflies, fountain displays and more. *Staplers Road, Wootton* 🖥www.butterflyworldiow.com ☎01983 883430 **10 B2**

Dinosaur Expeditions A conservation facility and museum of locally and internationally discovered dinosaur remains, with an exhibition of palaeoart. The centre runs fossil hunting expeditions. *Military Road (A3055), nr Brighstone* 🖥www.dinosaurexpeditions.co.uk ☎01983 740844 **38 G6**

Dinosaur Isle A purpose-built attraction with life-sized models of some of the Isle's dinosaur types in a recreated landscape, interactive exhibits, and the opportunity to see volunteers working on new fossil finds. *Culver Parade, Sandown* ☎01983 404344 🖥www.dinosaurisle.com **36 B4**

Donkey Sanctuary A donkey-rescue charity housing more than 100 donkeys over 50 acres, with opportunities to interact with the animals, and offering an 'Adopt a Donkey' scheme. *Lower Winstone Farm, Whiteley Bank, Wroxall* 🖥www.iowdonkeysanctuary.org ☎01983 852693 **42 B7**

Isle of Wight Reptilarium 'Micro' zoo devoted to reptiles and invertebrates, with four themed rooms – desert, rainforest, nocturnal and a turtle zone – and children's activities, set in the remains of a Victorian fort. *Fort Victoria Country Park, near Yarmouth.* 🖥www.reptilarium.org ☎01983 761582 **14 F6**

Newtown National Nature Reserve The island's only national nature reserve, popular with birdwatchers, with ancient woodlands, wildflower meadows, rare wildlife and views over the peaceful Newtown harbour. There are walking routes and a trail suitable for canoeists or paddleboarders. *Newtown.* 🖥www.nationaltrust.org.uk ☎01983 531785 **6 D2**

Monkey Haven Animal sanctuary, mainly housing rescued monkeys, including marmosets, mangabeys and lar gibbons, as well as birds of prey, reptiles and meerkats, with keeper talks and opportunities to feed the animals. *Staplers Road, Newport.* ☎01983 530885 🖥www.monkeyhaven.org **21 C8**

Shanklin Chine An historic gorge, once the haunt of smugglers, with waterfalls, nature trails (with the chance of red squirrels), nature hide, rare plants, a Heritage Centre with exhibitions, and a Victorian tea garden. It is part of The Chines, a special coastal feature (see also Blackgang Chine xv). *Old Village, Shanklin* ☎01983 866432 🖥www.shanklinchine.co.uk **43 C7**

West Wight Alpacas and Llamas Breeding farm for alpacas and llamas, also home to other farm animals, where visitors can interact with the animals, view the birthing field and take an alpaca or llama for a walk. *Wellow.* ☎01983 760900 🖥www.westwightalpacas.co.uk **16 E5**

Wildheart Animal Sanctuary Wildlife park and animal sanctuary, with a collection of rare and endangered big cats. The zoo also features lemurs and monkeys, spiders, reptiles and amphibians, plus a children's play area and pets' corner. *Seafront, Yaverland, Sandown* 🖥www.wildheartanimalsanctuary.org ☎01983 403883 **36 B4**

Activities

Adgestone Vineyard A vineyard and winery offering tastings and tours of the cellars and the 10-acre site. *Adgestone*

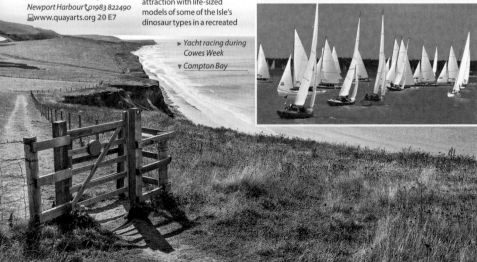

▶ Yacht racing during Cowes Week

▼ Compton Bay

☎*01983 402882* 🖳*www.
adgestonevineyard.co.uk* **23 F2**

Bembridge Trail A 10-mile
walking trail from the middle of
the island to its eastern tip, over
downland and past marshes,
historic houses and the village
of Brading. *From Newport to
Bembridge* **22 E2**

Blackgang Chine Dramatic
40-acre landscaped clifftop
gardens with a range of
family attractions, including
Cowboy Town, Dinosaurland,
Underwater Kingdom, with
sunken shipwreck, and a roller
coaster and other rides. *Chale,
near Ventnor* ☎*01983 730330*
🖳*www.blackgangchine.com*
44 C4

Compton Bay Long sandy
beach, good for swimming and
surfing, backed by multi-col-
oured cliffs, and known for its
dinosaur fossils and footprints.
There are walking trails on the
chalky grassy downs above.
Military Road, Compton. ☎*01983
741020.* 🖳*www.nationaltrust.
org.uk* **28 A7**

Cowes Week The world's
most famous sailing regatta,
held annually in early August
since 1826. There are 8 or 9 days
of racing involving about 900
craft, and a host of social events,
including balls and a fireworks
finale. *Cowes* ☎*01983 295744*
🖳*www.cowesweek.co.uk*

Fort Victoria Country Park
A country park with seashore
and woodland walks, a nature
trail, ranger tours, and fine
views over the Solent, and
containing a reptilarium (see
page xiv) and a planetarium
(see page xiv). *Fort Victoria, near
Yarmouth* ☎*01983 760111*
🖳*www.fortvictoria.co.uk*
14 F6

▶ *A replica dinosaur at
The Needles Park*

Freshwater Bay Golf Club
One of two 18-hole courses
on the island, with panoramic
views of the Solent and English
Channel, and Neolithic and
Bronze Age burial mounds
forming natural 'hazards', set
on a Site of Special Scientific
Interest with many rare and
endangered plant and animal
species. *Afton Down, Freshwater*
🖳*www.freshwaterbaygolfclub.
co.uk* ☎*01983 752955* **27 E6**

Hamstead Trail A 7-mile
walking trail crossing the island
from north to south, passing
saltwater marshes and ancient
burial grounds, including the
Long Stone (see page xii). At
the south coast the remains of
a fossil forest can be seen at low
tide. *From Hamstead to Brook*
16 F3

**Island Brass Rubbing
Centre.** A craft centre with
reproduction medieval brasses
depicting chivalrous scenes;
tuition is provided. *The Coach
House, St George's Church,
Arreton* ☎*01983 526290* 🖳*www.
geocities.ws/islandbrass* **21 E2**

Island Sailing Club A friendly
family yachting club with excellent facilities. *70 High Street,
Cowes* 🖳*www.islandsc.org.uk*
☎*01983 296621* **3 B5**

Isle of Wight Steam Railway
5-mile country trips in restored
Victorian and Edwardian
steam trains, plus a museum,
woodland walk and play area.
Railway Station, Havenstreet
🖳*www.iwsteamrailway.co.uk*
☎*01983 882204* **22 E8**

The Needles Park A park
offering views of the spectacu-
lar Needles Rocks and lighthouse. Features a chairlift to the
beach with its coloured sand,
children's attractions, a
pier with shopping
arcade, glass manufac-
tory, sand shop, Jurassic

▲ *Isle of Wight Steam Railway*

golf and boat trips, as well as
summer fireworks displays.
Alum Bay ☎*01983 752401* 🖳*www.
theneedles.co.uk* **26 D5**

**Robin Hill Countryside
Adventure Park** A large
country park with activities for
all ages, including woodland
trails, treetop canopy walkway,
a falconry centre, rides – including a toboggan run – and
plenty of opportunities for
adventure play. *Downend,
Arreton* ☎*01983 527352*
🖳*www.robin-hill.com* **21 F4**

Rosemary Vineyard One of
Britain's biggest vineyards, with
both guided walks and self-
guided trails, and free tastings.
Smallbrook Lane, Ryde ☎*01983
811084* 🖳*www.rosemary
vineyard.co.uk* **12 C2**

**Round the Island Cycling
Route** A route taking in
dedicated cycleways, disused
railway lines, bridleways and
quiet country lanes. Maps are
available from tourist centres.
☎*01983 813818* 🖳*www.visitisle-
ofwight.co.uk/things-to-do/
cycling/round-the-island-route*

St Helens Beach One of
the island's 13 award-winning
beaches, adjoining some
National Trust land that is
home to a variety of interesting
wildlife. A calm spot with won-
derful views over Bembridge
Harbour, it is excellent for
swimming. *St Helens* **25 B7**

▼ *The Needles*

Solent Cruises Half-hour
Cowes Harbour sightseeing
trips, cruises taking in Cowes,
Yarmouth and the Needles,
full-day trips to Portsmouth
and more. *Thetis Wharf, Cowes*
☎*01983 564602* 🖳*www.solent-
cruises.co.uk* **3 B4**

Tennyson Trail A 12½-mile
walk across the downs and
through forests, passing ancient
burial sites and the Tennyson
Monument, and affording
excellent views.
*From Carisbrooke Castle to the
Needles* **20 A3**

Walking Festival The UK's
biggest walking festival, held
each May, with more than 130
themed volunteer-led walks,
including castles, red squirrels,
storytime walks, lanternlit
strolls, ghost walks, a pram walk
and a 70-mile three-day walk
around the island. ☎*01983 813818*
🖳*www.isleofwightwalking
festival.co.uk*

Waltzing Waters An indoor
synchronised water, light and
music show. *Westridge, Ryde*
☎*01983 811333* 🖳*www.waltzing
waters.co.uk* **12 F1**

Wightlink Warriors
Motorcycle speedway races.
*Smallbrook Stadium, Ashey
Road, Ryde* 🖳*www.warriors-
speedway.com* ☎*03335 774458*
12 C1

Worsley Trail A 12½-mile
walk past pine forests and
farm buildings, over chalk
downlands, fields and a disused
railway line. *From Mottistone
Down to Old Shanklin* **30 C5**

Major administrative and Postcode boundaries

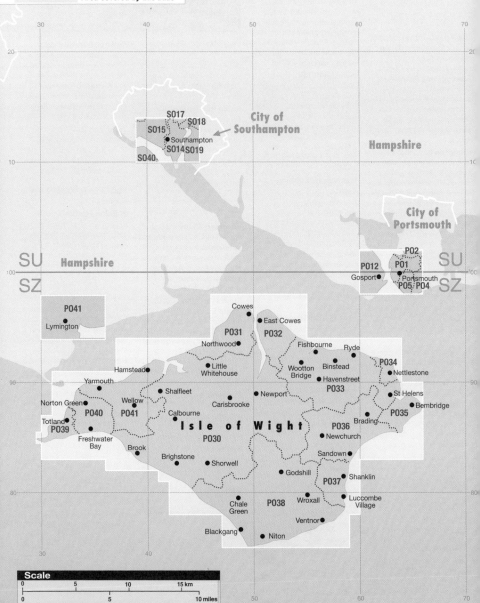

County and unitary authority boundaries

Postcode boundaries

Area covered by this atlas

S017
S018
S015
City of Southampton
Hampshire
Southampton
S014 S019
S040

City of Portsmouth

SU
Hampshire
P012
P02
P01
Gosport
Portsmouth
P05 P04
SZ

P041
Lymington
Cowes
East Cowes
P031
P032
Northwood
Fishbourne
Ryde
Hamstead
Little
Whitehouse
Wootton
Bridge
Binstead
P034
Nettlestone
Yarmouth
Shalfleet
Havenstreet
Newport
St Helens
Bembridge
Norton Green
Wellow
Carisbrooke
P033
P035
Totland
P040
P041
Calbourne
Isle of Wight
Brading
P036
Freshwater
Bay
Brook
P030
Newchurch
P039
Brighstone
Shorwell
Sandown
Godshill
P037
Shanklin
Chale
Green
P038
Wroxall
Luccombe
Village
Ventnor
Blackgang
Niton

Scale
0   5   10   15 km
0   5   10 miles

Key to map symbols

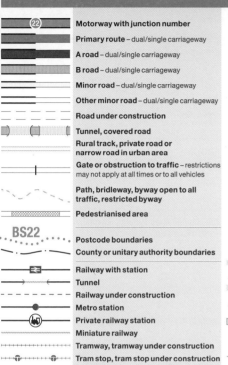

	Motorway with junction number
	Primary route – dual/single carriageway
	A road – dual/single carriageway
	B road – dual/single carriageway
	Minor road – dual/single carriageway
	Other minor road – dual/single carriageway
	Road under construction
	Tunnel, covered road
	Rural track, private road or narrow road in urban area
	Gate or obstruction to traffic – restrictions may not apply at all times or to all vehicles
	Path, bridleway, byway open to all traffic, restricted byway
	Pedestrianised area
BS22	Postcode boundaries
	County or unitary authority boundaries
	Railway with station
	Tunnel
	Railway under construction
	Metro station
	Private railway station
	Miniature railway
	Tramway, tramway under construction
	Tram stop, tram stop under construction
	Bus, coach station

◆		Ambulance station
◆		Coastguard station
◆		Fire station
◆		Police station
✚		Accident and Emergency entrance to hospital
	Ⓗ	Hospital
	✛	Place of worship
	ⓘ	Information centre
🛒	Ⓟ	Shopping centre, parking
P&R	PO	Park and Ride, Post Office
Ⅹ	🚐	Camping site, caravan site
▶	✕	Golf course, picnic site
Church	ROMAN FORT	Non-Roman antiquity, Roman antiquity
	Univ	Important buildings, schools, colleges, universities and hospitals
		Woods, built-up area
River Medway		Water name
		River, weir
		Stream
		Canal, lock, tunnel
		Water
		Tidal water
58 ◀	87	Adjoining page indicators and overlap bands – the colour of the arrow and band indicates the scale of the adjoining or overlapping page (see scales below)
246		The dark grey border on the inside edge of some pages indicates that the mapping does not continue onto the adjacent page
		The small numbers around the edges of the maps identify the 1-kilometre National Grid lines

Enlarged maps only

	Railway or bus station building
	Place of interest
	Parkland

Abbreviations

Acad	**Academy**	Meml	**Memorial**	
Allot Gdns	**Allotments**	Mon	**Monument**	
Cemy	**Cemetery**	Mus	**Museum**	
C Ctr	**Civic centre**	Obsy	**Observatory**	
CH	**Club house**	Pal	**Royal palace**	
Coll	**College**	PH	**Public house**	
Crem	**Crematorium**	Recn Gd	**Recreation ground**	
Ent	**Enterprise**			
Ex H	**Exhibition hall**	Resr	**Reservoir**	
Ind Est	**Industrial Estate**	Ret Pk	**Retail park**	
IRB Sta	**Inshore rescue boat station**	Sch	**School**	
		Sh Ctr	**Shopping centre**	
Inst	**Institute**	TH	**Town hall / house**	
Ct	**Law court**	Trad Est	**Trading estate**	
L Ctr	**Leisure centre**	Univ	**University**	
LC	**Level crossing**	W Twr	**Water tower**	
Liby	**Library**	Wks	**Works**	
Mkt	**Market**	YH	**Youth hostel**	

The map scale on the pages numbered in blue is 2⅔ inches to 1 mile
4.2 cm to 1 km • 1:23 810

0	¼ mile	½ mile	¾ mile	1 mile
0	250m	500m	750m	**1km**

The map scale on the pages numbered in red is 5⅓ inches to 1 mile
8.4 cm to 1 km • 1:11 900

0	220yds	440yds	660yds	½ mile
0	125m	250m	375m	**500m**

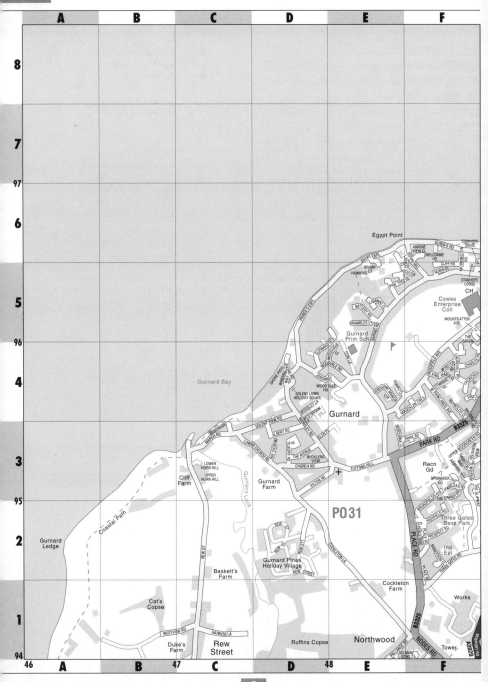

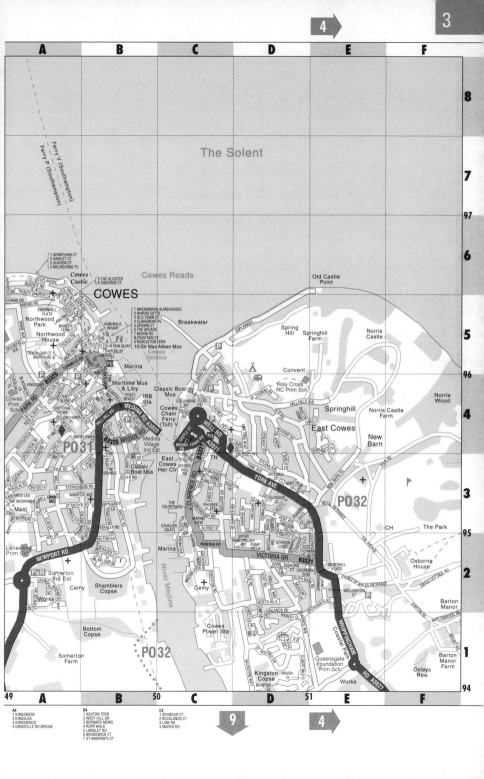

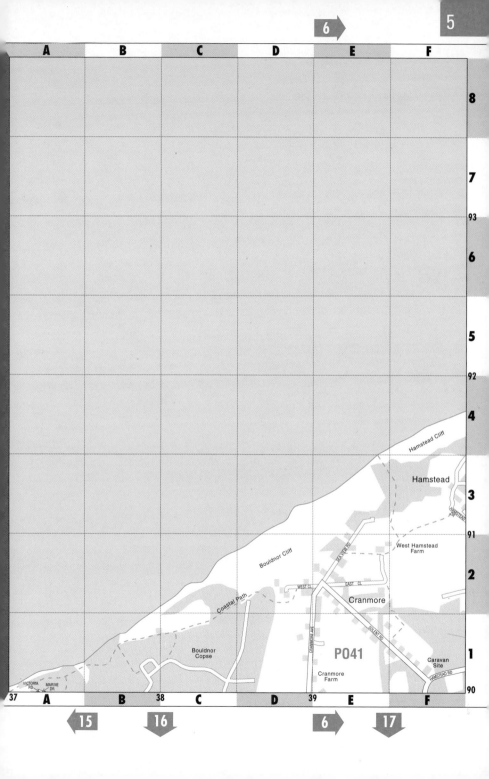

A B C D E F

8

7

93

6

5

92

4

Hamstead Cliff

Hamstead

3

HAMSTEAD DR

91

West Hamstead
Farm

SEA VIEW RD

Bouldnor Cliff

2

WEST CL

EAST CL

Cranmore

Coastal Path

SOLENT RD

1

Bouldnor
Copse

CRANMORE AVE

P041

Caravan
Site

Cranmore
Farm

HAMSTEAD RD

90

VICTORIA
RD

MARINE
DR

37 A B 38 C D 39 E F

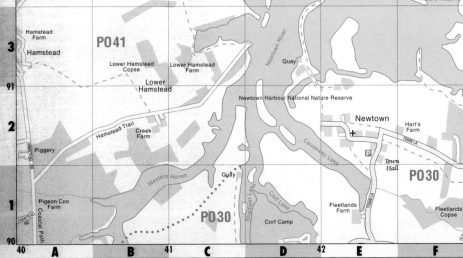

A B C D E F

8

7

93

6

5

92

4

91

3

2

1

90

DANGER AREA

Newtown Bay

Brickfield Farm
House

PO30

Hamstead Point

Hamstead
Ledge

Hamstead Dover

Coastal Path

Clamerkin Lake

Newtown Marshes
Nature Reserve

Hamstead
Farm

Hamstead

PO41

Newtown River

Lower Hamstead
Copse

Lower Hamstead
Farm

Quay

Lower
Hamstead

Newtown Harbour National Nature Reserve

Newtown

Hart's
Farm

Hamstead Trail

Creek
Farm

TOWN LA

Causeway Lake

Town
Hall

PO30

Piggery

HAMSTEAD RD

Western Haven

Quay

Fleetlands
Farm

TOWN LA

Pigeon Coo
Farm

Coastal Path

HAMSTEAD RD

PO30

Shalfleet Lake

Corf Lake

Corf Camp

Fleetlands
Copse

OLD VICARAGE LA

40   A   B   41   C   D   42   E   F

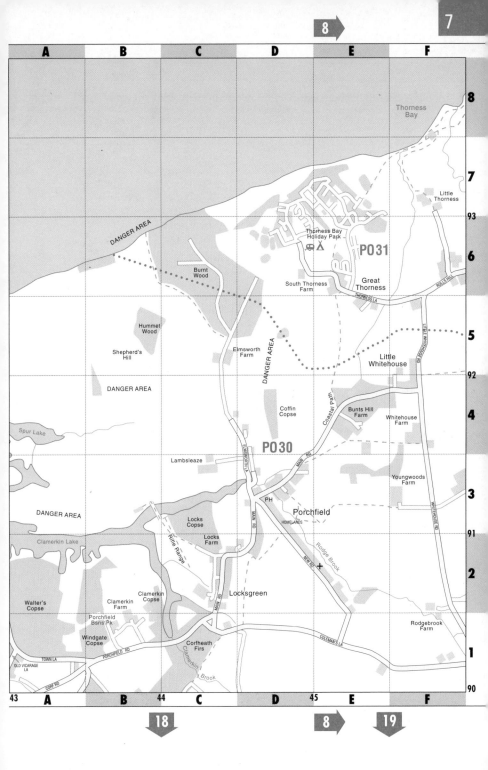

7 2

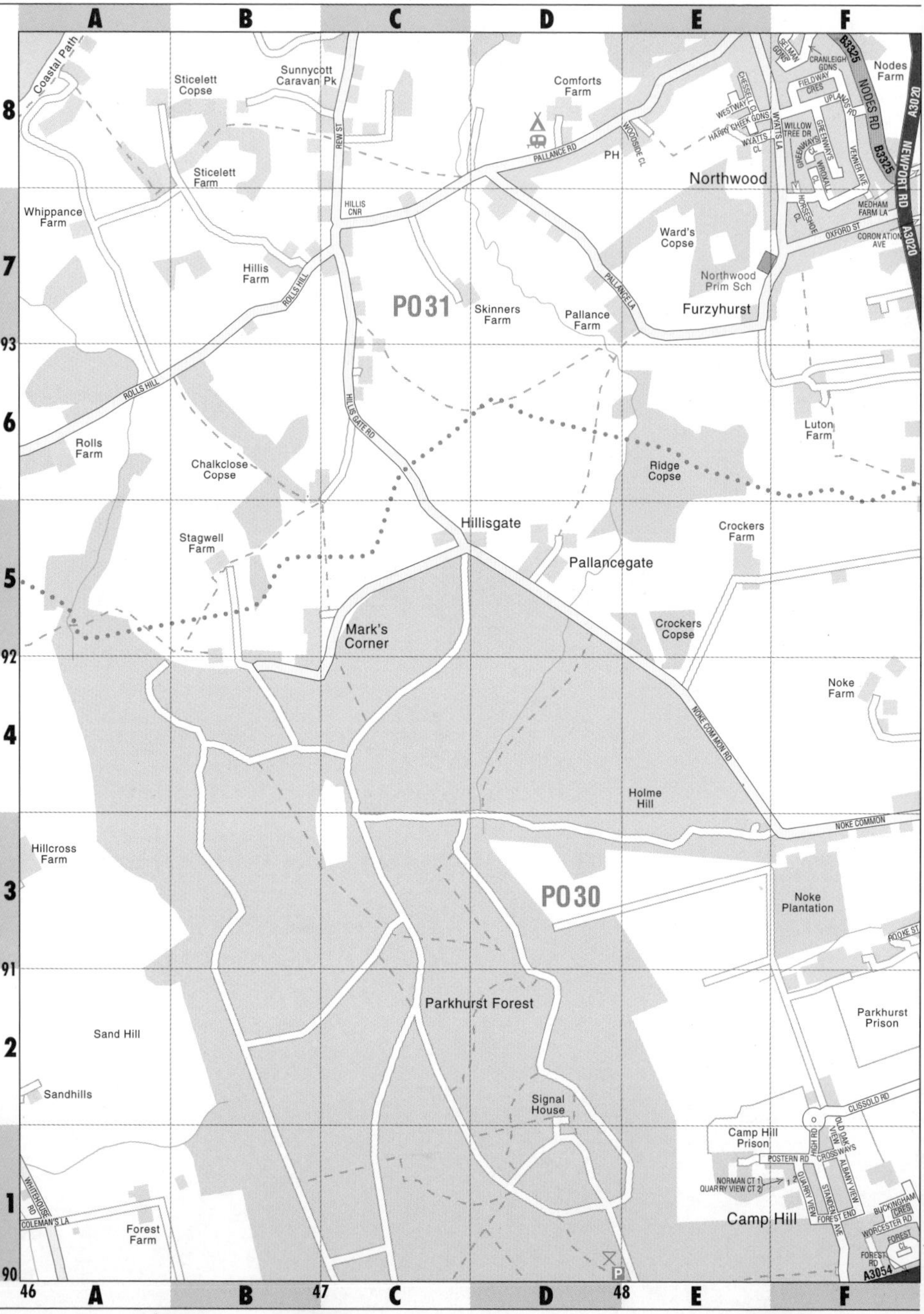

A B C D E F

8

Coastal Path

Sticelett Copse

Sunnycott Caravan Pk

Comforts Farm

REW ST

Nodes Farm

B3325

CRANLEIGH GDNS
FIELDWAY
UPL4
WYATTS CL
WILLOW TREE DR
WEST WATS
HARKY CREEK GDNS
PALLANCE RD
PH
Northwood
MEDHAM FARM LA

Sticelett Farm

Whippance Farm

HILLIS CNR

7

Hillis Farm

PO31

Skinners Farm

Pallance Farm

PALLANCE LA

Ward's Copse

Northwood Prim Sch

Furzyhurst

OXFORD ST
CORONATION AVE
A3020

ROLLS HILL

93

ROLLS HILL

6

Rolls Farm

HILLS GATE RD

Chalkclose Copse

Ridge Copse

Luton Farm

Crockers Farm

Stagwell Farm

Hillisgate

Pallancegate

5

Crockers Copse

92

Mark's Corner

Noke Farm

NOKE COMMON RD

4

Holme Hill

NOKE COMMON

Hillcross Farm

3

PO30

Noke Plantation

POOLE RD

91

Parkhurst Forest

Parkhurst Prison

2

Sand Hill

CLISSOLD RD

Sandhills

Signal House

Camp Hill Prison

POSTERN RD
HIGH PK RD
CROSSWAYS
NORMAN CT 1
QUARRY VIEW CT 2
ALBANY RD
STANLEY END
FOREST SIDE
WORCESTER RD
BUCKINGHAM
FOREST
FOREST RD
A3054

WHITEHOUSE RD

1

COLEMAN'S LA

Forest Farm

Camp Hill

90

46 A 47 B C 48 D E F

7 19 20

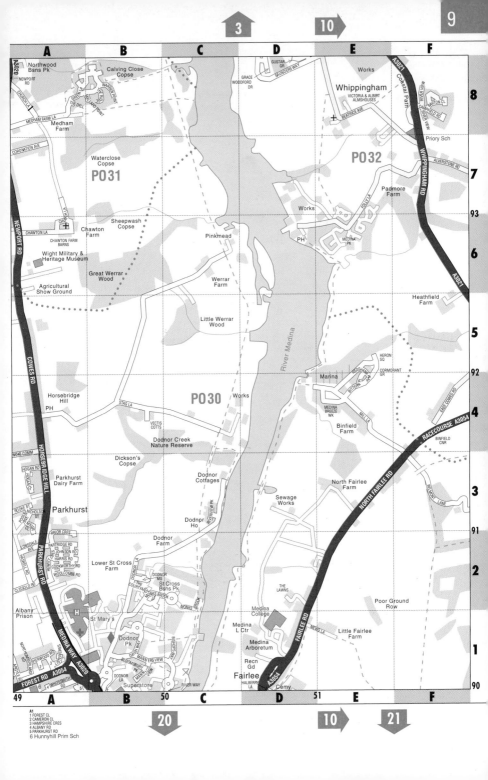

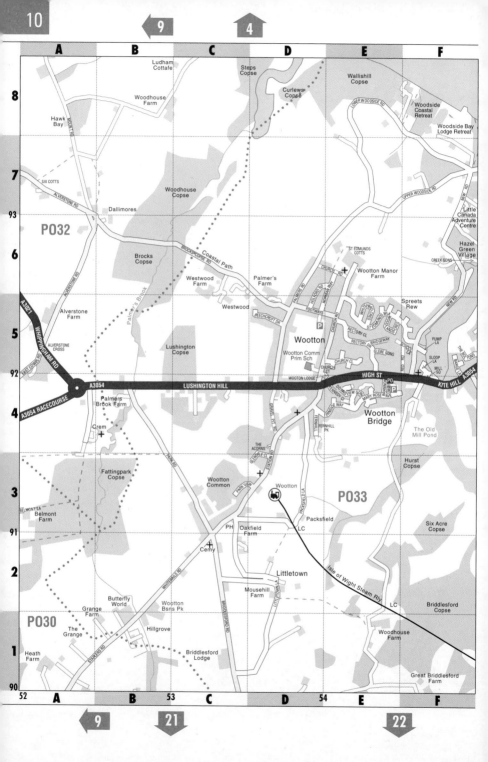

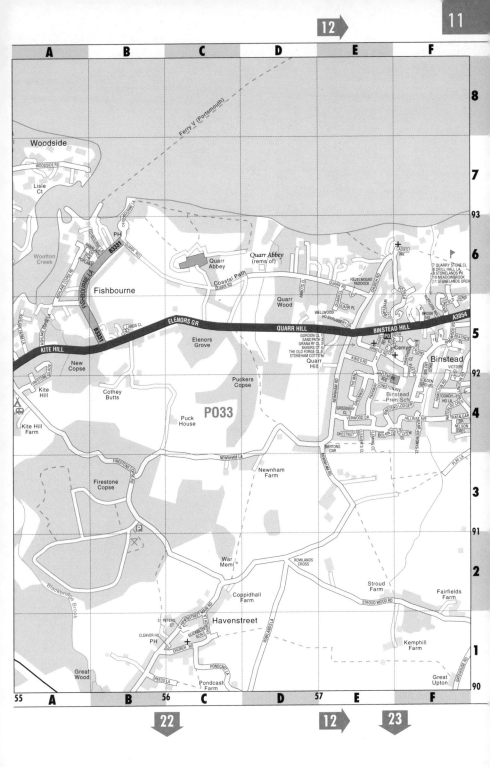

11

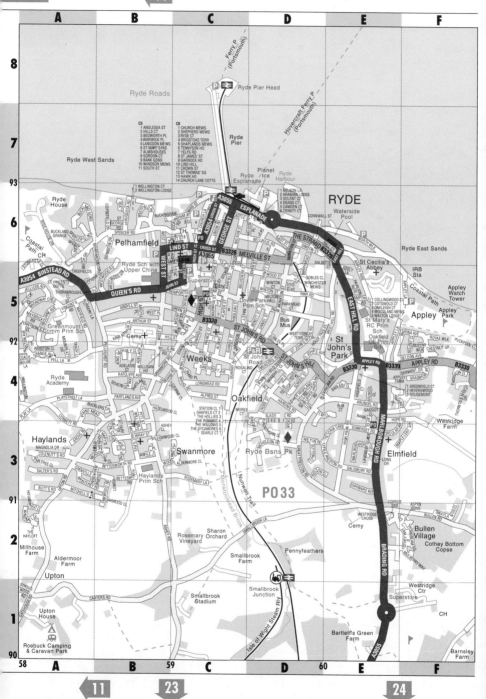

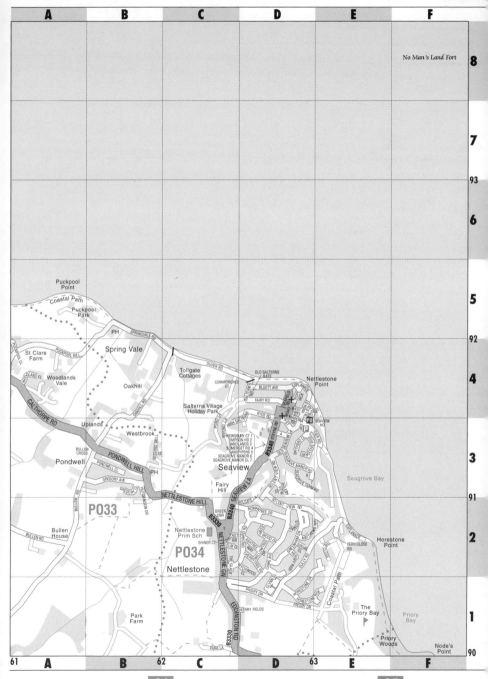

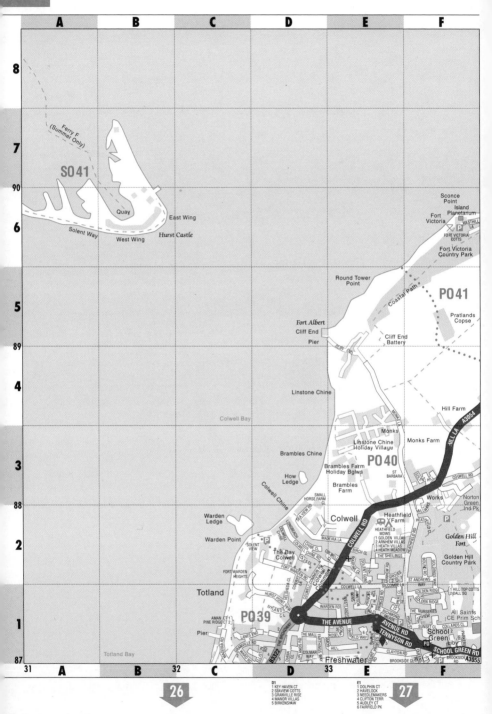

D1
1 KEY HAVEN CT
2 SEAVIEW COTTS
3 GRANVILLE RISE
4 MANOR VILLAS
5 BIRKENSHAW

E1
1 DOLPHIN CT
2 HAVELOCK
3 NEEDLEMAKERS
4 CLIFTON TERR
5 AUDLEY CT
6 FAIRFIELD PK

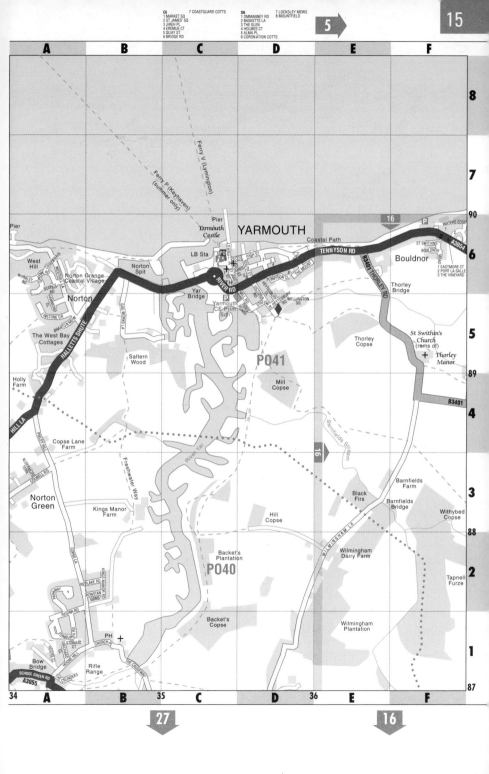

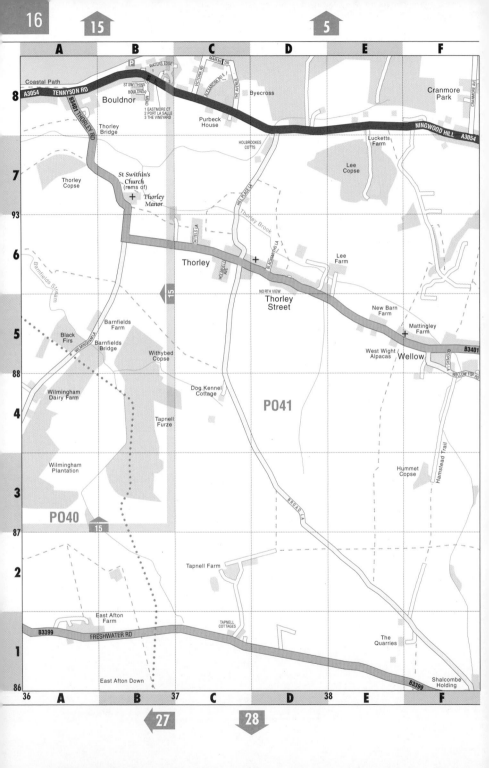

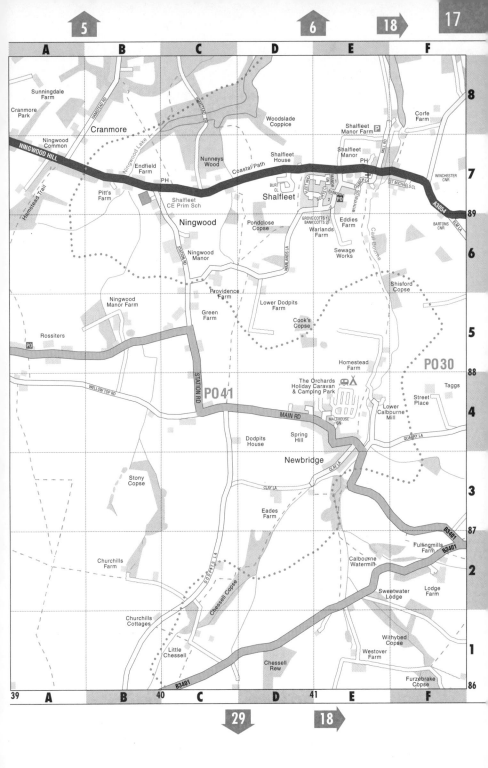

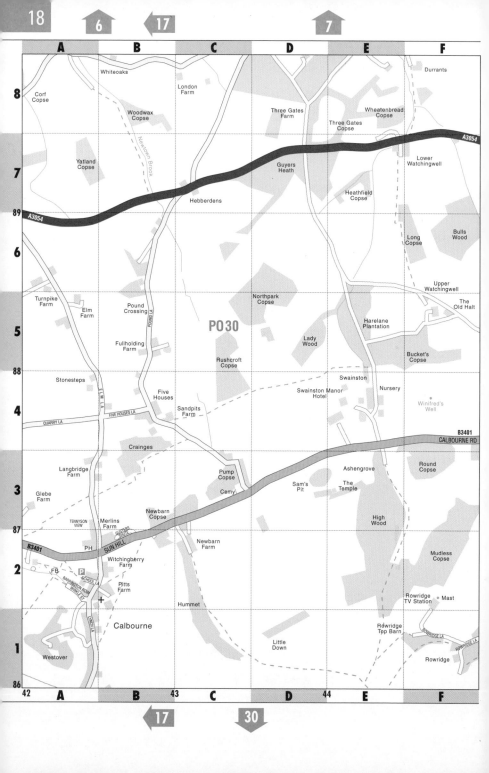

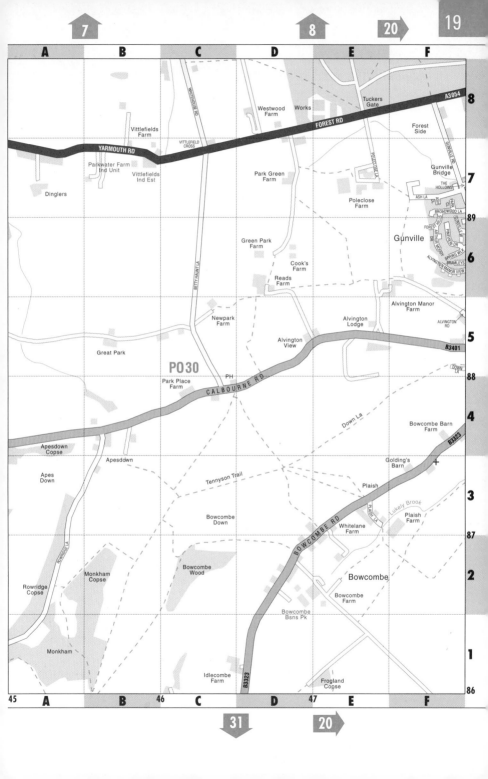

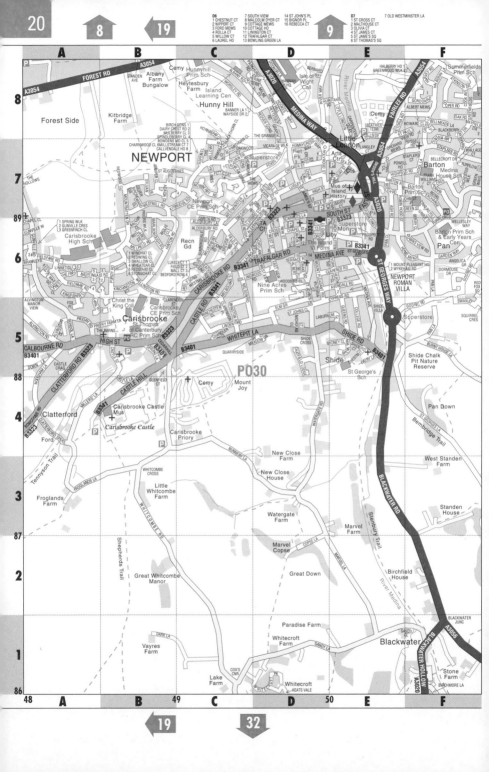

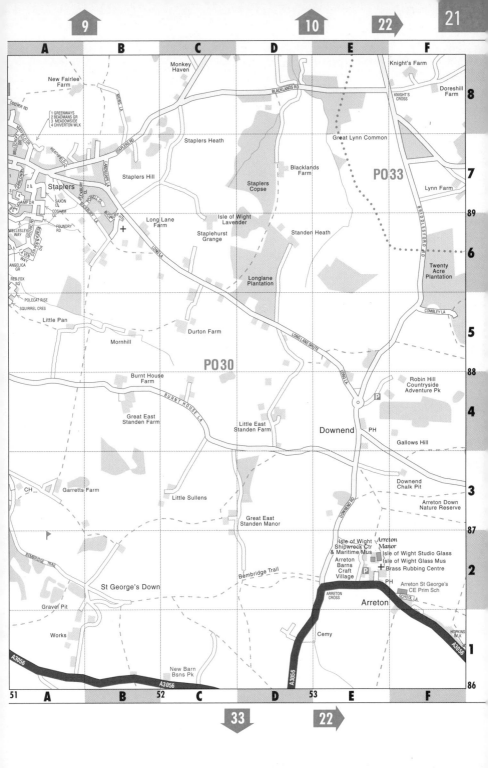

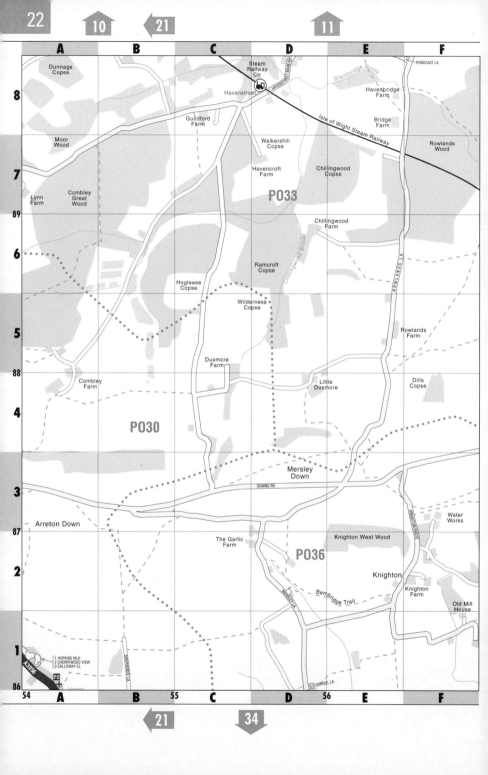

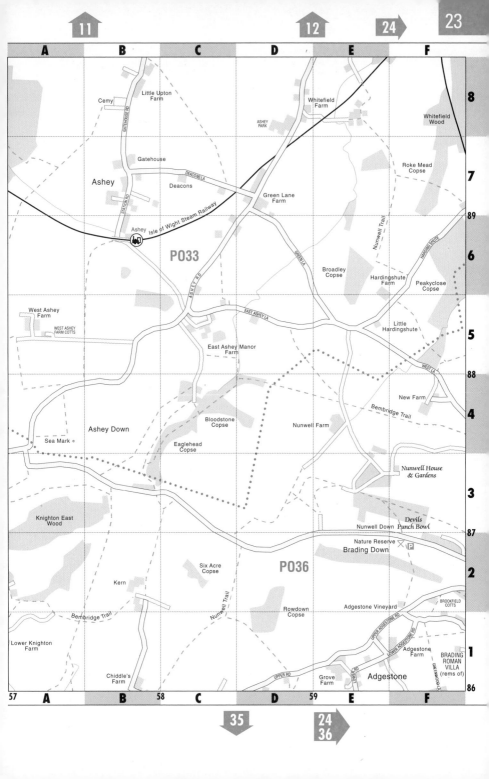

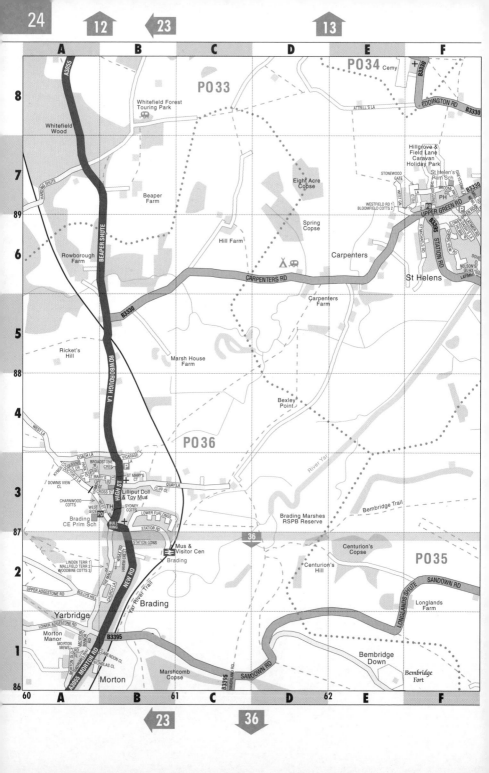

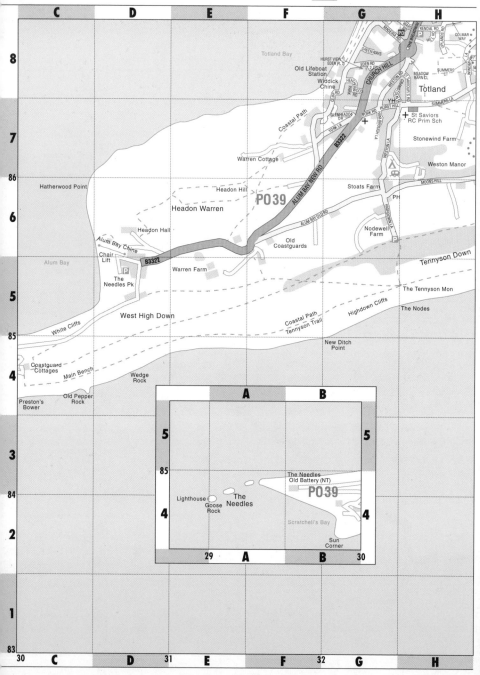

Map labels:

C D E F G H

8
7
86
6
5
85
4
3
84
2
1
83

Totland Bay
Old Lifeboat Station
Widdick Chine
Hurst View
Eden Pl
Church Hill
Totland
St Saviours RC Prim Sch
Stonewind Farm
Weston Manor
Moons Hill
Coastal Path
Warren Cottage
Headon Hill
Hatherwood Point
Headon Warren
PO39
Stoats Farm
PH
Headon Hall
Alum Bay Chine
Chair Lift
Alum Bay
B3322
The Needles Pk
Warren Farm
Old Coastguards
Nodewell Farm
White Cliffs
West High Down
Tennyson Down
The Tennyson Mon
The Nodes
Highdown Cliffs
Coastal Path
Tennyson Trail
New Ditch Point
Coastguard Cottages
Main Bench
Wedge Rock
Preston's Bower
Old Pepper Rock
Alum Bay New Rd
Alum Bay Old Rd
B3322

Inset map:

A B

5
85
4

Lighthouse
Goose Rock
The Needles
The Needles Old Battery (NT)
PO39
Scratchell's Bay
Sun Corner

29 A B 30

30 C D 31 E F 32 G H

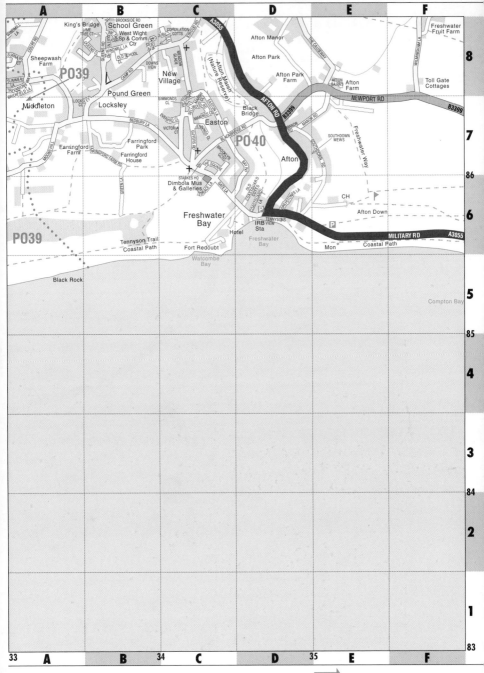

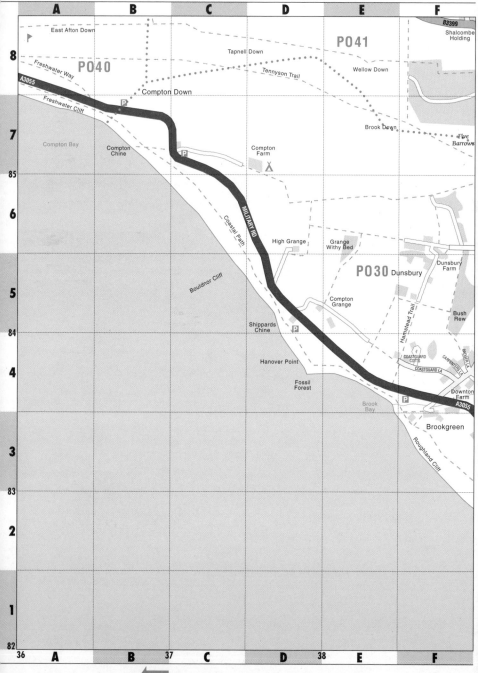

East Afton Down

PO40

PO41

Tapnell Down

Shalcombe
Holding

B3399

Freshwater Way

A3055

8

Tennyson Trail

Wellow Down

Compton Down

Freshwater Cliff

7

Compton Bay

Brook Down

Five
Barrows

Compton
Chine

85

Compton
Farm

Coastal Path

MILITARY RD

6

High Grange

Grange
Withy Bed

PO30 Dunsbury

Bouldnor Cliff

5

Dunsbury
Farm

Compton
Grange

Bush
Rew

Hamstead Trail

Shippards
Chine

84

CARPENTERS

BADNELLS

COASTGUARD
COTTS

COASTGUARD LA

4

Hanover Point

Fossil
Forest

Downton
Farm

A3055

Brook
Bay

Brookgreen

3

Roughland Cliff

83

2

1

82

| 36 | A | | B | 37 | C | | D | 38 | E | | F |

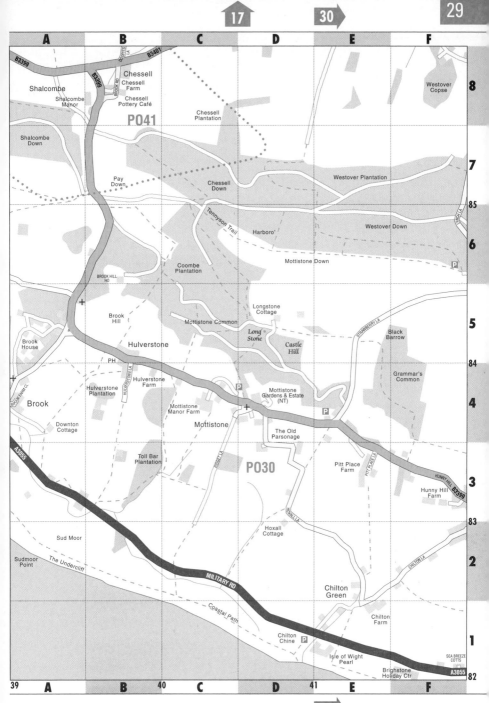

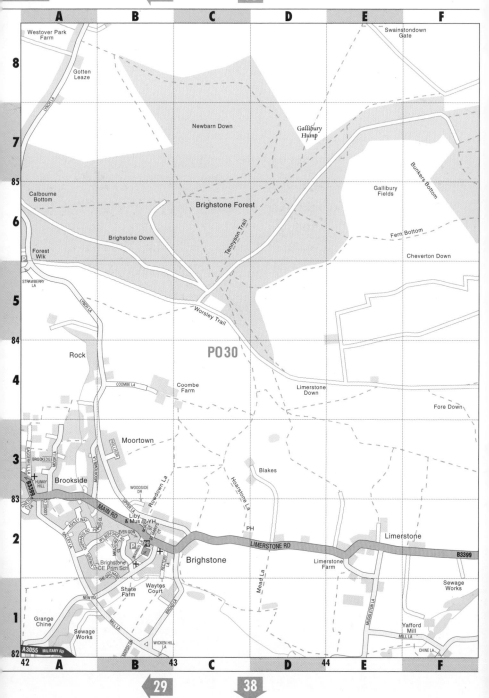

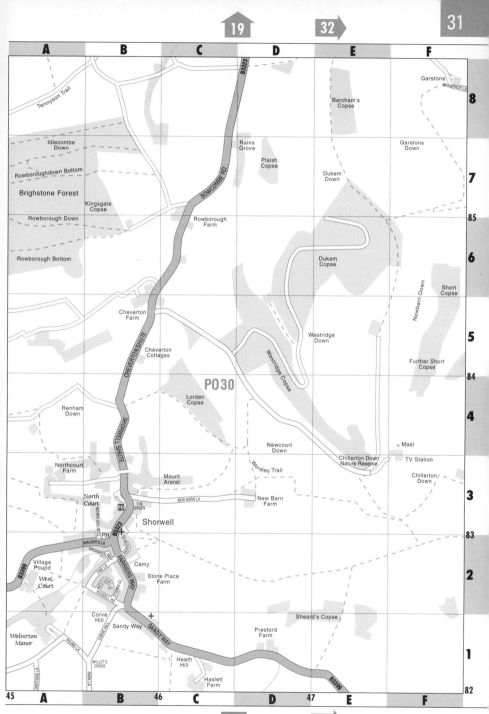

A **B** **C** **D** **E** **F**

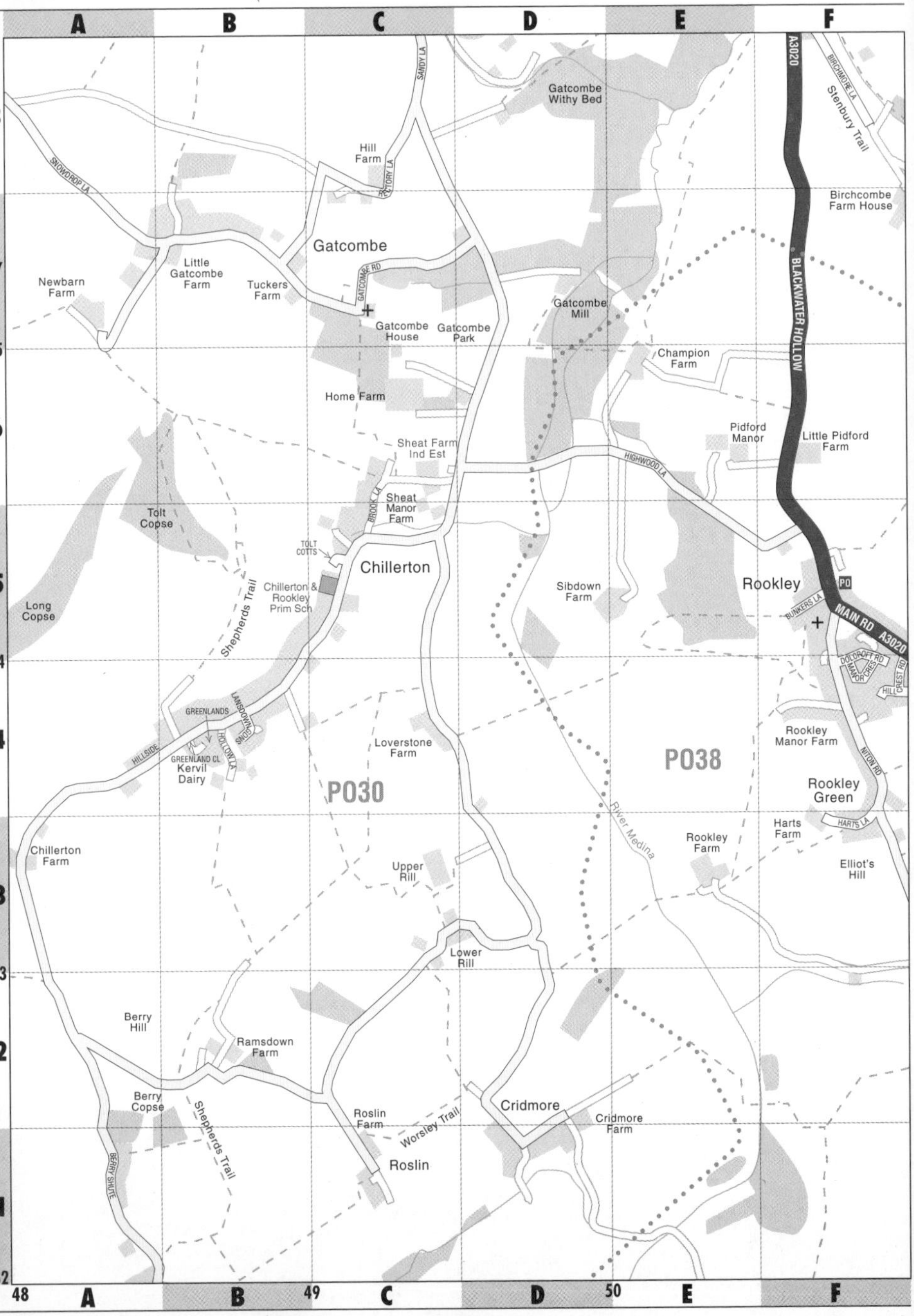

8

SNOWDROP LA

Newbarn
Farm

HILL HOLLOW LA

SANDY LA

Hill
Farm

Gatcombe
Withy Bed

A3020

BEACHMORE LA

Stenbury Trail

7

Little
Gatcombe
Farm

Tuckers
Farm

GATCOMBE RD

Gatcombe

Gatcombe
House

Gatcombe
Park

Gatcombe
Mill

Champion
Farm

Birchcombe
Farm House

BLACKWATER HOLLOW

85

Home Farm

Pidford
Manor

Little Pidford
Farm

6

Sheat Farm
Ind Est

BROCK LA

HIGHWOOD LA

Tolt
Copse

Sheat
Manor
Farm

TOLT
COTTS

Chillerton

Sibdown
Farm

Rookley

PO

5

Long
Copse

Shepherds Trail

Chillerton &
Rookley
Prim Sch

BUNKERS LA

MAIN RD

A3020

OAKCROFT RD

84

GREENLANDS

HOLLOW LA

LANESEND RD

Greenland Cl
Kervil
Dairy

HILLSIDE

Loverstone
Farm

Rookley
Manor
Farm

Rookley
Green

WROXALL RD

NIT CROFT RD

4

PO30

River Medina

Rookley
Farm

Harts
Farm

HARTS LA

Elliot's
Hill

PO38

3

Chillerton
Farm

Upper
Rill

83

Berry
Hill

Ramsdown
Farm

Lower
Rill

2

Berry
Copse

BERRY SHUTE

Shepherds Trail

Roslin
Farm

Worsley Trail

Cridmore

Cridmore
Farm

1

Roslin

82

48 **A** **B** **49** **C** **D** **50** **E** **F**

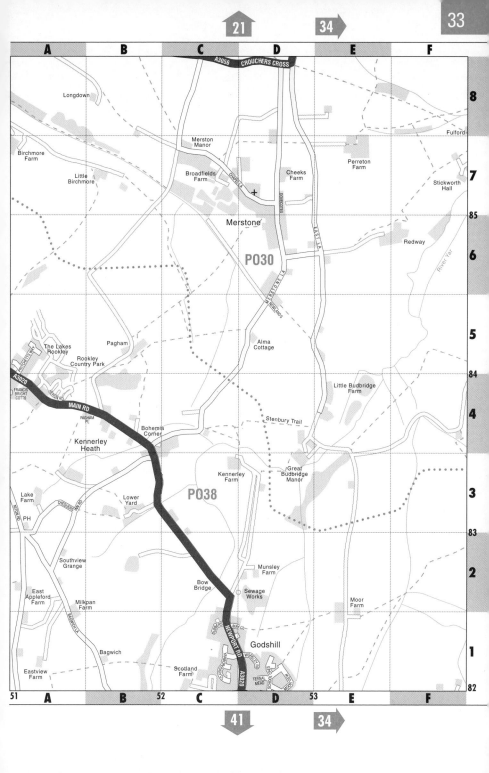

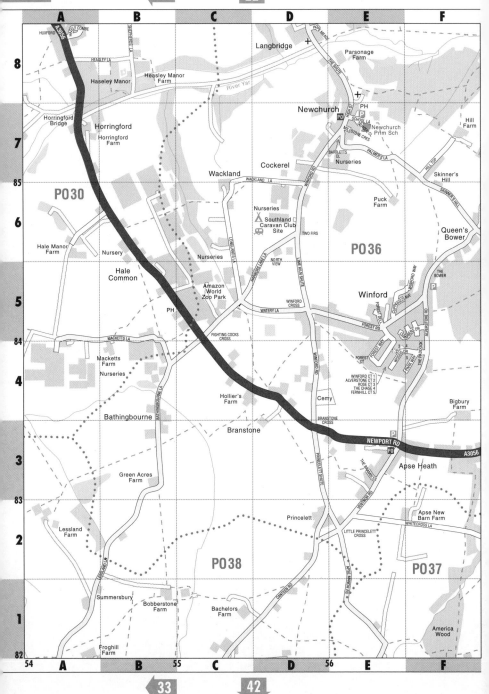

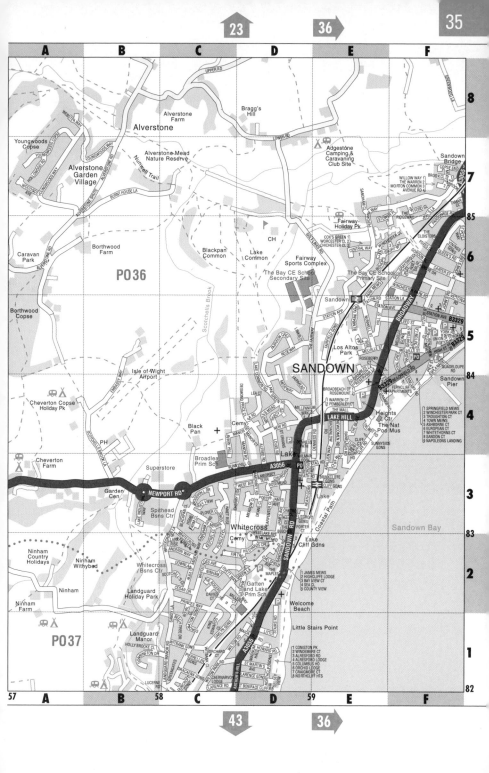

A B C D E F

8

Aircraft Works

B3395

Kingswood & Camp Beaumont Centre

Long Ledge

Bembridge Airport
PH
P

SANDOWN RD

HILLWAY RD

CENTRE STREETS LA

Whitecliff Bay Holiday Pk

B3395

Hillway

PO35

7

Bembridge Farm

Peacock Hill Farm

Coastal Path

PEACOCK HILL

Glover's Farm

Sandhills Holiday Pk

86

Whitecliff Bay

25

PO36

6

Mon
PH P
P

Culver Down

COASTGUARD COTTS

Whitecliff Ledge

The Nostrils

Culver Cliff

5

85

4

3

84

2

1

83

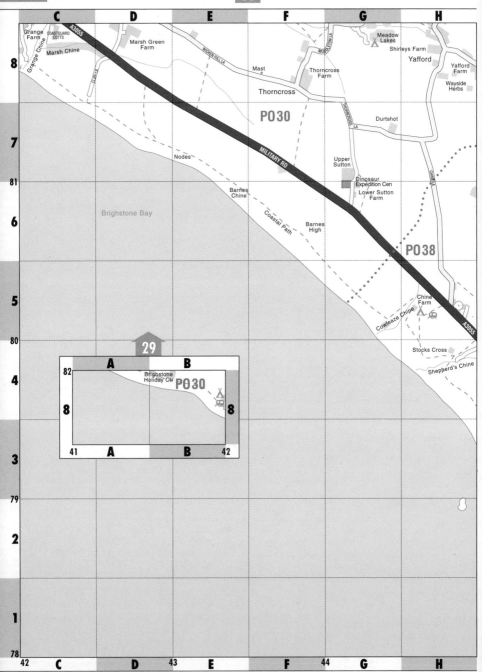

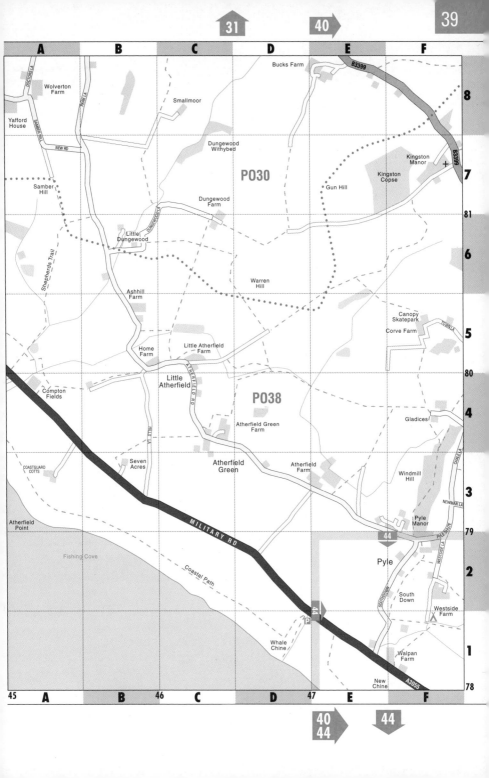

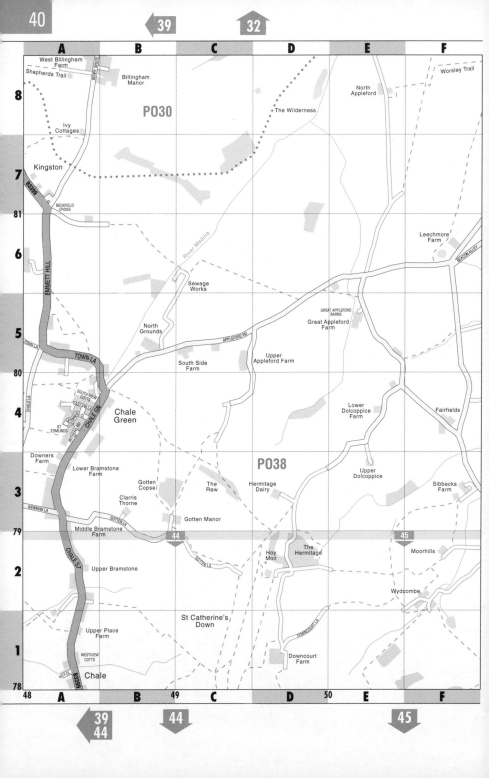

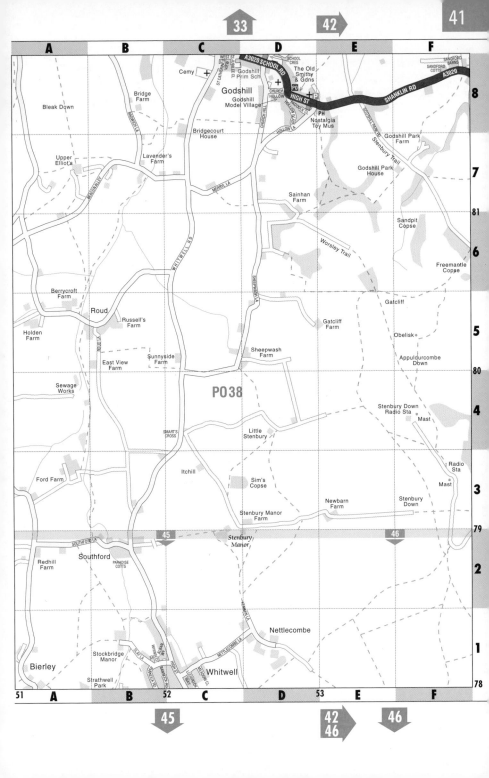

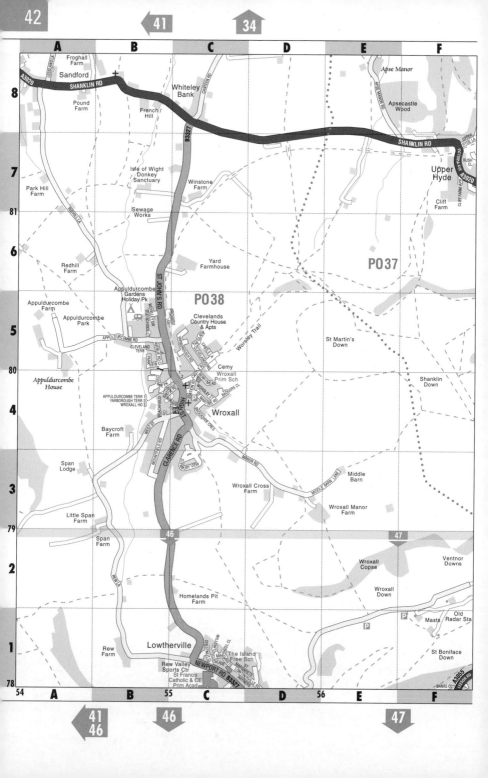

35

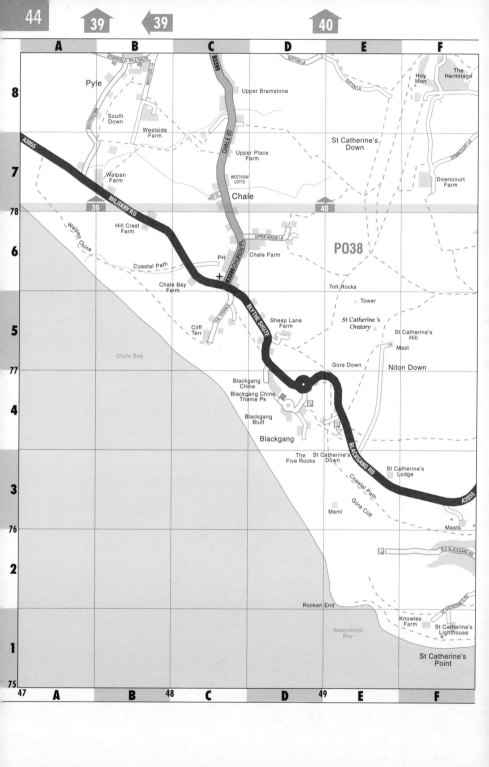

Pyle

The Hermitage

Hoy Mon

South Down

Westside Farm

Upper Bramstone

St Catherine's Down

Downcourt

Downcourt Farm

A3055

Walpan Farm

CHALE ST

Upper Place Farm

WESTVIEW COTTS

Chale

MILITARY RD

39

40

Hill Crest Farm

Walpan Chine

Coastal Path

PH

B3399 CHURCH PL

UPPER HOUSE LA

Chale Farm

PO38

Chale Bay Farm

HOY LA

Tolt Rocks

Tower

Cliff Terr

THE TERRACE

BLYTHE SHUTE

Sheep Lane Farm

St Catherine's Oratory

St Catherine's Hill

Mast

Chale Bay

Gore Down

Niton Down

Blackgang Chine

Blackgang Chine Theme Pk

P

Blackgang Bluff

P

Blackgang

The Five Rocks

St Catherine's Down

Coastal Path

Gore Cliff

St Catherine's Lodge

BLACKGANG RD

A3055

Meml

Masts

P

OLD BLACKGANG RD

Rocken End

ST CATHERINE'S RD

Knowles Farm

Watershoot Bay

St Catherine's Lighthouse

St Catherine's Point

47 A B 48 C D 49 E F

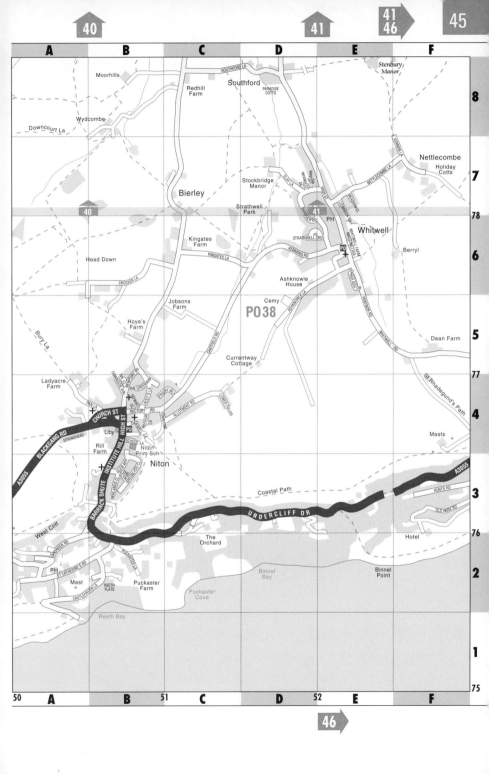

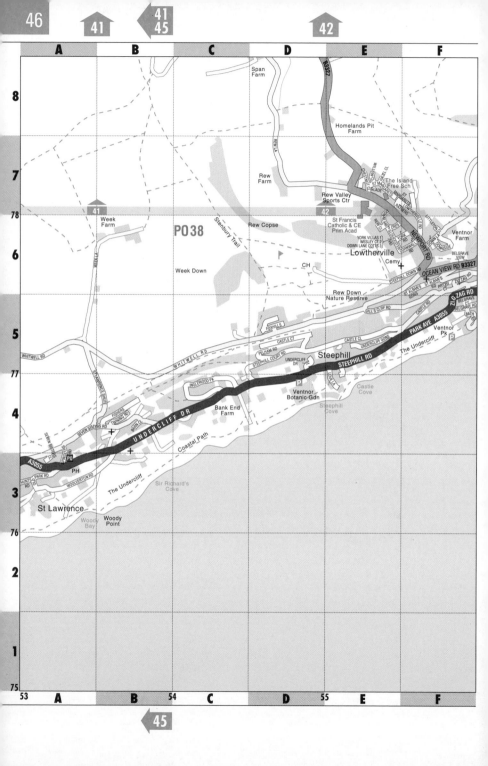

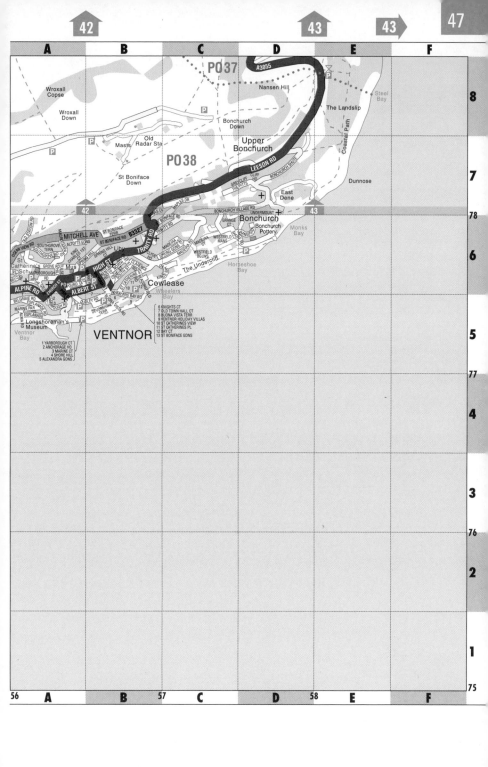

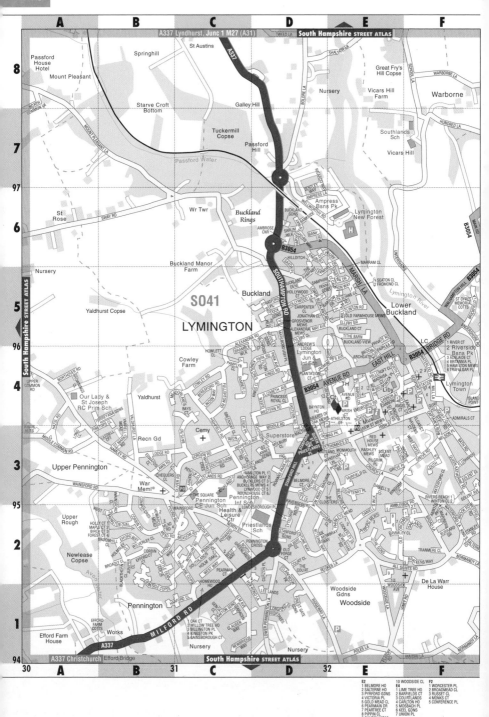

E3
1 BELMORE HO
2 SALTERNE HO
3 PYRFORD GDNS
4 VICTORIA PL
5 GOLD MEAD CL
6 PEARMAIN DR
7 PEARTREE CT
8 PIPPIN CL
9 CHURCH MEAD

10 WOODSIDE CL
E4
1 LIME TREE HO
2 BARFIELDS CT
3 COURTLANDS
4 CARLTON HO
5 MOSBACH PL
6 KEEL GDNS
7 UNION PL

F2
1 WORCESTER PL
2 BROADMEAD CT
3 RUSSET CL
4 MONKS CT
5 CONFERENCE PL

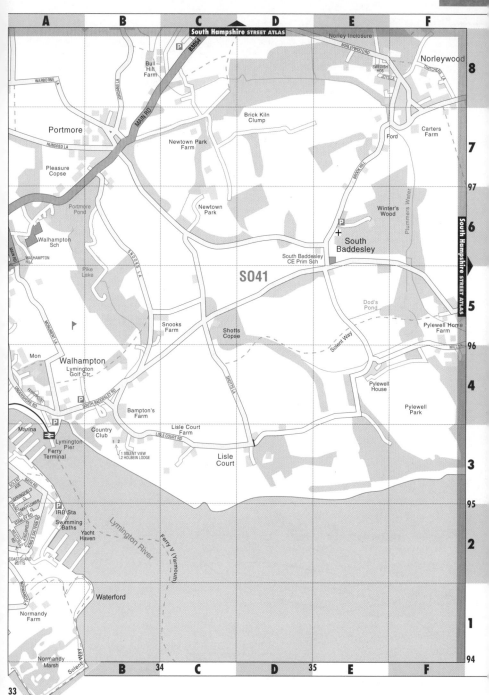

A **B** **C** **D** **E** **F**

Norley Inclosure

Norleywood

NORLEYWOOD RD

SWEDISH HOS

JOYS LA

THATCHERS LA

8

Bull Hill Farm

WARBORNE LA

KINGSTON LA

MAIN RD

Carters Farm

Ford

BROCK HILL

Brick Kiln Clump

Newtown Park Farm

Portmore

HUNDRED LA

7

97

Pleasure Copse

Newtown Park

Winter's Wood

Plummers Water

South Baddesley

Portmore Pond

Walhampton Sch

WALHAMPTON HILL

MAIN RD

Pike Lake

STROKE LA

South Baddesley CE Prim Sch

SO41

6

5

Dod's Pond

Pylewell Home Farm

MILL LA

96

Mon

MONTAGU LA

Walhampton

Lymington Golf Ctr

Snooks Farm

Shotts Copse

Solent Way

Pylewell House

4

UNDERSHORE RD

SOUTH BADDESLEY RD

SHOTTS LA

Bampton's Farm

Pylewell Park

Marina

Lymington Pier Ferry Terminal

Country Club

1 2

Lisle Court Farm

LISLE COURT RD

Lisle Court

1 1 SOLENT VIEW
2 HOLBEIN LODGE

3

95

IRB Sta

Swimming Baths

Yacht Haven

Lymington River

Ferry v (Yarmouth)

2

COASTGUARD COTTS

NORMANDY LA

SOLENT WAY

Waterford

1

94

Normandy Farm

Normandy Marsh

Solent Way

B 34 **C** **D** 35 **E** **F**

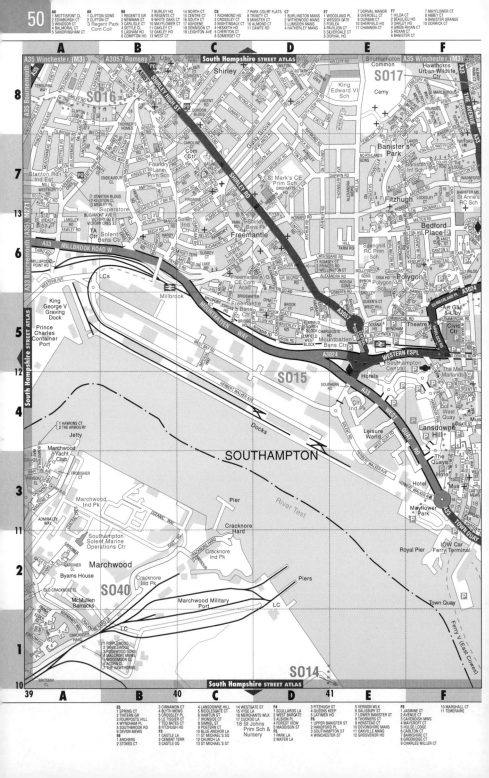

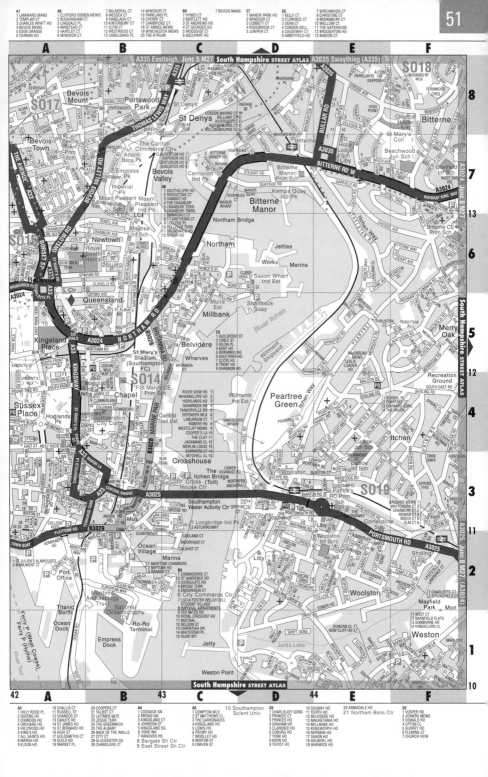

A7
1 LAMWARD MANS
2 TEMPLAR CT
3 CHARLES WYATT HO
4 BEVOIS MEWS
5 EDEN GRANGE
6 DARNAN HO

A8
1 CLIFFORD DIBBEN MEWS
2 BUCKINGHAM CT
3 LINGDALE PL
4 MINSTEAD CT
5 HARTLEY CT
6 WINDSOR CT

B6
14 WINDSOR CT
15 PARKLAND PL
16 CHERRY CT
17 CAMBRIDGE CT
18 ST ANNES MEWS
19 WINCHESTER MEWS
20 THE ATRIUM

B7
1 HYNES CT
2 BARTLETT HO
3 ST ANDREWS HO
4 ST GEORGES HO
5 ASCUPART HO

7 BEVOIS MANS

E7
1 MANOR PARK HO
2 WINDSOR CT
3 COBBETT CT
4 ROSEBROOK CT
5 JUNIPER CT

E8
1 KELLY CT
2 FLORENCE CT
3 DEAN CT
4 COBDEN DELL
5 CAUSEWAY CT
6 BAYSFIELD HO

F7
7 BIRCHWOOD CT
8 CHRISTINE CT
9 MANDABURY CT
10 WELLOW CT
11 THE GATEHOUSE
12 BROUGHTON HO
13 BINDON CT

A3
1 HOLY ROOD PL
2 QUEENS HO
3 CHANDOS HO
4 ORCHARD HO
5 HOLYROOD HO
6 KING'S HO
7 ALL SAINTS HO
8 MARSH HO
9 ELDON HO
10 CHALLIS CT
11 RUSSELL ST
12 CHANDOS ST
13 CANUTE HO
14 ST JAMES HO
15 ST BERNARD HO
16 HIGH ST
17 GOLDSMITHS CT
18 GUILD HO
19 MARKET PL
20 COOPERS CT
21 TALBOT CT
22 LATIMER GATE
23 JESSIE TERR
24 THE GREENWICH
25 THE ALBANY
26 BACK OF THE WALLS
27 CITY CT
28 GLOUCESTER SQ
29 CHANDLERS CT

A4
1 COSSACK GN
2 BROAD GN
3 KINGSLAND CT
4 JOHNSON ST
5 KINGSLAND SQ
6 YORK WK
7 HANOVER HO
8 Bargate Sh Ctr
9 East Street Sh Ctr

A5
1 COMPTON WLK
2 ST MATTHEWS CL
3 THE CARRONADES
4 KINGSLAND HO
5 LEWIS HO
6 PRIORY HO
7 WOOLLEY HO
8 WINTON ST
9 CRAVEN ST

10 Southampton
Solent Univ

C6
1 CHARLIEJOY GDNS
2 PRINCES CT
3 PRINCES HO
4 GRAHAM HO
5 CLARENCE HO
6 COBURG HO
7 YORK HO
8 AVON HO
9 TEVIOT HO

D6
10 SOLWAY HO
11 FORTH HO
12 BELVIDERE HO
13 MAURETANIA HO
14 MILLBANK HO
15 CLARENCE HO
16 NORMAN HO
17 SAXON HO
18 WARWICK HO

20 ARMADALE HO
21 Northam Bsns Ctr

D2
1 VOSPER RD
2 JOINERS MEWS
3 OSWALD RD
4 UPTON CL
5 SURREY RD
6 FLEMING CT
7 CHURCH VIEW

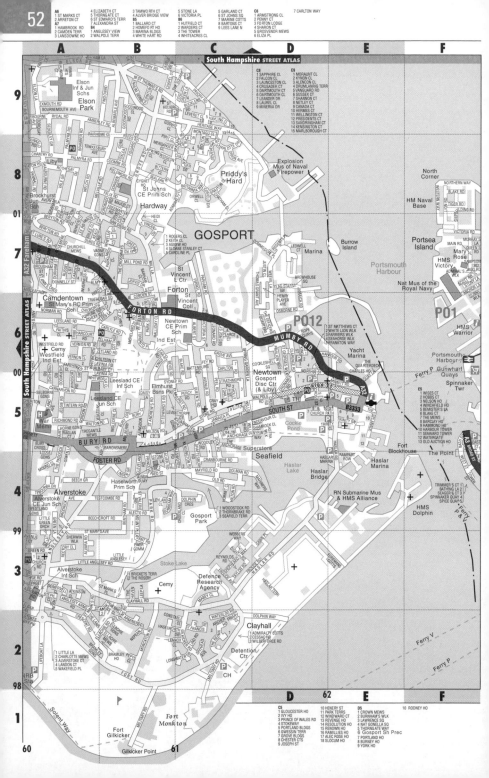

A6
1 ST MARKS CT
2 ARRETON CT

A7
1 HAMBROOK RD
2 CAMDEN TERR
3 LANSDOWNE HO

B4
1 ANGLESEY VIEW
2 WALPOLE TERR

B5
1 BALLARD CT
2 HOMEFORT HO
3 MARINA BLDGS
4 WHITE HART RD

B6
1 HUTFIELD CT
2 WARDERS CT
3 THE TOWER
4 WHITEACRES CL

4 ELIZABETH CT
5 THORNGATE CT
6 ST EDWARD'S TERR
7 ALEXANDRA ST

3 TAMWO RTH CT
4 ALVER BRIDGE VIEW

STONE LA
1 VICTORIA PL

5 GARLAND CT
6 ST JOHNS SQ
8 BARTONS CT
10 LEES LANE N

C6
1 ARMSTRONG CL
2 PENNY CT
3 FORTON LODGE
4 SHARON CT
5 GROSVENOR MEWS
6 ELIZA PL

7 CARLTON WAY

C8
1 SAPPHIRE CL
2 FALCON CL
3 LAUNCESTON CL
4 CRUSADER CT
5 DARTMOUTH CT
6 DARTMOUTH CL
7 LEANDER DR
8 LAUREL CL
9 MINERVA DR

C9
1 MORAUNT CL
2 KYNON CL
3 ALENCON CL
4 DRUMLANRIG TERR
5 VANGUARD RD
6 SUSSEX CT
7 SHANNON CT
8 NETLEY CT
9 CANADA CT
10 HERMES CT
11 WELLINGTON CT
12 PRESIDENTS CT
13 SANDRINGHAM CT
14 KENSINGTON CT
15 MARLBOROUGH CT

C6
1 ST MATTHEWS CT
2 WHITE LION WLK
3 FARRIERS WLK
4 SEAHORSE WLK
5 FRANKTON WAY

E5
1 WISES CT
2 HOBBS CT
3 NELSON HO
4 WINCHFIELD HO
5 BEMISTER'S LA
6 BLAKE CT
7 THE MEWS
8 BARCLAY HO
9 HAMMOND HO
10 HARBOUR TOWER
11 SEAWARD TOWER
12 WATERGATE
13 OLD AUCTION HO

F4
1 TRIMMER S CT
2 BATHING LA
3 SEAGER S CT
4 SPINNAKER QUAY
5 SPICE QUAY

D5
1 GLOUCESTER HO
2 IVY HO
3 PRINCE OF WALES RD
4 STOKEWAY
5 PORTLAND BLDGS
6 GWESSIN TERR
7 GROVE BLDGS
8 CHESTER CTS
9 JOSEPH ST
10 HENERY ST
11 PARK TERRS
12 WINDWARD CT
13 REVENGE HO
14 RESOLUTION HO
15 RENOWN HO
16 RAMILLIES HO
17 ALEC ROSE HO
18 SLOCUM HO

D5
1 CROWN MEWS
2 BURNHAM'S WLK
3 LAWRENCE SQ
4 NAT GONELLA SQ
5 THORNGATE WAY
6 Gosport Sh Prec
7 PORTLAND HO
8 BURNEY HO
9 YORK HO

10 RODNEY HO

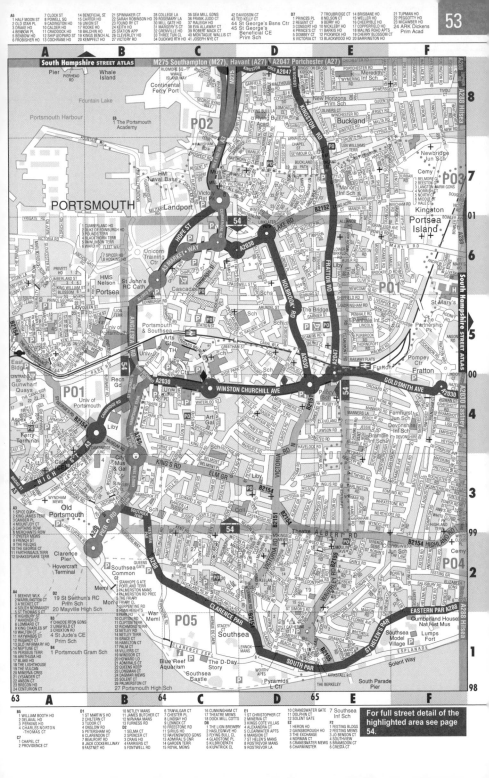

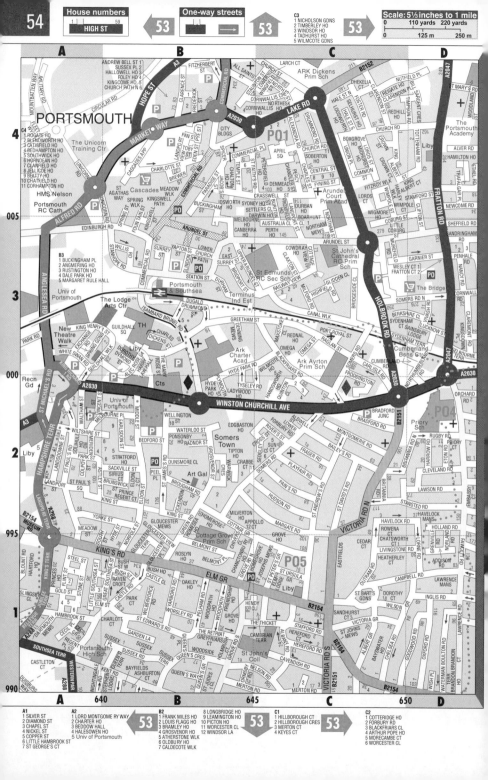

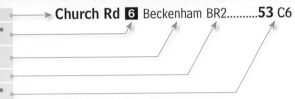

55

Index

Place name May be abbreviated on the map

Location number Present when a number indicates the place's position in a crowded area of mapping

Locality, town or village Shown when more than one place has the same name

Postcode district District for the indexed place

Page and grid square Page number and grid reference for the standard mapping

Church Rd 6 Beckenham BR2.........**53** C6

Cities, towns and villages are listed in CAPITAL LETTERS   **Public and commercial buildings** are highlighted in magenta
Places of interest are highlighted in blue with a star★

Abbreviations used in the index

Acad	**Academy**	Comm	**Common**	Gd	**Ground**	L	**Leisure**	Prom	**Promenade**
App	**Approach**	Cott	**Cottage**	Gdn	**Garden**	La	**Lane**	Rd	**Road**
Arc	**Arcade**	Cres	**Crescent**	Gn	**Green**	Liby	**Library**	Recn	**Recreation**
Ave	**Avenue**	Cswy	**Causeway**	Gr	**Grove**	Mdw	**Meadow**	Ret	**Retail**
Bglw	**Bungalow**	Ct	**Court**	H	**Hall**	Meml	**Memorial**	Sh	**Shopping**
Bldg	**Building**	Ctr	**Centre**	Ho	**House**	Mkt	**Market**	Sq	**Square**
Bsns, Bus	**Business**	Ctry	**Country**	Hospl	**Hospital**	Mus	**Museum**	St	**Street**
Bvd	**Boulevard**	Cty	**County**	HQ	**Headquarters**	Orch	**Orchard**	Sta	**Station**
Cath	**Cathedral**	Dr	**Drive**	Hts	**Heights**	Pal	**Palace**	Terr	**Terrace**
Cir	**Circus**	Dro	**Drove**	Ind	**Industrial**	Par	**Parade**	TH	**Town Hall**
Cl	**Close**	Ed	**Education**	Inst	**Institute**	Pas	**Passage**	Univ	**University**
Cnr	**Corner**	Emb	**Embankment**	Int	**International**	Pk	**Park**	Wk, Wlk	**Walk**
Coll	**College**	Est	**Estate**	Intc	**Interchange**	Pl	**Place**	Wr	**Water**
Com	**Community**	Ex	**Exhibition**	Junc	**Junction**	Prec	**Precinct**	Yd	**Yard**

Index of towns, villages, streets, hospitals, industrial estates, railway stations, schools, shopping centres, universities and places of interest

A

Abbey Ct **8** SO15........... 50 F7
Abbeyfield Ho **6** SO18.... 51 E8
Abbey La PO33........... 12 E5
Abbots Brook SO41....... 48 F2
Abbots Cl PO33........... 11 D6
A'Becket Ct **3** PO1....... 53 A4
Abingdon Cl PO12........ 52 B5
Abingdon Rd PO12....... 12 C5
Above Bar St SO14....... 50 F5
Acacia Cl PO30........... 20 B7
Acacia Rd SO19........... 51 F5
Acorn Cl SO40........... 50 A1
Acorn Gdns PO32........ 3 D2
Acorns The PO33........ 10 D4
Acorn Bsns Pk SO14.... 51 B7
Adames Rd PO1......... 53 E6
Addison Rd PO4......... 54 D1
Adelaide Ct
  Lymington SO41........ 48 F4
  Ryde PO33........... 12 B4
Adelaide Gr PO32........ 3 C3
Adelaide Pl PO33........ 12 B4
Adelaide Rd SO17........ 51 C8
ADGESTONE........... 23 E1
Adgestone Vineyard★
  PO36........... 23 F2
Admiral's Cnr **13** PO5.... 53 D2
Admirals Ct
  Lymington SO41........ 48 F4
  7 Portsmouth PO5....... 53 C2
Admiral's Wharf PO31.... 3 B5
Admiral's Wlk PO1........ 52 F7
Admiralty Cl PO12........ 52 C8
Admiralty Cotts PO12.... 52 C2
Admiralty Ho SO14....... 51 A2
Admiralty Rd PO1........ 53 A5
Admiral War PO31........ 2 F3
Afton Barns PO40........ 27 E8
Afton Marsh Nature
  Reserve★ PO40........ 27 C8
Afton Park Gdns★ PO40.. 27 D7
Afton Rd PO40........... 27 D7
Agincourt Rd PO2....... 53 D7
Agnew Ho PO12........ 52 B7
Ailsa La SO19........... 51 D4
Alan Way PO38........ 45 D7
Albany Ct PO12........ 52 B6
Albany Park Ct SO17.... 50 F8
Albany Rd
  East Cowes PO32....... 3 C5

Albany Rd continued
  Newport PO30........ 20 C8
  Portsmouth PO5........ 54 C1
Albany The **22** SO14.... 51 A3
Albany View PO30........ 20 D6
Albemarle Ave PO12.... 52 B9
Albert Gr PO5........... 54 C1
Albert Mews PO30........ 20 F8
Albert Rd
  Gurnard PO31........... 2 D3
  Portsmouth PO4, PO5.. 53 E2
  Sandown PO36........ 36 A3
  Shanklin PO37........ 43 B7
Albert Road N SO14.... 51 B3
Albert Road S SO14.... 51 B3
Albert St
  Cowes PO31........... 3 A4
  Gosport PO12........ 52 C6
  Newport PO30........ 20 D6
  Ryde PO33........... 12 C6
  Ventnor PO38........ 47 B6
Albert Way PO32........ 3 D1
Albion Pl **3** SO14........ 50 F4
Albion Rd PO36........ 36 A3
Albion Towers SO14.... 51 A3
Alcantara Cres SO14.... 51 B3
Alderbury La PO30........ 20 C6
Alderbury Rd PO30...... 20 C6
Aldermore Cl PO33...... 12 C3
Aldermore Terr PO40.... 15 A3
Aldrich Rd PO1........ 53 A6
Aldwell St **17** PO5...... 54 C2
Alec Rose Ho   PO12.... 52 C5
Alec Rose La PO1....... 54 B3
Alecto Rd PO12........ 52 B4
Alec Wintle Ho PO2.... 53 B8
Alencon Cl **3** SO41.... 52 C9
Alexandra Ct
  Southampton SO15.... 50 D6
  Southampton, Woolston
  SO19........... 51 D3
Alexandra Ct **4** PO4.... 53 E1
Alexandra Gdns PO38.... 47 A5
Alexandra La PO30........ 20 D6
Alexandra Mews
  Lymington SO41........ 48 D5
  Southampton SO15.... 50 E7
Alexandra Rd
  Cowes PO31........... 3 A3
  Lymington SO41........ 48 C5
  Portsmouth PO1........ 54 C4
  Ryde PO33........... 12 E4

Alexandra Rd continued
  Shanklin PO37........ 43 C7
  Southampton SO15.... 50 E6
Alexandra Road E PO41.. 16 C8
Alexandra St **7** PO12.... 52 A7
Alfred Rd
  Portsmouth PO1....... 54 A4
  Sandown PO36....... 35 D4
Alfred St
  East Cowes PO32....... 3 C3
  Ryde PO33........... 12 C4
  Southampton SO14.... 51 B6
Alhambra Rd PO4....... 53 E1
Allen's Rd PO4........ 53 E2
Alliance Ho PO1........ 53 E6
Allotment Rd PO38....... 45 C4
All Saints CE Prim Sch
  PO40........... 14 F1
All Saints Ho **7** SO14.. 51 A3
All Saints Rd SO41....... 48 F2
All Saint's Rd PO1....... 53 D7
All Saints' St PO1....... 54 B4
Alma Ho SO14........ 51 A4
Alma Pl **5** PO41........ 15 D6
Alma Rd
  Southampton SO14.... 51 A8
  Ventnor PO38........ 47 A5
Almond Cl **10** SO15.... 50 C6
Almond Rd SO15....... 50 C6
Almshouses **7** PO33.... 12 C5
Alpine Rd PO38........ 47 A6
Alresford Lodge PO37.. 35 D1
Alresford Rd PO37....... 35 D1
Altofts Gdns PO38....... 47 A6
Alton Ho SO18........ 51 E8
Alum Bay New Rd PO39.. 26 E6
Alum Bay Old Rd PO39.. 26 F6
Alvara Rd PO12........ 52 A3
Alver Bridge View **4**
  PO12........... 52 B4
Alver Quay PO12........ 52 B4
Alver Rd
  Gosport PO12........ 52 C6
  Portsmouth PO1........ 53 E6
ALVERSTOKE........... 52 A4
Alverstoke CE Jun Sch
  PO12........... 52 A4
Alverstoke Cl **1** SO41.. 52 A3
Alverstoke Inf Sch PO12.. 52 A3
ALVERSTONE........... 23 A8
Alverstone Cross SO32.. 10 A5
Alverstone Ct PO36........ 34 E4

**ALVERSTONE GARDEN
VILLAGE**........... 35 B7
Alverstone Rd
  Alverstone Garden Village
  PO36........... 35 B7
  Winford PO36........ 34 F5
  Wootton PO32........ 10 A6
Alverstone Shute PO36.. 35 B7
Alverston Mead Nature
  Reserve★ PO36....... 35 B7
Alvington Cl PO30........ 20 A5
Alvington Manor View
  PO30........... 19 F6
Alvington Rd PO30....... 20 A5
Alyne Ho SO15........ 50 F8
Aman Ct PO39........ 14 C1
Amazon World Zoo Park★
  PO36........... 34 C5
Amberley Rd PO37....... 43 B7
Amberley Rd PO12....... 52 A9
Ambleside Rd SO41...... 48 F3
Ambrose Cnr SO41...... 48 D6
Amherst Pl PO33........ 12 E4
Amos Hill PO39........ 14 E1
Amoy St SO15........ 50 F6
Ampress La SO41....... 48 D6
Ampress Bsns Pk SO41.. 48 D6
Ampthill Rd
  Ryde PO33........... 12 E5
  Southampton SO15.... 50 B7
Ancasta Rd SO14....... 51 B7
Anchorage Rd PO38.... 47 A5
Anchorage The PO12.... 52 C5
Anchorage Way
  East Cowes PO32....... 3 C2
  Lymington SO41........ 48 D3
Anchor Cl PO30........ 20 D6
Anchor Gate Rd PO1.... 53 A6
Anchor La PO1........ 53 A6
Anchor Mews SO41...... 48 E4
Anchor Way PO12....... 52 C2
Anderson's Rd SO14.... 51 B3
Andes Cl SO41........ 51 C3
Andover Rd
  Portsmouth PO4....... 53 F2
  Southampton SO15.... 50 D6
Andrew Bell St PO1.... 54 B4
Andrew Cl PO1........ 53 F6
Andrew's Lodge SO41.. 48 D5
Angel Ct SO41........ 48 E4
Angelica Grove PO30.... 20 F6
Angeleas Rd PO1........ 53 B5
Anglesea Rd PO1........ 54 A3
Anglesea St **1** PO33.... 12 C5

Abb–Arl

Anglesea Terr SO14....... 51 B3
Anglesey Arms Rd PO12.. 52 A3
Anglesey Rd PO12....... 52 A3
Anglesey View **1** PO12.. 52 B4
Angmering Ho **2** PO1.. 54 B3
Ann's Hill Rd PO12....... 52 A6
Ansells PO34........... 13 D2
Anson Ct **22** PO1........ 53 A4
Anson Ho SO14........ 51 B3
Appleford RdPO38....... 40 C5
APPLEY........... 12 F5
Appley Farm PO33....... 12 E4
Appley La PO33........ 12 E5
Appley Rd PO33........ 12 F4
Appley Rise PO33....... 12 F5
Appley Twr★ PO33....... 12 F5
Appollo Cl PO5........ 54 B2
Appuldurcombe Ho★
  PO38........... 42 B5
Appuldurcombe Rd PO38.. 42 B5
Appuldurcombe Terr
  PO38........... 42 C4
April Sq PO1........ 54 C4
APSE HEATH........... 34 F3
Aquitania Ho **6** SO14.. 51 C5
Arabian Lodge PO33.... 12 D8
Araluen Way PO36........ 35 E3
Arcade The PO31........ 3 A4
Archer Ho PO12........ 52 C2
Archers **1** SO15........ 50 E6
Archers Rd SO15........ 50 F7
Archery Gdns SO19.... 51 F2
Archery Gr SO19........ 51 F1
Archery Rd SO19........ 51 E1
Archgate SO41........ 48 E4
Arctic Rd PO31........ 3 B4
Arethusa Ho **16** PO1.... 53 A4
Argyle Rd
  Newport PO30........ 9 A1
  Southampton SO14.... 51 B5
Argyll Pl PO33........ 12 B5
Argyll St PO33........ 12 B5
Ariel Rd PO1........ 53 E5
Ark Ayrton Prim Sch PO5.. 54 C2
Ark Charter Acad PO5.... 54 B2
ARK Dickens Prim Acad
  PO1........... 54 C4
Arlott Ct SO15........ 50 E7

Armadale Ho **20** S014.........51 C6
Arminers Cl **11** P012........52 B2
Armory La P01............53 A4
Armoury The S040.........50 A3
Armstrong Cl **11** P012.....52 C6
Arnaud Cl P02.............53 D7
Arnhem Rd P040...........14 E2
Arnhem Villas P040.........14 E2
Arnold Rd
  Cowes P031.............3 A3
  Ryde P033.............11 E5
ARRETON.................21 E2
Arreton Barns Craft Village*
  P030.................21 E2
Arreton Cross P030........21 E1
Arreton Ct **2** P012......52 A6
Arreton St George's CE Prim
  Sch P030..............21 F2
Arrow Cl S019............51 D1
Arthur Cott P032..........3 E2
Arthur Moody Dr P030.....19 F6
Arthur Pope Ho P05.......54 C2
Arthur Rd S015............11 E5
Arthur's Hill P037.........35 D1
Arthur St
  Portsmouth P02.........53 E7
  Ryde P033.............12 E4
Arundel Cl P033...........12 E4
Arundel Ct Prim Acad
  P01..................54 C4
Arundel Ho
  Southampton, Banister's Pk
  S015................50 F8
  18 Southampton, Northam
  S014................51 C6
Arundel Rd P033..........12 E4
Arundel St P01............54 C3
Ascupart Ho **6** S017....51 B8
Ascupart St S014..........51 B4
Ashborne Ct P036.........35 F5
Ashburnham Cl S019.......51 D5
Ashburton Ct P05.........54 B1
Ashburton Rd P05.........54 B1
Ashby Pl P05.............53 C2
Ash Cl
  Gosport P012...........52 B5
  Newport P030..........20 C7
Ashdene **17** S015.......50 B8
ASHEY...................23 B7
Ashey Cl P033............12 B3
Ashey Pk P033............23 D8
Ashey Rd P033............23 C6
Ashey View P036..........35 C3
Ash Gr
  Cowes P031.............3 A2
  Shanklin P037..........43 C4
Ashknowle La P038........45 D5
Ash La P030..............19 F7
Ashlake Copse La P033....11 A5
Ashlake Copse Rd P033....11 A6
Ashlake Farm La P033.....11 A5
Ashley Ct P012...........52 A6
Ashley Pl P033...........12 E3
Ashley Way P030..........30 A2
Ash Rd P030.............20 E7
Ashridge Cl S015.........50 F8
Ashton Ho S019...........51 F1
Ashton Terr **1** P031....3 B4
Ashtree Way P034.........13 D2
Aspen Cl P030............20 C7
Aspen Gdns P033.........12 F2
Aspen (Gall)* P01........53 A4
Astley St P05.............54
Aston Rd P033............53
Astra Wlk P012...........52 A2
Asturias Way S014........51 F3
Asylum Rd S015..........51 D5
Athelstan Rd S019........51 C3
Athelston Ct S041.........48 A6
ATHERFIELD GREEN.......39 E6
Atherfield Rd P038.......39 D3
Atherley Cross Rd P037...43 C3
Atherley Ct
  Shanklin P037..........43 C4
  Southampton S015.......50
Atherley Pk Cl P037.......43 B8
Atherley Pk Way P037.....43 B8
Atherley Rd
  Shanklin P037..........43 C8
  Southampton S015.......50 D6
Atherstone Wlk **5** P05..54 A2
Atkinson Cl P012..........52 A3
Atkinson Dr P016.........20 F8
Atlantic Cl S014..........51 B2
Atrium The **20** S017.....51 A8
Attrill's La P033, P034.....24 E8
Auckland Road E P05......53 C2
Auckland Road W P05.....53 C2
Audley Ct **5** P040......14 E1
Augusta Rd P033..........12 B6
Augustine Rd S014........51 B6
Augustus Ho S018.........51 C7
Australia Cl P01...........54 C3
Autumn Rd S040..........50 A1
Avenue Ct
  Gosport P012...........52 A3
  2 Southampton S017..51 B8
Avenue De Caen P05.......53 C1
Avenue Nurseries P036....36 A4
Avenue Rd
  Freshwater P040........14 E1
  Gosport P012...........52 C5
  Lymington S041.........48 E4
  Sandown P036..........36 A4
  Shanklin P037..........43 C8

Avenue Rd continued
  Southampton S014.......51 A8
  Wroxall P038...........42 B5
Avenue Slipway P036......36 A3
Avenue The
  Boulnor P041...........16 C8
  East Cowes P032.........3 E2
  Gosport P012...........52 A4
  Gurnard P031............2 D3
  Totland P039............14 E1
  Avery La P012...........52 A8
Avon Cl S041.............48 C3
Avondale Rd
  Newport P030...........20 E6
  Portsmouth P01.........53 F7
  Avon Ho **8** S014......51 C6
Avro Cl S015.............50 A7
Aylesbury Rd P02.........53 F8
Aylett Cl P035...........36 A6
Aylward St P01...........53 A5
Aynsley Ct S015..........50 D7

B

Back of the Walls **28**
  S014.................51 A3
Bacon Cl S019............51 F1
Badger La P030...........28 F4
Badgers Cl P038..........42 C4
Badger Terr P03...........3 A5
Bagshot Mews S019.......51 F3
Bagwich La P038..........33 A1
Bailey Cl P033...........12 D5
Bailey's Rd P05...........54 C2
Bakers Ct P033...........11 F5
Baker St P01.............53 D7
Balchin Ho **18** P01......53 A5
Ballard Ct **1** P012......52 B5
Balliol Rd P02............53 E8
Balmoral Ct
  4 Southampton, Millbrook
  S015................50 A6
  7 Southampton S017..51 A8
Banas Cl P038............47 B7
Banbury Cl P033..........12 E4
Bangor Rd S015..........50 B6
Banister Ct **6** S015.....50 F7
Banister Gdns S015.......50 F7
Banister Grange **9** S015.50 F7
Banister Inf Sch S015......50 F7
Banister Mews S015.......50 F7
BANISTER'S PARK........50 E7
Bank Cotts P030..........17 E7
Bank Gdns **9** P033.....12 C5
Bankhill Dr S041.........48 D5
Bank Pl P033............12 C5
Bankside
  Lymington S041.........48 D6
  Shalfleet P030.........17 E7
Bankview S041...........48 D6
Banner La P030...........20 C8
Bannock Rd P038.........45 D6
Barclay Ho **8** P012.....52 E5
Barfield P033............12 C5
Barfields S041...........48 E4
Barfields Ct **2** S041....48 E4
Bargate Mon Mus* S014..51 A4
Bargate Sh Ctr **8** S014..51 A4
Bargate St S014..........50 F4
Barge La P033...........10 F5
Barham Ct P012..........52 B7
Barham Dr P031..........3 A5
Baring Rd P031...........2 E5
Barkis Ho **8** P01.......53 D7
Barkshire Ct **7** S015....50 F7
Barn Cl P038............46 B4
Barnes Rd P01...........53 E6
Barnfield Cl S019........51 E1
Barnfield Ct S019........51 F1
Barnfield Flats P035......51 F1
Barnfield Rd
  Portsmouth S019.......25 E4
  Southampton S019......51 F1
Barnfield Way S019.......51 F1
Barns The P030..........20 B5
Baronsmere P012.........52 A5
Barrack Shute P038.......45 B3
Barrington Ho **20** P01...53 D7
Barrington Row P030.....18 A2
Bars Hill P031............3 A5
Bartlett Ho **2** S017.....51 B8
Bartletts Cl P036.........34 E7
BARTON.................20 F7
Barton Cl P02.............9 F8
Barton Prim Sch P030.....20 F7
Barton Prim Sch & Early
  Years Ctr P030.........20 F6
Barton Rd
  East Cowes P032.........3 F2
  Newport P030..........20 E7
Bartons Cnr
  Ryde P033.............11 E4
  Shalfleet P030.........17 F6
Bartons Ct **8** P012.....52 B6
Bartonwood Rd P032......4 A1
Basepoint Ent Ctr S014...51 B3
Basing Ho S015...........50 C7
Basin St P02.............52 F5
Baskets La **2** P041.....11 D6
BATHINGBOURNE........34 B4
Bathingbourne La P036...34 B4
Bathing La P01...........52 F5
Bath Rd
  Cowes P031.............3 B5
  Lymington S041.........49 A3
  Portsmouth P04.........53 F3

Bath Rd continued
  Ventnor P038...........46 F5
Bath Sq P01.............52 F5
Bath St S014.............51 A7
Battenburg Rd P012.......52 C6
Battery Rd P01...........53 A3
Battery Row P01..........52 E5
Batts Rd P037............33 B7
Bay CE School Prim Site The
  P036.................35 E6
Bay CE School Sec Site The
  P036.................35 E6
Bay Ct P038.............47 B6
Bayfields P05............54 B1
Baynton Ho S041.........48 D4
Bay Rd P040.............20 F7
Bays Ct S041............48 C4
Bays Rd S041............48 C3
Bayswater Ho P05........54 C1
Baythorn Rd P02.........53 D7
Bay View Ct P036.........35 D2
Bay View Rd P031.........2 D3
Beachfield Rd
  Bembridge P035........25 F3
  Sandown P036.........35 F5
  Wroxall P038..........42 B4
Beach House La P035.....25 F5
Beach Rd
  Bembridge P035........25 C6
  Portsmouth P05........53 D1
Beachside P031...........3 C1
Beacon Alley P030........41 B7
Beaconsfield Rd P038.....47 B6
Beadmans Cr P030.......21 A7
Beaper Shute P033, P036..24 B6
Beatrice Ave
  Cowes P032.............9 E8
  Shanklin P037..........43 D8
Beatrice Cl P033.........11 F5
Beatrice Rd
  Portsmouth P04........53 E2
  Southampton S015......50 C7
Beatrice Terr P030........20 E8
Beatty Ho **9** P01.......54 C4
Beauchamp Dr P030......21 A7
Beaufort Rd **7** P05.....53 D1
Beaulieu Ho **2** S015....50 F7
Beaumont Ct P012.......52 A9
Beckfield Cross P038......40 A7
Beckford Rd P031.........3 B4
Beck St P01.............53 B5
Bedbury La P040.........27 B7
Beddow Hall **3** P05....54 A2
Bedford Ave S019........51 E2
Bedford Pl S015..........50 F6
BEDFORD PLACE........50 F6
Bedford Row P030........20 C6
Bedford St
  Gosport P012...........52 A7
  Portsmouth P05........54 B2
Bedhampton Ho **4** P04..54 C4
Bedhampton Rd P02......53 F8
Bedworth Pl **3** P033....12 C5
Beecham Rd P01.........53 F7
Beech Ave S018..........51 E7
Beechcroft Dr P033.......10 D5
Beechcroft Rd P012.......52 B4
Beech Ct
  Shanklin P037..........43 C6
  Southampton S019......51 F3
Beeches The P036.........35 D3
Beechfield Ct S015........50 B8
Beech Gr
  Gosport P012...........52 A4
  Ryde P033.............12 A6
Beech Rd
  Newport P030..........20 E7
  Southampton S015......50 B6
Beech Tree Dr P037.......35 C1
Beechwood Gdns S018....51 F8
Beechwood Ho S017......51 C8
Beechwood Jun Sch S018..51 F7
Beehive Wlk **1** P01.....53 A4
Beeston Ct P01...........53 E7
Behrendt Cl P012.........54 B1
Belgrave Cr P038.........46 F5
Belgrave Rd P038.........47 A5
Bellamy Ct S017.........51 D8
Bellecroft Dr P030........20 F7
BELLEVUE...............51 A6
Bellevue Rd
  Cowes P031.............3 A3
  Ryde P033.............12 D6
  Southampton S015......51 A6
Bellevue Terr
  Portsmouth S015.......54 A1
  10 Portsmouth P05...54 A1
Bellmeade La P030........20 F8
Bell St S041.............51 A3
Belmont La P032..........9 F3
Belmont Pl P05...........54 A2
Belmont Rd S041.........54 B1
Belmore Cl P01...........53 E7
Belmore Cl S014.........48 D3
Belmore Ho **1** S041....48 E2
Belmore La S041.........48 E4
Belmore Rd S041.........48 D3
Belvedere St P033........12 C5
BELVIDERE..............51 C5
Belvidere Ho **2** S014...51 C5
Belvidere Rd S014........51 C5
Belvidere Terr S014.......51 C5
BEMBRIDGE.............25 C4
Bembridge Airport P035...25 A2
Bembridge CE Prim Sch
  P035.................25 D4
Bembridge Cres P04......53 E1

Bembridge Her Str*
  P035.................25 C5
Bembridge House Cl
  P035.................25 C4
Bembridge Trail P030.....21 A2
Bembridge Windmill*
  P035.................25 B3
Bemister's La **5** P012...52 E5
Benbow Ho **6** P01......53 A5
Benbow Pl P01...........53 A5
Beneficial St **14** P01....53 A5
Benett St P033...........12 D5
Benjamen Mews P036.....35 F5
Benson Rd S015..........50 B8
Bentham Rd P012........52 B4
Bentley Way S041.........48 D6
Bently Way S041.........48 D7
Benton Cl P032...........3 D3
Beresford Rd S041........48 C4
Berkeley Cl S015.........50 E7
Berkeley Rd S015........50 F6
Berkeley The P05.........53 E1
Berkshire Cl P01..........54 D3
Bernard Mews **8** P031..3 B4
Bernard Rd P033..........3 B4
Bernard St S014..........51 A3
Bernard Way P030........20 D8
Berry Cl P030............20 F6
Berry Hill P036...........35 C4
Berry Ho **9** P01........53 D7
Berrylands P035..........35 D7
Berrymead P036.........42 C4
Berry Shute P030.........32 A1
Beryton Cl P012..........52 A7
Beryton Rd P012.........52 A7
Bettesworth Rd
  Portsmouth P01........53 E7
  Ryde P033.............12 B3
Betty Haunt La P030......19 C6
Bevan Cl S019...........51 E1
Bevis Rd P012...........52 B6
Bevois Gdns S014........51 B8
Bevois Hill S014..........51 B8
Bevois Mans **7** S014...51 B8
Bevois Mews **4** S014...51 B8
BEVOIS MOUNT.........51 A8
BEVOIS TOWN...........51 A8
Bevois Town Prim Sch
  S014................51 A7
BEVOIS VALLEY.........51 B7
Bevois Valley Rd S014.....51 B7
Biddlesgate Ct **5** S014..50 F3
BIERLEY.................41 A1
Bignor Pl **15** P030......20 D6
Billington Pl S041.........48 D2
Bill Sargent Cres P01......54 D4
Bindon Ct **13** S018.....51 F8
Binfield Cnr P032..........9 F4
Bingham Dr S041.........48 E3
BINSTEAD...............11 F5
Binstead Hill P033........11 F5
Binstead Lodge Rd
  P033.................11 F4
Binstead Prim Sch P033...11 F4
Binstead Rd P033........12 A5
Birch Cl S041............48 B3
Birch Gr
  East Cowes P032.........3 D3
  Freshwater P040.......14 E2
Birch Ct S041............48 B2
Birch Gdns
  Newport P030..........20 C7
  Ryde P033.............11 F5
Birchmore La P030.......32 F8
Birchwood Cl **7** S018...51 E8
Birdham Ct P033.........11 F5
Birkenshaw **8** P031....14 D1
Birmingham Rd P031......3 B4
Bishops Cl P036..........35 E6
Bishops Cres S019........51 F4
Bishops Rd S019.........51 E4
Bishop St P01............53 A5
Bishops Way P030........9 C1
Bittern Cl P012...........52 B8
BITTERNE................51 F8
Bitterne CE Prim Sch
  S019................51 F7
Bitterne Manor Ho S018..51 C7
Bitterne Manor Prim Sch
  S018................51 D7
Bitterne Road E S018.....51 E7
Bitterne Sta S018.........51 D7
Bitterne Way
  Lymington S041........48 D2
  Southampton S019......51 D7
Bittern Pl P030...........9 E4
Blackberry Cl P030.......20 F8
Blackberry La P031........3 A4
Blackberry Terr S014......51 B7
Blackbridge Rd P040.....27 C7
Blackfriars Cl **3** P05....54 C3
Blackfriars Rd P05........54 C3
BLACKGANG..............44 D4
Blackgang Chine* P038...44 E4
Blackgang Rd P038.......44 E4
Blackgang Chine Theme Pk*
  P038.................44 D4
Blacklands
  P030, P033............21 D8
Blackman Cl P036.........35 C3
Blacksmiths La P041......16 D6
Blackthorn Cl
  Lymington S041........48 B2
  Newport P030..........20 C7
  Ryde P033.............12 D4
  Southampton S019......51 F5
Blackthorn Rd S019......51 F5

Blackthorn Terr P01.......53 A6
BLACKWATER.............20 E1
Blackwater Hollow P030,
  P038.................32 F7
Blackwater Junc P030.....20 F1
Blackwater Rd P033......20 E1
Blackwood Ho **13** P01..53 D7
Blake Cl **6** P012........52 E5
Blake Ho **5** P01........53 A4
Blake Rd
  Gosport P012...........52 C6
  Portsmouth P01........53 A4
Blechynden Terr S015.....50 E5
Blendworth Ho **2** P01..54 C4
Blenheim Gdns P012......52 B9
Blighmont Ave S015.......50 B6
Blighmont Cres S015......50 B6
Bloomfield Cotts P033....24 F7
Bloomsbury Pk P030......9 B1
Bloomsbury Wlk S019....51 C2
Blossom Sq P01..........53 B4
Blount Rd P01............53 B3
Blue Anchor La **10** S014..50 F3
Blue Reef Aquarium*
  P05.................53 C1
Bluett Ave P034..........13 D4
Blythe Shute P038........44 D5
Blythe Way P037.........43 A8
Blyth Mews **2** S015.....50 E6
Boardwalk Way S040.....50 A3
Boarhunt Cl P01..........54 C3
Boldens Rd P012.........52 B2
Boldre La S041...........48 D8
Bolton Dr P012...........52 C8
Boltons The P033.........10 F5
BONCHURCH.............47 D6
Bonchurch Pottery*
  P038.................47 C7
Bonchurch Shute P038....47 D7
Bonchurch Village Rd
  P038.................47 C7
Bond St S014.............51 C6
Bonfire Cnr P01..........53 A6
Bosham Rd P02..........53 F8
BOULDNOR..............15 F6
Bouldnor Mead P041......15 F6
Boulton Rd P05..........54 D1
Boundary Dr P032........4 B3
Bound Rd P040..........14 F2
Bourn Cl P033............11 E4
Bournemouth Ave P012...52 A9
Bourne Rd S015..........50 D5
BOWCOMBE..............19 E2
Bowcombe Bsns Pk P030..19 C2
Bowcombe Rd P030......19 E3
Bowdens Mead Cl P030...19 C7
Bower Cl S019............51 F1
Bower The P034..........34 F5
Bower Ave P01...........53 F6
Bowler Ct P01............53 F6
Bowling Green La **13**
  P030.................54 C4
Boxgrove Ho P01.........54 C4
Bracken Dell P037........43 C4
Brackens Way S041.......48 F2
Bracklesham Cl S019.....51 F3
Bradford Junc P05........54 C4
Bradford Rd P05..........54 C2
BRADING................24 B2
Brading CE Prim Sch
  P036.................24 A3
Brading Marshes RSPB
  Reserve* P035........25 D4
Brading Museum & Visitor
  Ctr * P036...........24 B2
Brading Rd P033.........12 E2
Brading Sta P036.........24 A2
Braeside Cl S019.........51 E5
Braeside Cres S019.......51 E5
Braeside Rd S019.........51 E5
Bramber Rd P012.........52 A4
Bramble Inf Sch P05......53 E4
Bramble Rd P04..........53 E4
Brambles La P031..........2 E5
Brambles The
  Apse Heath P036......34 E3
  Bembridge P035.......25 E4
Bramble Wlk S041........48 C4
Bramdean Mews S019....51 C1
Bramley Cl S041..........48 E2
Bramley Gdns P012......52 B2
Bramley Ho
  Gosport P012...........52 B2
  3 Portsmouth P05...54 B2
Bramleys P030...........20 A6
Bramsdon Ct **5** P04....53 F2
Bramshott Rd P04........53 F4
Bramston Rd S015.......50 C8
Brandon Ct P05..........54 D1
Brandon Ho P05..........54 D1
Brandon Rd P05..........53 D2
Brannon Way P033.......10 F4
BRANSTONE.............34 D3
Branstone Cross P036....34 D3
Braxton Mdw P041.......15 A5
Brecon Ho P01...........53 A4
Brewer St P01............54 B4
Brewhouse Sq P012......52 D7
Briary Ct P031............2 E5
Brickets Terr P012........52 B3
Brickfield La
  Freshwater P039.......27 A8
  Lymington S041.......48 F5
Brickfields Way P036.....36 A4
Briddlesford Rd P030,
  P033.................21 F6

Bridge Ho S015. . . . . .50 C5
Bridge Rd
  Cowes PO31. . . . . .3 B4
  East Cowes PO32 . . . . .3 C4
  Lymington S041. . . . . .48 F5
  Southampton S019 . . . . .51 D3
  6 Yarmouth PO41 . . . . . . .15 C6
Bridge Sh Ctr The PO1 . . . . .54 C3
Bridgeside CI PO1 . . . . .54 C3
Bridge Sq PO32. . . . . .3 C4
Bridge Terr **8** S014 . . . . . .51 B3
Bridgeway PO33 . . . . .10 E5
Bridgeway The S019 . . . . . . .51 E3
Bridgwater Ct S015. . . . . . . .50 D5
Bridlington Ave S015 . . . . . .50 D8
Bridport Ct S015. . . . . .50 C5
Bridport St PO1 . . . . .54 B3
BRIGHSTONE. 30 C2
Brighstone CE Prim Sch
  PO30 . . . . .30 B2
Brighstone Forest Wlk*
  PO30 . . . . .30 A6
Brighstone Mus* PO30 . . . . .30 B2
Brighton Rd S041 . . . . .50 F7
Brigstoke Terr PO13. . . . . . . .12 C6
Brinkcliffe Gdns PO36. . . . . .35 E3
Brinton CI PO32 . . . . .3 D1
Brinton's Rd S014 . . . . .51 B5
Brinton's Terr S014 . . . . .51 A6
Brisbane Ho **14** PO1. . . . . .53 D7
Bristol Rd PO4. . . . . .53 F2
Britain St PO1. . . . . .53 A5
Britannia Ct S014. . . . . .51 C5
Britannia PI S041. . . . . .48 F4
Britannia Rd
  Portsmouth PO5 . . . . .54 C2
  Southampton S014 . . . . .51 B5
Britannia Road N PO5. . . . . .54 D2
Britannia Way
  East Cowes PO32 . . . . .3 C2
  Gosport PO12 . . . . .52 C8
Britannic Ho **5** S014 . . . . .51 C5
Briton St S014. . . . . .51 A3
Brittany CI S040 . . . . .50 A1
Broadbeach Ct PO36. . . . . . .35 E4
Broadfields Ave PO31 . . . . . .2 F2
Broad Gn **2** S014 . . . . . . .51 A4
Broad La
  Brighstone PO30 . . . . .30 B1
  Lymington S041. . . . . .48 F2
  Southampton S014 . . . . .50 F3
Broadlea Prim Sch PO36 .35 D3
Broadly CI S041 . . . . .48 B2
Broadmead Ct **2** S041 . . .48 F2
Broadsmith Ave PO32 . . . . . .3 D2
Broad St PO1. . . . . .52 F4
Broadstone Cres PO36 . . . . . .24 B3
Broadway PO36. . . . . .35 F5
Broadway Cres PO33. . . . . . .12 A5
Broadway The PO39. . . . . . . .14 D1
Broadwood La PO30 . . . . . . .19 F7
Brockhurst Jun Sch PO12 .52 A8
Brocks Copse Rd PO33 . . . . .10 D6
Brockwood Dr PO37 . . . . . . .43 C8
Brook Rd
  Lymington S041. . . . . .48 F8
  Shalcombe PO41 . . . . .29 B8
  Shanklin PO37 . . . . .43 C8
Brooks CI PO35. . . . . .25 E4
BROOKSIDE. 30 A3
Brookside CI PO40 . . . . .14 F1
Brookside Cres PO38. . . . . . .42 C4
Brookside Rd PO40 . . . . .14 F1
Broomfield La S041. . . . . . . .51 A8
Broomhill CI S041 . . . . .48 B2
Broomlands PO33 . . . . .24 F7
Brougham La PO12 . . . . .52 A7
Brougham Rd PO5. . . . . .54 C2
Brougham St PO12. . . . . .52 A7
Broughton Ho **8** S018. . . .51 E8
Brownings CI S041 . . . . .48 A4
Brownlow CI PO1 . . . . .53 D7
Brownlow Rd PO36. . . . . .35 E4
Bruce Rd PO4 . . . . .53 F2
Brunswick Ct **6** PO31. . . . .3 B4
Brunswick Ho **11** S015 . . .51 A6
Brunswick PI
  Lymington S041. . . . . .48 E4
  Southampton S015 . . . . .51 A6
Brunswick Rd PO31 . . . . .3 B4
Brunswick Sq S014. . . . . . . .51 A3
Brunswick St S014 . . . . .54 B2
Bryanston Rd S019. . . . . . . .51 E5

Buckbury CI PO30. . . . . .21 A7
Buckbury Hts PO30 . . . . .21 B6
Buckbury La PO30 . . . . .21 B7
Buckingham CI PO33. . . . . . .12 B6
Buckingham Cres PO30 . . . . .8 F1
Buckingham Ct **2** S017. . .51 A8
Buckingham Gn PO1. . . . . . .53 D7
Buckingham Rd PO33 . . . . . .12 C6
Buckingham St PO1. . . . . . . .54 B4
BUCKLAND
  Lymington 48 D5
  Portsmouth. 53 E8
Buckland Ct S041. . . . . .48 E5
Buckland Dene S041. . . . . . .48 D5
Buckland Gdns
  Lymington S041. . . . . .48 D6
  Ryde PO33 . . . . .11 E6
Buckland Grange PO33. . . . .12 A6
Buckland Path PO2 . . . . .53 D7
Bucklands Ct **2** PO32. . . . .3 C4
Buckland View S041 . . . . . . .48 E5
Bucklers Ct S041 . . . . .48 D3
Bucklers Dr PO33 . . . . .12 B4
Bucklers Mews S041 . . . . . . .48 D3
Bucklers Rd PO33 . . . . .12 B4
Bucklers View PO31. . . . . . . .52 C9
Bugle St S014 . . . . .50 F3
Bullar Rd S018 . . . . .51 E8
Bullar St S014 . . . . .51 B6
Bullen Cross PO33 . . . . .13 B3
Bullen Rd PO33 . . . . .12 F2
BULLEN VILLAGE 12 F2
Bull Ring PO30 . . . . .20 A6
Bullys Hill PO36. . . . . .24 A2
Bunkers La PO38. . . . . .32 F5
Buona Vista Rd PO38. . . . . . .47 B5
Buona Vista Terr PO38. . . . . .47 B5
Burgoyne Rd PO5 . . . . .53 D1
Buriton Ct S019 . . . . .51 E3
Buriton St PO1 . . . . .54 C4
Burleigh Rd PO2 . . . . .53 F7
Burley Ho **7** S016 . . . . . . .50 B8
Burlington Mans **1** S015 . .50 C7
Burlington Rd S015. . . . . . . .50 C6
Burnaby Rd PO1 . . . . .53 B4
Burney Ho **8** PO12 . . . . . .52 C5
Burnham's Wlk **2** PO12. . .52 D5
Burnt House La
  Alverstone PO36. . . . . .35 B7
  Downend PO30 . . . . .21 C4
Burrard Gr S041. . . . . .48 F2
Burt CI PO30. . . . . .17 D7
Burton Rd S015 . . . . .50 E6
Bury CI PO12 . . . . .52 B5
Bury Cres PO12. . . . . .52 B5
Bury Cross PO12. . . . . .52 A5
Bury Rd PO12 . . . . .52 A5
Bush Ho PO5 . . . . .54 B1
Bush St E PO5 . . . . .54 B1
Bush St W PO5 . . . . .54 A1
Butcher St PO1. . . . . .53 A5
Butler Gdns S041. . . . . .48 D6
Butterfly World* PO33. . . . . .10 B2
Butt's Rd PO33 . . . . .12 A3
Byams La S040 . . . . .50 A2
Byerley Rd PO1 . . . . .53 F5
Byron CI S015. . . . . .50 E6
Byron Rd PO2 . . . . .53 F8

C

Cable St **2** S014 . . . . .51 C5
Cadets Wlk PO32 . . . . .3 D2
Cadington Ho **9** PO1 . . . .53 A5
Cadland CI S041 . . . . .51 C2
Caernarvon Lodge PO37. . . . .35 C1
Caesars Rd PO30 . . . . .20 C7
Cairo Terr PO1. . . . . .53 D7
CALBOURNE 18 B1
Calbourne Rd PO30 . . . . .19 D4
Calbourne Water Mill*
  PO30 . . . . .17 E2
Caldecote Wlk **7** PO5 . . . .54 B2
Calder Ho **10** PO1. . . . . . .53 A5
Calloway CI PO30 . . . . .22 A1
Callvendale Ho PO30. . . . . . .20 C7
Calshot Ct S014 . . . . .51 C2
Calthorpe Rd PO33. . . . . . . .13 A4
Camber PI **1** PO1 . . . . . . .53 A3
Cambrian Terr PO1. . . . . .53 D7
Cambridge Ct **17** S014. . .51 A8
Cambridge Junc PO1 . . . . . . .53 B4
Cambridge Rd
  East Cowes PO32 . . . . .3 C5
  Portsmouth PO1. . . . . .53 D7
  Southampton S014 . . . . .51 A8
Camden Ct PO33. . . . . .12 D6
Camden St PO12. . . . . .52 A7
Camden Terr **2** PO12 . . . . .52 A7
CAMDENTOWN 52 A6
Cameron CI
  Freshwater PO40. . . . . .27 B8
  2 Newport PO30 . . . . . . .9 A1
Camley CI S019. . . . . .51 E1
Campbell Rd PO5. . . . . .54 D1
Campbell St S014. . . . . .51 C6
Campfield Rd PO32 . . . . .9 F8
CAMP HILL 8 E1
Campion Way S041. . . . . . . .48 E5
Camp Rd PO40. . . . . .27 B8
Canada Ct **8** PO12 . . . . . .52 C9
Canada Rd S014 . . . . .51 E2
Canalside The PO1. . . . . .53 A4
Canal Wlk
  Portsmouth PO1. . . . . .54 C3

Southampton S014 . . . . .51 A3
Canberra Ho PO1 . . . . .54 B3
Candlemas PI **13** S017 . . .51 A8
Cannon Ho S014 . . . . .48 E4
Cannon St
  Lymington S041. . . . . .48 E4
  Southampton S015 . . . . .50 C8
Canteen Rd PO38. . . . . .34 D1
Canterbury Rd PO4 . . . . .53 F3
Canute Ct S015. . . . . .50 F6
Canute Ho **10** S014 . . . . .51 A3
Canute Rd S014 . . . . .51 B3
Captains PI S014 . . . . .51 B3
Captains Row **5** PO1 . . . . .53 A3
Captain's Row S041 . . . . . . .48 F4
CARISBROOKE 20 B5
Carisbrooke Castle*
  PO30 . . . . .20 B4
Carisbrooke Castle Mus*
  PO30 . . . . .20 B4
Carisbrooke CE Prim Sch
  PO30 . . . . .20 B5
Carisbrooke Dr S019 . . . . . . .51 F6
Carisbrooke High Sch
  PO30 . . . . .20 A6
Carisbrooke Rd
  Gosport PO12 . . . . .52 C6
  Newport PO30. . . . . .20 C6
Carlisle Ct **3** S016 . . . . . .50 B8
Carlisle Rd
  Portsmouth PO5 . . . . .54 C3
  Southampton S016 . . . . .50 B8
Carlton Commerce Ctr The
  S014 . . . . .51 B7
Carlton Cres S015 . . . . .50 F6
Carlton Ct **6** S015. . . . . . .50 F8
Carlton Ho **4** S041 . . . . . .48 E4
Carlton Ho **6** S015. . . . . . .50 F6
Carlton Rd
  Gosport PO12 . . . . .52 C6
  Portsmouth PO2 . . . . .53 F8
  Southampton S015 . . . . .50 F7
Carlton Way **7** PO12. . . . . .52 C6
Carlyle Rd PO12 . . . . .52 B6
Carnarvon Rd
  Gosport PO12 . . . . .52 A5
  Portsmouth PO2 . . . . .53 F8
Caroline Ct S015 . . . . .50 B7
Caroline PI PO12 . . . . .52 B7
Carolyn CI S019 . . . . .51 E2
Carpathia Dr **19** S014. . . .51 B3
Carpenter CI
  Lymington S041. . . . . .48 D5
  Sandown S036. . . . . .35 D3
CARPENTERS 24 E6
Carpenters La PO30 . . . . .20 B4
Carpenters Quay PO30 . . . . .20 E8
Carpenters Rd PO33, PO36 .24 D6
Carronades The **3** S014 . . .51 A5
Carter Ave PO37 . . . . .43 B8
Carter Ho **18** PO1 . . . . . . .53 A5
Carters Rd PO33. . . . . .43 C8
Carter St PO36 . . . . .35 F6
Carval Ct PO31 . . . . .3 B5
Carvel La PO31 . . . . .3 B5
Cascades App PO1. . . . . .54 B4
Cascades Sh Ctr PO1 . . . . . .54 B4
Castle CI
  Portsmouth PO5 . . . . .54 B1
  Ventnor PO38 . . . . .46 E5
Castle Crag PO30 . . . . .20 A5
Castle Ct
  Southampton, Millbrook
    S015. . . . . .50 A6
  Ventnor PO38 . . . . .46 D5
Castlehaven La PO38. . . . . . .45 A2
Castle Hill
  Carisbrooke PO30 . . . . .20 B4
  1 East Cowes PO32. . . . .3 C4
  Wroxall PO38. . . . . .42 C5
Castle La
  Carisbrooke PO30 . . . . .20 B4
  1 East Cowes S014. . . . .50 F3
  Wroxall PO38. . . . . .42 C5
Castle Mews S014 . . . . .50 F3
Castle Rd
  Cowes PO31 . . . . .3 B5
  Newport PO30. . . . . .20 C5
  Ventnor PO38 . . . . .46 F5
  Wroxall PO38. . . . . .42 C5
Castle Sq **4** S014 . . . . . . .50 F3
Castle St
  Carisbrooke PO30 . . . . .20 B5
  East Cowes PO32 . . . . .3 C4
  Ryde PO33 . . . . .12 C6
Castleton Cr PO5 . . . . .54 A1
Castle View PO12 . . . . .52 B9
Castle Way S041 . . . . .50 F3
Catherine Terr PO30 . . . . . . .20 D8
Catisfield Ho **3** PO1 . . . . .54 C4
Causeway Ct **5** S018 . . . . .51 E8
Causeway The PO40. . . . . . . .27 E8
Cavalier Quay PO32 . . . . .3 C3
Cavendish Gr S017 . . . . .50 F8
Cavendish Mews **3** S015 . .50 F8
Cavendish PI PO30 . . . . .20 C6
Cavendish Rd PO5 . . . . .54 C1
Caws Ave PO34 . . . . .13 D2
Cawte Rd **11** S015 . . . . . .50 C6
Cecil Gr PO5 . . . . .54 A1
Cecil PI PO5 . . . . .54 A1
Cedar Ave S015 . . . . .50 D8
Cedar Ct PO37. . . . . .35 C2
Cedar Gdns S014 . . . . .51 A8
Cedar Hill PO30. . . . . .20 B5

Cedar Rd S014 . . . . .51 A7
Cedar Wood Dr PO34 . . . . . .13 D2
Ceder Ho S014 . . . . .51 B3
Cement Terr **2** S014. . . . . .50 F3
Cemetery Rd
  Ryde PO33. . . . . .11 E5
  Sandown PO36. . . . . .35 D2
  Southampton S015 . . . . .50 F8
Centaur St PO2 . . . . .53 D8
Central Bridge S014 . . . . . . .51 B3
Central Cres S040 . . . . .50 A3
Central Rd S014 . . . . .51 A2
Central Sq PO1 . . . . .53 A4
Central St PO1 . . . . .54 C4
Central Station Bridge
  S015. . . . . .51 C5
Central Trading Est S014. . . .51 C4
Central Way PO36. . . . . .35 C6
Centurion Ct **24** PO1 . . . .53 A4
Centurion Ho S018. . . . . . . .51 C7
Centurion Ind Pk S018. . . . .51 C7
Cessac Ho PO12 . . . . .52 C2
Chadderton Gdns **1** PO1. .53 B3
Chafen Rd S018 . . . . .51 D7
Chain La PO30. . . . . .20 D7
CHALE. 44 C7
Chale Gn PO38 . . . . .40 A4
CHALE GREEN. 40 A4
Chale La PO38. . . . . .40 A4
Chale St PO38 . . . . .44 C7
Challenger Dr PO12. . . . . . . .52 C8
Challis Ct **10** S014 . . . . . .51 A3
Chalton Ho PO1 . . . . .54 B4
Chambers Dr PO36. . . . . .34 F5
Chanctonbury Ho PO5 . . . . .54 B3
Chandler CI PO30. . . . . .20 C5
Chandlers Ct **22** S014 . . .51 A3
Chandlers The PO31 . . . . . . .2 F3
Chandos Ho **3** S014 . . . . .51 A3
Chandos Sq **12** S014 . . . .51 A3
Channel Way S014. . . . . .51 C2
Channon Ct **11** S015 . . . .50 E7
Chantry Rd
  Gosport PO12 . . . . .52 A8
  Portsmouth PO2 . . . . .53 F7
CHAPEL. 51 B4
Chapel CI PO30 . . . . .20 A6
Chapel Ct **1** PO1. . . . . . . .54 C1
Chapel La PO30. . . . . .33 C7
Chapel Rd
  Ryde PO33 . . . . .11 E5
  Southampton S014 . . . . .51 B4
Chapel St
  Gosport PO12 . . . . .52 B9
  Newport PO30. . . . . .20 D6
  Portsmouth, Buckland PO2 .53 D8
  3 Portsmouth PO5. . . . . .54 A1
  Southampton S014 . . . . .51 B4
Charlecote Ho S015 . . . . . . .50 C5
Charles Dickens' Birthplace
  Mus* PO1 . . . . .53 C7
Charles Dickens St PO1. . . . .53 B4
Charles Knott Gdns S015. . . .50 F7
Charles Miller Ct **9** S015 .50 F8
Charles Norton-Thomas Ct
  4 PO1. . . . . .53 B5
Charles Rd PO31. . . . . .2 F4
Charles St
  Portsmouth PO5 . . . . .54 C4
  Southampton S014 . . . . .51 A3
Charles Wyatt Ho **8**
  S014 . . . . .51 A7
Charliejoy Gdns **1** S041 . .51 C6
Charlott Ct PO5. . . . . .54 B1
Charlotte Ct S019. . . . . .51 F2
Charlotte Dr PO12 . . . . .52 C8
Charlotte Mews PO12. . . . . . .52 A3
Charlotte PI S014. . . . . .51 A6
Charlotte St PO1. . . . . .51 B4
Charlton House Sch S018 .51 E8
Charlton Rd S015 . . . . .50 D7
Charnwood CI PO30. . . . . . . .20 C7
Charnwood Cotts PO36. . . . .24 A3
Charter Ho **2** PO5. . . . . . .54 A2
Chase The PO36 . . . . .34 F4
Chatfield Ave PO2 . . . . .53 A8
Chatfield Ho PO1. . . . . .54 C4
Chatfield Lodge PO30. . . . . .20 D5
Chatfield Rd PO38 . . . . .45 C5
Chatham CI PO12. . . . . .52 C8
Chatham Dr PO1 . . . . .53 B3
Chatsworth Ave PO37 . . . . . .43 A7
Chatsworth Ct PO5. . . . . .54 D1
Chatsworth Mews PO36. . . . .36 A4
Chawton Farm Barns PO31 .9 A6
Chawton La PO31 . . . . .9 A6
Cheddar CI S019. . . . . .51 E3
Cheeryble Ho **16** PO1 . . . .53 D7
Chelsea Rd PO5 . . . . .54 C1
Chelsfield Ave PO36. . . . . . . .35 D2
Chequers CI S041. . . . . .48 B3
Chequers Inn Rd PO38 . . . . .33 A3
Cheriton CI **5** S015 . . . . . .50 C6
Cherry Blossom Ct **8**
  PO1. . . . . .53 D7
Cherry Ct **16** S017 . . . . . .51 A8
Cherry Side PO36 . . . . .35 D3
Cherrytree Rd PO34. . . . . . . .13 D2
Cherry Wlk S015 . . . . .50 C8
Cherrywood View PO30. . . . .22 A1
Cheshell Ave S019 . . . . .51 F7
Chessel Cres S019 . . . . .51 F7
CHESSELL. 29 B8
Chessell CI PO31. . . . . .8 E8
Chessell Pottery* PO41. .29 B8

Chester Cts **8** PO12 . . . . . .52 C5
Chester PI PO7. . . . . .53 D2
Chestnut Ave PO4. . . . . .53 F4
Chestnut CI
  Newport PO30. . . . . .20 E5
  Ryde PO33. . . . . .11 E4
  Ventnor PO38 . . . . .46 E7
Chestnut Ct **1** PO30 . . . . .20 D6
Chestnut Gr PO33. . . . . .12 F4
Chestnut Mews PO37. . . . . . .43 C6
Chetwynd Rd PO4 . . . . .53 F3
Cheverton Shute PO30. . . . . .31 B5
Chewter CI PO4. . . . . .53 E1
Chichester CI PO36 . . . . .35 E4
Chichester Rd PO2 . . . . .53 E8
Chichester Wlk PO30 . . . . . .20 F7
CHILLERTON 32 C5
Chillerton & Rookley Prim
  Sch PO30 . . . . .32 C5
Chiltern Ct
  Gosport PO12 . . . . .52 B6
  2 Portsmouth PO5. . . . . .53 D1
CHILTON GREEN. 29 E2
Chilton La PO30 . . . . .29 F2
Chilworth Gr PO12. . . . . .52 A6
Chine Ave
  Shanklin PO37 . . . . .43 C7
  Southampton S019 . . . . .51 E6
Chine Ct PO40 . . . . .14 C2
Chine La PO30 . . . . .38 H7
Chivers CI PO5. . . . . .54 B1
Chiverton Wlk PO30 . . . . . . .21 A7
Christie Ct S018 . . . . .51 E8
Christ the King Coll PO30 .20 B5
Church Ct PO33. . . . . .10 E5
Church Ct S033. . . . . .10 E5
Church End S015 . . . . .50 C8
Church Hill
  Godshill PO38 . . . . .41 D8
  Totland PO39 . . . . .26 G8
Church Hollow PO30 . . . . . . .41 D8
Churchill CI
  Cowes PO31 . . . . .2 F4
  Sandown PO36 . . . . .35 D3
Churchill Mews PO12 . . . . . .52 A7
Churchill Rd PO31 . . . . .2 F4
Church La
  Brading PO36. . . . . .24 B2
  Cowes PO31 . . . . .9 A6
  Cowes PO31 . . . . .9 A8
  Lymington S041. . . . . .48 E3
  Ryde PO33. . . . . .12 C6
  Shalfleet PO30 . . . . .17 E7
  12 Southampton S014 . .50 F3
Church Lane Cotts **14**
  PO33 . . . . .12 C6
Church Litten PO30 . . . . . . .20 E6
Church Mead **3** S041. . . . .48 E2
Church Mews **1** PO12 . . . .52 C5
Church Path
  East Cowes PO32 . . . . .3 C4
  Gosport PO12 . . . . .52 D5
Church Path N PO1 . . . . .54 B4
Church PI
  Chale PO30. . . . . .44 C6
  Freshwater PO40. . . . . .15 B1
Church Rd
  Bembridge PO35. . . . . .25 C5
  Cowes PO31 . . . . .3 A5
  Gosport PO12 . . . . .52 A3
  Gurnard PO31 . . . . .2 D3
  Havenstreet PO33. . . . . .11 C1
  Portsmouth PO1. . . . . .54 C4
  Ryde PO33. . . . . .11 E6
  Shanklin PO37 . . . . .43 B6
  Southampton S019 . . . . .51 D2
  Wootton PO33 . . . . .10 E5
Church St
  Niton PO38 . . . . .45 B4
  Portsmouth PO1. . . . . .54 C4
  Seaview PO34 . . . . .13 D3
  Ventnor PO38 . . . . .47 A6
Church View S019 . . . . .51 D2
Cinnamon Ct **3** S015 . . . .50 E6
Circle The PO5. . . . . .53 D2
Circular Rd
  Portsmouth PO1. . . . . .53 C7
  Ryde PO33. . . . . .12 E3
  Seaview PO34 . . . . .13 D4
City Bldgs PO1 . . . . .54 B4
City Commerce Ctr **6**
  S014 . . . . .51 B3
City Ct **2** S014 . . . . .51 A3
City Ind Pk S015. . . . . .50 C4
Civic Centre Rd S014 . . . . . .51 A4
Clanfield Ho **7** PO1 . . . . . .54 C4
Claremont Cres S015 . . . . . .50 A7
Claremont PI PO31. . . . . .3 B5
Claremont Rd
  Portsmouth PO1. . . . . .54 D3
  Southampton S017 . . . . .50 A7
Clarence Espl PO5 . . . . .53 C1
Clarence Gdns PO37 . . . . . . .35 D1
Clarence Ho **5** S014. . . . . .51 C6
Clarence Par PO5 . . . . .53 C2
Clarence Rd
  East Cowes PO32 . . . . .3 C3
  Gosport PO12 . . . . .52 D6
  Newport PO30. . . . . .20 E6
  Portsmouth PO5 . . . . .53 C1
  Shanklin PO37 . . . . .35 C1
  Ventnor PO38 . . . . .47 B6
  Wroxall PO38. . . . . .42 C3
Clarence St PO1 . . . . .54 B4
Clarendon CI PO36. . . . . .24 B1

Clarendon Ct 6 P05......53 D1
Clarendon Pk S041......48 D2
Clarendon Pl
  Newport P030......20 C5
  Portsmouth P01......54 C4
Clarendon Rd
  Portsmouth, Southsea
    P05......53 D2
  Shanklin P037......43 C8
  Southampton S016......50 A8
Clarendon St
  Newport P030......20 C6
  Portsmouth P01......54 C4
Clarkes Rd P01......53 F6
Classic Boat Mus*
  P04......3 B3
  East Cowes P033......3 C4
CLATTERFORD......20 A4
Clatterford Rd P030......20 A5
Clatterford Shute P030......20 A4
Clausentum Ho S018......51 C7
Clausentum Rd S014......51 B7
Clausen Way S041......48 C1
Claxton St P01......54 C3
CLAYHALL......52 D2
Clayhall Rd P012......52 B3
Clay La P041......17 E3
Clayton Rd P040......14 E1
Clearwater Apartments 5
  P04......53 E1
Cleaver Ho P033......11 C1
Cleaver's Cl P033......11 E4
Cleveland Rd
  Gosport P012......52 B4
  Portsmouth P05......53 D2
Clevelands Rd P038......42 C5
Cleveland Terr P038......42 B5
Cleverley Ho 20 P01......53 A8
Cliff Cl P036......24 B3
Cliff Ct P036......35 E4
Cliff End P040......14 E4
Cliff Farm App P037......42 F7
Cliff Gdns P036......35 E3
Cliff Ho
  Sandown P036......35 E4
  Ventnor P038......47 D7
Cliff La P030......28 C8
Clifford Dibben Mews 1
  S014......51 A8
Clifford St
  Newport P030......20 C6
  Southampton S014......51 B5
Cliff Rd
  Cowes P031......2 F5
  Sandown P036......35 E4
  Southampton S015......50 D5
  Totland P039......26 C8
Cliff The S019......51 D3
Cliff Way P036......35 E3
Clifton Ct 2 S015......50 A8
Clifton Gdns 1 S015......50 A8
Clifton Lodge S015......50 A8
Clifton Rd
  10 Portsmouth P05......53 C2
  Southampton S015......50 A8
Clifton St P01......54 D4
Clifton Terr
  4 Portsmouth P05......53 C2
  4 Totland P040......14 E1
Clinton Rd S041......48 E5
Clissold Rd P030......9 A2
Clive Rd P01......53 E6
Clock St 7 P01......53 E6
Cloisters The
  Lymington S041......48 E3
  Sandown P036......35 E5
Close The P034......13 E2
Clovelly Rd S014......51 B6
Clydebank Rd P02......53 D8
Clyde Ho
  7 Southampton S014......51 C6
  Ventnor P038......47 B6
Coach House La P033......12 A4
Coach House Mews P037......43 C8
Coach La P036......24 A3
Coastal Visitors Ctr*
  P038......47 A5
Coastguard Cotts
  Bembridge P035......37 A6
  Brighstone P030......38 C8
  Brook P030......28 F4
  Little Atherfield P038......39 A3
  Lymington S041......49 A2
  7 Yarmouth P041......15 C6
Coastguard La
  Brook P030......28 F4
  Freshwater Bay P040......27 D6
Cobbett Ct 3 S041......51 E7
Cobbett Rd S018......51 E8
Cobden Ave S018......51 E8
Cobden Cres S018......51 E8
Cobden Ct S018......51 E8
Cobden Dell 3 S018......51 E8
Cobden Marine Ct S017......51 D8
Cobden St P012......52 B6
Coburg Ct S041......51 C6
Coburg Ho 6 S014......51 C6
Coburg St
  Portsmouth P01......54 C4
  Southampton S014......51 C6
Cochrane Ho 18 P01......53 A8
COCKEREL......34 D7
Cockerell Rise P032......3 D2
Cockleshell Sq P012......52 B6
Cockleton La P031......2 E2

Colborne Cl S041......48 E5
Coleman's La
  P030......7 E1
Coleman St S014......51 B4
Colenutt's Rd
  P033......12 A3
Coles Cl P040......14 D2
Coleson Rd S018......51 E8
Collards Cl P040......14 F1
College Cl P036......36 A4
College Keep S014......51 B3
College La 28 P01......53 A5
College Pl 9 S015......51 A4
College Rd
  Newport P030......20 E5
  Portsmouth P01......53 A5
  Southampton S019......51 E2
College St
  Portsmouth P01......53 A5
  Southampton S014......51 A3
College Way P032......3 D2
Collier Cl S017......51 C8
Collingwood Ct P033......12 E5
Collingwood Rd
  Newport P030......20 D6
  Portsmouth P05......53 D2
  Shanklin P037......43 B8
Colmar Way P039......14 D1
Colonnades The P037......43 B6
Colonnade The S019......51 D3
Colpoy St P05......54 A2
Columbine Rd P032......3 C4
Columbus Ho P037......35 D1
COLWELL......14 E2
Colwell Chine P040......14 D2
Colwell Cl P040......14 E2
Colwell Ct P040......14 E2
Colwell Common Rd
  P039......14 D1
Colwell La P040......14 E1
Colwell Rd
  Freshwater P039......14 E2
  Norton Green P040......15 A3
Combley La P030......21 F5
Comforts Farm P031......8 D7
Commercial Pl P01......54 B4
Commercial Rd
  Portsmouth P01......54 B4
  Southampton S015......50 E5
Commodore Cl 2 S014......51 B3
Commodore Pl P012......52 B7
Commodores Ct P034......13 C4
Compass The S014......51 B4
Compton Ho 6 S016......50 B8
Compton Wlk 1 S014......51 A5
Condor Cl S019......51 D3
Conference Pl 5 S041......48 F2
Conifer Cres S041......48 B3
Coniston Ave P033......11 E4
Coniston Dr P033......12 B6
Coniston Pk P037......35 D1
Connaught Rd P032......3 D3
Consort Ho 3 P01......53 D7
Consort Rd P031......3 B4
Constable Cl P012......52 C2
Consulate Ho 3 S014......51 B3
Conway La P039......14 D2
Cook Ave P030......20 F8
Cook St S014......51 A4
Cookworthy Rd P030......9 A2
Coombe La P030......30 B4
Coombe Pk P030......42 B4
Coombe Rd P012......52 B8
Cooper Rd P030......20 F8
Coopers Cl P040......14 E1
Coopers Ct 20 S014......51 A3
Coopers La P041......16 F5
Cooper's La S019......51 E2
Copperfield Ho 1 P01......53 D7
Copper St 13 P05......54 A1
Coppice End P033......12 E2
Coppins Ct P030......20 E7
Copse Butt P035......25 E4
Copse End P036......35 F7
Copsefield Dr P033......12 B6
Copse La
  Blackwater P030......20 D2
  Portsmouth P01......15 A2
Copse Rd P037......43 B8
Corbett Rd P033......12 A3
Corbin Cl S041......48 B2
Corbin Rd S041......48 B2
Corf Rd P030......7 A1
Corhampton Ho 11 P01......54 C4
Cormorant Grove P032......9 F5
Cornaway La P016......51 F5
Cornwall Cres S041......54 C4
Cornwallis Ho P01......54 C4
Cornwall Rd
  Portsmouth P01......53 E5
  Ventnor P038......46 F6
Cornwall St P033......12 D6
Coronado Rd P012......52 B8
Coronation Ave P031......9 A7
Coronation Cotts
  Freshwater P040......27 C8
  7 Yarmouth P040......15 D4
Coronation Gdns P037......35 C1
Coronation Rd P031......3 A4
Corve Hill P030......31 B1
Cosham Cl P030......21 A7
Cossack Gn 1 S014......51 A4
Cotley Way S041......12 F2
Cotswold Cv P033......15 F8
Cottage Gr
  Gosport P012......52 B6
  Portsmouth P05......54 B2

Cottage Grove Prim Sch
  P05......54 B1
Cottage Ho 16 P030......20 D6
Cottage Mews 9 P030......20 D6
Cottage View P01......54 C3
Cotteridge Ho 1 P05......54 C2
Cotton Cl P031......3 A3
Coulmere Rd P012......52 A7
County View P037......35 D2
Court Cl S041......42 C8
Courtenay Pl S041......48 E3
Courtlands 3 S041......48 E4
Court Rd
  Freshwater P040......27 A8
  Southampton S015......50 F7
Court Royal Mews S015......50 F8
Court The S041......48 D2
Courtyard The
  East Cowes P032......3 C3
  Newport P030......9 B2
Cousins Gr P04......53 F2
Coventry Rd S015......50 F6
Cowdray Ho P01......54 C3
COWES......3 B6
Cowes Enterprise Coll
  P031......2 F5
Cowes Prim Sch P031......3 A4
Cowes Maritime Mus*
  P031......3 B4
Cowes Rd P030......9 A5
Cow La P031......3 A4
COWLEASE......47 B6
Cowleaze Hill P037......43 B4
Cowley Rd S041......48 C4
Cowper Rd P01......53 E7
Cox's Cnr P030......20 C1
Cox's Green P036......35 E6
Cox's La S019......51 D3
Cozens Cl S019......51 E1
Crabbe Ct P05......54 B2
Cracknore Hard S040......50 A1
Cracknore Hard La S040......50 A1
Cracknore Ind Pk S040......50 C2
Cracknore Rd S015......50 D5
Craddock Ho P01......54 C3
Craig Ho 8 P05......53 D2
Craigmore Ct P037......35 D1
Cranbourne Rd P012......52 C4
Cranbury Ave S014......51 B6
Cranbury Ct S019......51 F3
Cranbury Pl S014......51 A6
Cranbury Rd S019......51 F3
Cranbury Terr S014......51 A6
Cranbury The 5 S014......51 A6
Cranbury Twrs 6 S014......51 A6
Craneswater Ave P04......53 E2
Craneswater Gate 10 P04......53 E2
Craneswater Jun Sch P04......53 F2
Craneswater Mews 5
  P04......53 E2
Craneswater Pk P04......53 E2
Cranleigh Ave P01......53 B8
Cranleigh Gdns P031......8 F8
Cranleigh Rd S017......51 A8
Cranleigh Rd S016......51 E6
CRANMORE......17 B8
Cranmore Ave P041......5 D1
CRANMORE PARK......16 F8
Cranstoun Cl P039......26 G8
Crasswell St P01......54 C4
Craven St 9 S014......51 A5
Cray Ho P021......52 D5
Creek Gdns P033......10 F6
Creek Rd P012......52 D5
Crescent Ct P037......43 D8
Crescent Rd
  Gosport P012......52 A2
  Sandown P036......36 A3
  Shanklin P037......43 D8
Cressy Rd P02......53 D7
Cresta Ct P04......53 F2
Crocker La P038......45 B6
Crocker St P030......20 D7
Cromwell Ave P032......3 D1
Cromwell Rd S015......50 F7
Crossfield Ave P031......2 F4
CROSSHOUSE......13 C3
Cross House Ctr S014......51 C3
Crosshouse Rd S014......51 C3
Cross La S019......20 F8
Crossland Cl P012......52 C4
Crossley Ct 2 S015......50 C6
Crossley Pl 1 S015......50 E6
Cross Rd
  Sandown P036......35 D3
  Shanklin P037......43 C8
  Southampton S019......51 E7
Cross St
  Brading P036......24 B3
  Cowes P031......3 B4
  Newport P030......20 D6
  Portsmouth P05......54 C2
  Portsmouth, Portsea P01......53 A6
  Ryde, Oakfield P033......12 C6
  Ryde P033......12 C6
  Sandown P036......36 A4
  Shanklin P037......43 C7
Crossway P05......25 E4
Crossways Rd
  Camp Hill P030......8 F1
  East Cowes P032......3 E2
Crossways The P012......52 B7
Crouchers Cross P030......33 D8
Crown Cl
  Cowes P031......3 B5
  Portsmouth P01......54 C4
Crown Mews 1 P012......52 D5

Crown St
  Portsmouth P01......54 C4
  11 Ryde P033......12 C6
  Southampton S015......50 B8
Croxton Rd P01......53 B3
Crozier Rd P041......15 A6
Crundles The P040......15 A1
Crusader Ct 4 P012......52 C8
Cuckoo La 17 S014......50 F3
Culver Parr P036......36 A4
Culver Rd P033......43 D8
Culver Way P036......36 B5
Cumberland Bsns Ctr
  P01......53 A6
Cumberland Ho P01......53 A6
Cumberland House Natural
History Mus* P04......53 F1
Cumberland Pl S015......50 F8
Cumberland Rd P05......54 D3
Cumberland St
  Portsmouth P01......53 A6
  Southampton S014......51 B4
Cunard Ave S015......50 C8
Cunard Rd S014......51 A2
Cunningham Ct 16 P05......53 C2
Cupressus Ave P036......34 E5
Currie Rd P036......35 E4
Curzon Howe Rd P01......53 A5
Curzon Pl S041......48 D2
Cuthbert Rd P01......53 F6
Cut The P031......3 B5
Cygnet Ho P012......52 B8
Cynthia Gr P030......20 F8
Cypress Ave S019......51 F5
Cypress Rd P030......20 E5
Cyprus Rd P02......53 E8

D

Dagmar Mews 24 P05......53 C2
Dairy Crest Rd P030......20 C7
Dairy La P030......20 E5
Daish's La P033......11 F8
Daish Way P030......9 B1
Daisy La P012......52 B5
Dale Park Ho 4 P01......54 B3
Dall Sq P030......14 F1
Dalmally Gdns S018......51 F8
Dame Anthonys Cl P033......11 F4
Daneshill Flats P032......3 E2
Daniell's Cl S041......48 E3
Daniell's Wlk S041......48 E3
Daniel St P033......12 B1
Dark Lane P030......20 D5
Dapple Pl S040......50 A1
Darlington Rd P04......53 E3
Darnan Ho 6 S041......51 A7
Dart Ho S018......51 F8
Dartmouth Cl 6 P012......52 C8
Dartmouth Ct 8 P012......52 C8
Dartmouth Mews P05......54 D3
Darts La P035......25 D5
Darwin Ho P01......54 C4
Darwin Rd S015......50 E7
Daulston Rd P01......53 F7
Davidson Ct 42 P01......53 A5
Davies Ct P037......35 C2
Dawlish Ave S015......50 D8
D-Day Story*P05......53 C1
Dean Cl S015......50 D8
Dean Ct 18 S018......51 E8
Dean Ct P033......35 D3
Deans Ct P033......12 D6
Dean St P01......53 A5
Debourne Cl P031......2 E3
Debourne Manor Dr P031......2 E4
Deepdene
  Shanklin P037......43 B7
  Southampton S018......51 E8
Deeping Cl S019......51 F1
Defender Rd S019......51 D3
Defender Wlk S019......51 D3
Delamere Rd P04......53 F3
Delaval Ho 2 S041......51 B5
Dell The
  Cowes P031......9 A8
  Southampton S015......50 F6
Delphi Cl P037......43 D8
Delphi Rd P037......43 D8
De Mowbray Way S041......48 D2
Deneside Copse S041......48 B1
Denmark Rd P031......3 A4
Denmead Ho P01......54 C4
Denness Path P036......35 D4
Denness Rd P036......35 E4
Dennett Rd P035......25 C5
Denning Mews P05......54 B3
Dennison Ct 18 S015......50 B8
Denny Gdns P037......43 B8
Denton Gdns P032......3 D4
Denzil Ave S014......51 B6
Derby Rd S014......51 B6
Derwent Dr P033......12 F4
Desmond Price Ct P036......35 D4
Devonia Gdns P030......36 A6
Devon Mews 8 S015......50 E5
Devonshire Inf Sch P04......53 F4
Devonshire Mans 10 S015......50 F6
Devonshire Rd S015......50 F6
Devonshire Sq P04......53 F4
Devonshire Terr P038......47 B5
Dhekelia Ct P01......54 C4
Diamond St 2 P05......54 A1
Diana Cl P039......14 D1
Dickens Cl P02......53 D7
Dickinson Rd P04......53 F5
Diggings The P033......24 F7

Dight Rd P012......52 C3
Dimbola Mus & Galleries*
  P040......27 D6
Dimond Rd S018......51 E7
Dinosaur Exhibition
  Centre*P030......38 G6
Dinosaur Isle* P036......36 B4
Disa Ho S015......50 E6
Ditchbury S041......48 D6
Dock Mill Cotts 18 P05......53 D2
Doctor La P036......24 A3
Doctors La P030......39 A8
Doctor's La P036......24 A3
Dodnor Creek Nature
Reserve* P030......9 B4
Dodnor La P030......9 A1
Dodnor Mews P030......9 B2
Dodnor Pk P030......9 B3
Dodnor La P030, P041......17 C2
Dolcroft Rd P030......32 F5
Dolman Rd P012......52 C4
Dolphin Cres P012......52 C4
Dolphin Ct
  1 Portsmouth P05......53 E1
  1 Totland P040......14 E1
Dolphin Way P012......52 D2
Dombey Ct 5 P01......53 D7
Donnelly St P012......52 A7
Donnington Dr P037......35 B1
Dorchester Ct S015......50 F8
Dormouse Dr P030......20 F6
Dorothy Ct P05......54 C1
Dorothy Dymond St P01......54 B3
Dorrick Ct 10 S015......50 F7
Dorrien Rd P012......52 B8
Dorrita Cl P04......53 F2
Dorset St S014......51 A6
Dorval Ho 8 S015......50 E7
Dorval Manor 7 S015......50 E7
Douglas Rd P01......53 F7
Dove Cl P033......24 F6
Dovecotes P030......33 D6
Dover Park Prim Sch
  P033......12 D5
Dover Rd P032......3 C4
Dover St
  Ryde P033......12 D6
  Southampton S014......51 A7
Downcourt La P038......44 F7
DOWNEND......21 E4
Downend Rd P030......21 E3
Down La
  Carisbrooke P030......20 A5
  Shanklin P037......46 F6
Downlands Cres P038......46 E6
Downland View P037......35 C2
Down Lane Cotts P038......46 F6
Downside Rd S018......45 B4
Downs Road P036......22 D3
Downs View P030......27 B8
Downs View P036......24 A3
Downsview Gdns P033......10 E4
Downsview Rd P035......25 D4
Downs View Rd
  Newport P030......20 F6
  St Helens P033......24 F6
Doyle Ct S019......51 F1
Drabbles La P036......35 E5
Dracaena Gdns P037......35 C1
Drake Cl S040......50 A2
Drake Rd 3 P02......53 A5
Drake Rd P030......20 D6
Drakes Ct S040......50 A3
Drill Hall La P033......11 F5
Drill Hall Rd P030......20 D7
Drive The P035......25 D5
Droffatts Ho S015......50 D7
Drummlanrig Terr 4 P012......52 C9
Drummond Cl S041......51 C8
Drummond Dr S014......51 E8
Drummond Rd P01......54 C4
Dubbers P038......33 C1
Ducie Ave P035......25 C5
Duckworth Ho 34 P01......53 A5
Dudley Rd P038......47 B5
Dugald Drummond St
  P01......54 B3
Duisburg Way P05......53 B2
Duke Cres P01......53 A6
Duke of Edinburgh Ho
  P01......53 A6
Dukes Rd
  Gosport P012......52 A7
  Southampton S014......51 B7
Duke St S014......51 B3
Dumbarton Cl P02......53 D8
Duncan Cl S019......51 E1
Duncan Rd P05......53 D2
Duncroft Gdns P037......35 C1
Dundonald Cl S019......51 D1
Dungewood La P030,
  P038......39 B6
Dunkeld Rd P012......52 A8
DUNSBURY......28 F5
Dunsmore Cl P05......53 D8
Durban Ct 3 S015......50 E7
Durban Ho P01......54 C4
Durban Rd P01......53 F7
Durham St
  Gosport P012......52 A7
  Portsmouth P05......54 B3
Durley Rd P012......52 A7
Durnford Rd S014......51 B6
Duver Rd
  Seaview P034......13 C4
  St Helens P033......25 A7
Dyer Rd S015......50 C7

Dymott Cl SO15..........50 D5

E

Earley Ct SO41..........48 F4
Earlsdon St PO5..........54 B2
Earls Rd SO14..........51 A7
East Ashey La PO33..........23 D5
East Bldg PO1..........53 A5
Eastbourne Ave SO15..........50 D8
East Cl PO41..........5 E2
Eastcliff Ct PO37..........43 D8
Eastcliff Prom PO37..........43 C7
Eastcliff Rd PO37..........43 C7
EAST COWES..........3 E4
East Cowes Heritage Ctr*
  PO32..........3 E4
East Cowes Rd PO32..........10 A5
East Ct PO1..........53 E7
Eastern Par PO4..........53 F2
Eastern Rd SO41..........48 D4
Eastern Villas Rd PO4..........53 D1
Eastfield Rd SO17..........51 C8
Eastfields PO5..........54 C1
Eastgate St SO14..........51 A3
East Gn PO34..........13 C2
East Hill
  Lymington SO41..........48 E4
  Ryde PO33..........12 E6
East Hill Rd PO33..........12 E5
East La PO30..........33 E6
East Mead PO37..........43 A7
Eastmore Ct PO41..........15 F6
East Mount Rd PO37..........43 D8
Easton La PO40..........27 C7
East Park Terr SO14..........51 A5
East Rd SO40..........50 B2
East St
  Newport PO30..........20 E7
  Portsmouth PO1..........53 A4
  Ryde PO33..........12 D6
  Southampton SO14..........51 A4
  Ventnor PO38..........47 B6
East Street Sh Ctr [9]
  SO14..........51 A4
East Surrey St PO1..........54 B3
East View PO30..........20 D6
East Yar Rd PO36..........26 A5
Easy View La PO38..........40 A4
Eddington Rd PO34..........24 F8
Eden Grange [5] SO14..........51 A7
Eden PO39..........26 G8
Eden Rd PO39..........26 A6
Eden St PO1..........54 B4
Edgbaston Ho PO5..........54 B2
Edinburgh Ct PO13..........3 A4
Edinburgh Ct [2] SO15..........50 A6
Edinburgh Rd
  Freshwater PO40..........15 A1
  Portsmouth PO1..........54 D3
Edith Haisman Cl SO15..........50 D5
Edmund Rd PO4..........53 F3
Edward Rd SO15..........50 C7
Edwards Cl SO41..........48 B3
Edward St PO33..........12 C5
Edwin Jones Gn SO15..........50 E8
Efford Cl SO41..........48 B2
Efford Farm Cotts SO41..........48 A1
Efford Way SO41..........48 A2
Egerton Rd PO35..........25 E4
Egypt Copse PO31..........2 F5
Egypt Espl PO31..........2 E6
Egypt Hill PO31..........2 F5
Elder Cl SO40..........50 A1
Eldon Ct PO5..........54 B2
Eldon Ho [9] SO14..........51 A3
Eldon St PO5..........54 B2
Elenors Gr PO33..........11 C5
Elfin Ct [11] SO17..........51 B7
Elgar Cl PO12..........52 A3
Elgar Ct SO41..........48 F4
Elgin St SO15..........50 D5
Elizabeth Ct
  Bembridge PO35..........25 C5
  [4] Gosport PO12..........52 A7
Elizabeth Gdns
  Havenstreet PO33..........11 C1
  Portsmouth PO4..........53 F2
Eliza Pl [3] PO12..........52 C6
Ellachie Gdns PO12..........52 B2
Ellachie Mews PO12..........52 B2
Ellachie Rd PO12..........52 B2
Ellery Gr SO41..........48 E5
Elliston Rd PO39..........14 D1
Elm Ave SO41..........54 E5
Embank Gdns PO36..........35 E5
Elm Cl
  Freshwater PO40..........14 E1
  Nettlestone PO34..........13 C2
  Ryde PO33..........12 D4
Elm Ct
  Ryde PO33..........12 E4
  Southampton, Sholing SO19..........51 F3
ELMFIELD..........12 E3
Elmfield North Block
  SO15..........50 D5
Elmfield West Block
  SO15..........50 D5
Elm Gr
  Cowes PO31..........3 A3
  Gosport PO12..........52 B6
  Newport PO30..........20 D5
  Portsmouth PO5..........54 B1
Elmhurst Bsns Pk PO12..........52 C5
Elmhurst Rd PO12..........52 C5
Elm La PO30..........18 B4
Elm Lodge PO5..........54 C1

Elms Cl PO35..........25 E5
Elm St
  Portsmouth PO5..........54 A1
  Southampton SO14..........51 B4
Elmsworth La PO30..........7 D3
Elm Terr SO14..........51 B3
Elphinstone Rd PO5..........53 C2
ELSON..........52 A9
Elson Inf Sch PO12..........52 A9
Elson Jun Sch PO12..........52 A9
Elson La PO12..........52 A9
Elson Rd PO12..........52 A9
Elstree Rd SO19..........51 E5
Emanuel St PO2..........53 D7
Embankment Rd PO33,
  PO35..........25 B5
Embassy Ct PO4..........54 D2
Embassy Way PO36..........35 B4
Emmadale Ct [7] SO14..........51 A6
Emperor No SO18..........40 A6
Emperor Way SO18..........51 C7
Empress Pk SO14..........51 B7
Empress Rd SO14..........51 B7
Empshott Rd PO4..........53 F4
Emsworth Rd
  Lymington SO41..........48 E4
  Southampton SO15..........50 B8
Endeavour Cl
  Gosport PO12..........52 D5
  Southampton SO15..........50 B7
Endeavour Ct [5] SO14..........51 B7
Endle St SO14..........51 C3
Enfield Gr SO19..........51 E3
Englefield Rd SO18..........51 D7
English Rd SO15..........50 B7
Ensign Cl PO31..........3 A3
Enterprise Way PO31..........3 A2
Eremue Ct [4] PO41..........15 C6
Ernest Rd PO1..........53 E7
Esplanade
  Cowes PO31..........3 A6
  East Cowes PO32..........3 D5
  Nettlestone PO34..........13 C2
  Ryde PO33..........12 D6
  Sandown PO36..........36 A3
  Seaview PO34..........13 C2
  Shanklin PO37..........43 D7
  Ventnor PO38..........47 A5
Esplanade Rd
  Sandown PO36..........36 A3
  Ventnor PO38..........47 A5
Esplanade The PO12..........52 E5
Esslemont Rd PO4..........53 F3
Ethel Ho PO2..........53 D8
Ethel Rd PO1..........53 E6
Eton Rd PO5..........54 D2
European Ct PO36..........35 F5
European Way SO14..........51 B2
Eva Allaway Ct [8] PO1..........53 A5
Evans St SO14..........51 A4
Evelyn Cres SO15..........50 D8
Everard Cl PO40..........27 C7
Everton La PO37..........43 C7
Ewart Rd PO1..........53 E7
Ewer Comm PO12..........52 B3
Exchange Rd PO1..........54 A3
Exchange The [3] PO4..........53 A2
Exeter Rd PO4..........53 F2
Exmoor Rd SO14..........51 B6
Exmouth Rd
  Gosport PO12..........52 A9
  Portsmouth PO5..........53 D2
Exmouth St SO14..........51 A5
Explosion Mus of Naval
  Firepower* PO12..........52 D8

F

Fairfield Cl SO41..........48 E3
Fairfield Gdns PO36..........35 E5
Fairfield Pk [6] PO39..........14 E1
Fairfield Way PO39..........14 E1
Fairhaven Ct PO33..........25 E4
Fairhome Cl PO12..........52 B8
Fairlead Rd PO31..........2 F3
Fairlea Rd SO41..........48 E5
FAIRLEE..........9 D1
Fairlee Rd PO30..........9 D1
Fairmead Ct SO14..........51 A5
Fairmount Dr PO30..........20 F8
Fairthorne Gdns PO12..........52 A5
Fairview Cres PO36..........35 E5
Fairway Cvn Site PO36..........35 C6
Fairway The PO36..........35 E5
Fairy Rd PO34..........13 D4
Fakenham Farm* PO33..........25 A7
Falcon Cl [4] PO12..........52 C8
Falcon Cross Rd PO37..........43 C8
Falcon Rd PO32..........3 C9
Falkland Rd SO15..........50 A8
Fanshawe St SO14..........51 A6
Farlington Rd PO2..........53 E8
Farm La PO12..........52 B2
Farnleys Mead SO41..........48 E2
Farriers Cl PO5..........54 D2
Farriers Wlk PO30..........31 B2
Farriers Wlk PO12..........52 C6
Farringford Farm Rd
  PO40..........27 B7
Farthingale Terr [11] PO1..........53 A3
Farthing Ct PO12..........52 A6
Farthing La PO1..........53 A3
Farthings Way PO39..........14 D1
Faulkner La PO30..........36 A5
Fawcett Rd PO4..........53 F2
Fawley Rd SO15..........50 A6

Felix Rd PO12..........52 B8
Fellows Rd PO31..........3 A4
Fennel Gdns SO41..........48 E5
Ferncliff Apartments
  PO36..........35 F4
Ferncliff Rd PO36..........35 F4
Fern Ct SO18..........51 E7
Ferndene Way SO18..........51 F8
Fernhill PO33..........10 D4
Fernhill Ct PO36..........34 F4
Fernhill Pk PO33..........10 D4
Fernhurst Jun Sch PO4..........53 F4
Fernhurst Rd PO4..........53 F4
Fernclose Rd PO34..........13 E2
Fern Rd SO19..........51 F2
Fernside Way PO34..........10 E4
Fernwood Cres SO18..........51 F8
Ferrol Rd PO12..........52 C7
Ferrypoint SO41..........49 A4
Ferry Rd PO32..........3 C3
Festing Bldgs [1] PO4..........53 F2
Festing Mews PO4..........53 F2
Festing Rd PO4..........53 F2
Fey Rd PO12..........52 C6
Field Ct PO30..........20 C6
Fieldfare Rd PO30..........20 A6
Field La PO33..........24 F7
Fieldmore Rd PO4..........53 F4
Field Pl PO30..........20 C6
Field View PO33..........12 B3
Fieldway Cres PO31..........8 F8
Field Wlk SO41..........48 D5
Fifth St PO1..........53 F6
Fighting Cocks Cross
  PO36..........34 C5
Filton Rd SO41..........48 D4
Finches The PO30..........20 A6
Findon Rd PO12..........52 B9
Fine La PO30..........31 B2
Firbank Lodge PO37..........43 C8
Firestone Copse Rd PO33..........11 B3
Firestone Glade PO33..........11 A4
Firgrove Ct SO15..........50 C7
Firgrove Rd SO15..........50 C7
Firs Cl PO33..........12 C4
Fir Tree Cl PO37..........35 D2
Fisgard Rd PO12..........52 B8
FISHBOURNE..........11 B6
Fishbourne La PO33..........11 A6
Fishermans Wlk PO5..........25 F5
Fishers PO38..........46 B4
Fitzherbert St PO1..........54 B4
FITZHUGH..........50 E7
Fitzhugh Ho [8] SO15..........50 E6
Fitzhugh St SO15..........50 E6
Fitzhugh St [3] SO15..........50 F5
Fitzroy St PO1..........53 F5
Fitzroy Wlk PO1..........54 C4
Five Houses La PO30..........18 A4
Five Post La PO12..........52 B7
Flagstaff Gn PO12..........52 D7
Flathouse Rd PO1..........53 C7
Flett Cl PO33..........11 F4
Fleet Way
  Portsmouth PO1..........53 B6
  Portsmouth PO1..........54 A4
  Shalfleet PO30..........17 D7
Fleming Cl PO33..........11 E4
Fleming Ct SO19..........51 D2
Flint St PO5..........54 A1
Flitcroft Gdns PO36..........35 D3
Floating Bridge Rd SO14..........51 C3
Florence Ct [2] SO18..........51 E8
Florence Rd
  Portsmouth PO5..........53 D1
  Shanklin PO37..........43 C7
  Southampton SO19..........51 D2
Flushards SO41..........48 F3
Flying Bull Cl [3] PO2..........53 D8
Flying Bull La PO2..........53 D8
Flying Bull Academy PO2..........53 D8
Foley Ho PO1..........54 B4
Fontwell Rd PO5..........53 D2
Footways PO33..........10 D5
Forbury Rd [2] PO5..........54 C2
Ford Mews [3] PO30..........20 D6
Foreland Farm La PO35..........25 F4
Foreland Rd PO35..........25 F4
Forelands Field Rd PO35..........25 F3
Foremans Cotts PO12..........52 E3
Forest Cl
  Lymington SO41..........48 B2
  Winford PO36..........34 E4
Forest Dell PO36..........34 E5
Forest End PO30..........8 F1
Forest Gate Gdns SO41..........48 D1
Forest Hills PO30..........19 F6
Forest Rd
  Newport PO30..........19 E8
  Winford PO36..........34 E5
FOREST SIDE..........20 A8
Forest View [4] SO14..........53 F4
Forest Way SO41..........48 E4
Forster Rd SO14..........51 B6
Forsythia Pl PO13..........51 F5
Forth Ho [11] SO14..........51 C6
Fort Mews PO36..........36 A4
FORTON..........52 C7
Forton Lodge [3] PO12..........52 C6
Forton Rd
  Gosport PO12..........52 B6
  Gosport PO12..........53 E6
Fort Rd
  Gosport PO12..........52 B2
  Southampton SO19..........51 E3
Fort Spinney PO36..........36 C5

Fort St PO36..........36 A4
Fortune Ho PO12..........52 A6
Fort Victoria Cotts PO41..........14 F6
Fort Victoria Country Pk*
  PO41..........14 F6
Fort Warden Hts PO39..........14 C2
Fort Warden Rd PO39..........14 D2
Forward Dr SO41..........48 C2
Foster Rd
  Gosport PO12..........52 B4
  Portsmouth PO1..........54 B4
Foundry Ct [2] PO1..........53 A5
Foundry La SO15..........50 B7
Foundry Lane Prim Sch
  SO15..........50 B7
Foundary Rd PO30..........21 A6
Fountain Ct PO31..........3 B5
Fountain Quay PO31..........3 B5
Fountain Rd PO1..........53 E7
Fountain St PO1..........54 B3
Fourposts Hill [3] SO15..........50 E5
Fourth St PO1..........53 F6
Foxes Cl PO36..........35 F6
Foxes Rd PO30..........20 D7
Foxhills PO38..........46 D5
Foxlea [3] SO15..........50 E7
Foxlea Gdns PO12..........52 B8
Fox PO30..........20 A6
Fox Pond La SO41..........48 D1
Foyes Ct SO15..........50 D6
Frampton Way PO35..........25 D5
Francis Ave PO4..........53 F3
Francis Bright Cotts PO38..........33 A4
Frank Judd Ct [36] PO1..........53 A5
Frank Miles Ho [1] PO5..........54 B2
Frank Rd PO36..........35 F6
Frank Williams Ct PO30..........20 F7
Fraser Cl PO13..........3 B2
Fraser Rd PO5..........54 C2
FRATTON..........53 F5
Fratton Ct PO1..........54 D3
Fratton Rd PO1..........54 D4
Fratton Sta PO1..........53 F5
Fratton Way PO4..........53 F5
Frederick St
  Portsmouth PO1..........54 B4
  Southampton SO14..........51 B6
FREEMANTLE..........50 C6
Freemantle Bsns Ctr
  SO15..........51 F6
Freemantle CE Community
  Acad SO15..........50 C6
Freemantle Cl SO19..........51 F5
Freemantle Common Rd
  SO19..........51 F6
Freemantle Rd PO12..........52 B8
Freestone Rd [10] PO5..........53 D2
French St
  [8] Portsmouth PO1..........53 A3
  Southampton SO14..........51 A3
Frensham Ct PO4..........53 F4
Frensham Rd PO4..........53 F4
Freshfield Rd SO15..........50 B7
Freshfield Sq SO15..........50 B7
FRESHWATER..........14 E1
FRESHWATER BAY..........27 C6
Freshwater Rd PO40..........16 A1
Friary Cl
  Gosport PO12..........52 C2
  [6] Portsmouth PO5..........53 C2
Friary The [5] PO5..........53 C2
Friendship Ho PO5..........54 B1
Frigate Rd PO1..........53 A6
Frobisher Ct SO40..........50 A3
Frobisher Ho [6] PO1..........53 A5
Froddington Rd PO5..........54 C2
Froglands La PO30..........20 A3
Frome Cl SO40..........50 A1
Fromond Cl SO41..........48 E5
Froude Ave PO12..........52 C2
Froude Rd PO12..........52 D3
Froxfield Ho PO1..........54 C4
Fullerton Rd SO41..........48 C4
Funtington Rd PO2..........53 F8
Furness Rd [19] PO5..........53 D1
Furlongs PO30..........20 E6
Furze Hill Rd PO37..........43 B7
FURZYHURST..........8 E7
Fyning St PO1..........54 C4

G

Gage Cl SO40..........50 A2
Gaggerhill La PO30..........30 A3
Gainsborough Ct SO41..........48 D2
Gainsborough Ho [2] PO4..........53 E2
Gainsford Rd SO19..........51 E5
Gain's Rd PO4..........53 E2
Galley La PO30..........30 A2
Gamble Cl SO19..........51 F4
Gamble Rd PO12..........53 D8
Garden La PO5..........54 B1
Garden Terr [14] PO5..........54 C2
Garden Way PO30..........20 F6
Gardiner Cl SO40..........50 A2
Garfield Rd
  Portsmouth PO5..........53 D8
  Ryde PO33..........12 C6
  Shanklin PO37..........43 B7
  Southampton SO19..........51 D3
Garland Ct [5] PO12..........52 B6
Garlic Farm The* PO36..........22 C2
Garner Ct PO1..........54 D3
Garnock Ho [9] PO33..........12 C6
Garnock Rd SO19..........51 D2
Garrow Dr SO41..........48 E5
Garton Rd SO19..........51 D3

Gassiot Cl PO33..........12 E4
Gas Works La PO41..........15 B5
GATCOMBE..........32 C7
Gatcombe Rd PO30..........32 C7
Gatehouse Rd PO33..........23 B8
Gatehouse The [11] SO18..........51 E8
Gate La PO40..........27 C6
Gatten & Lake Prim Sch
  PO36..........35 D2
Gawn Pl PO12..........52 A4
Gaynor Ho PO37..........43 C8
Genoa Cl SO41..........48 C1
George Byng Way PO2..........53 D8
George Ct PO5..........53 D2
George Ct The [10] PO1..........53 A3
George St
  Gosport PO12..........52 C6
  Portsmouth PO1, PO2..........53 F7
  Ryde PO33..........12 C6
  Sandown PO36..........35 F5
Gibbs Rd SO14..........50 F5
Gilbert Cl SO41..........48 D2
Giles Cl PO12..........52 A7
Gilkicker Rd PO12..........52 C2
Gill's Cliff Rd PO38..........46 E5
Glade The
  Nettlestone PO34..........13 C2
  Sandown PO36..........35 E4
  Wroxall PO38..........42 C5
Gladstone Pl [4] PO2..........53 D8
Gladstone Rd PO12..........52 A8
Glamis Gdns PO32..........3 D3
Glebe Gdns PO33..........10 E5
Glebe Rd SO14..........51 B3
Glen App PO38..........45 B3
Glencoe Rd PO1..........53 F7
Glendale Cl PO33..........10 D4
Glenfield Ave SO18..........51 F7
Glenfield Cres SO18..........51 F7
Glenfield Ct PO30..........20 B5
Glenfield Inf Sch SO18..........51 F7
Glenfield Way SO18..........51 F7
Glenheadon Dr PO39..........26 C7
Glenmore Ct SO17..........51 A8
Glen Pl PO31..........3 D2
Glen Rd SO19..........51 D2
Glen The
  Cowes PO31..........3 A4
  Niton PO38..........45 B3
  [3] Yarmouth PO41..........15 C6
Glidden Cl PO1..........54 C3
Glossop Cl PO2..........3 D3
Gloster The PO31..........3 A5
Gloucester Ho [1] PO12..........52 C8
Gloucester Mews PO5..........54 B2
Gloucester Pl PO5..........54 B1
Gloucester Rd
  Portsmouth PO1..........53 A6
  Ventnor PO38..........46 E6
Gloucester Sq [22] SO14..........51 A3
Gloucester Terr PO5..........54 B1
Gloucester View PO5..........54 B2
Glynn Cl PO4..........13 D1
Gobles Cl PO33..........12 D5
Godric Rd PO12..........20 F5
GODSHILL..........41 D8
Godshill Model Village*
  PO34..........41 D8
Goldash Ridge PO30..........41 D8
Goldshill Park Rd PO30..........41 D8
Godshill Prim Sch PO38..........41 D8
Godwit Cl PO12..........52 B9
Goldcrest Cl PO30..........20 A6
Golden Gr SO14..........51 B5
Golden Groves SO19..........51 F3
Golden Hill Country Pk*
  PO40..........14 F2
Golden Ridge PO40..........14 F1
Golden Villas PO40..........14 E1
Goldings Way PO41..........14 F2
Gold Mead Cl [5] SO41..........48 E2
Goldsmith Ave PO4..........53 F4
Goldsmiths Ct [17] SO14..........54 A1
Golf Links Rd PO36..........35 E6
Golf Course Cl PO12..........52 B9
Goodwood Rd
  Gosport PO12..........52 B9
  Portsmouth PO5..........54 C1
Gordon Ave SO14..........51 A8
Gordon Bldgs SO15..........50 C8
Gordon Cl
  Ryde PO33..........11 E5
  Sandown PO36..........35 F6
Gordon Ct [3] PO33..........12 C5
Gordon Lodge PO32..........3 D2
Gordon Rd
  Cowes PO31..........3 B4
  Gosport PO12..........52 A5
  Lymington SO41..........48 C3
  Newport PO30..........20 F8
  Portsmouth PO1..........53 B3
  Southampton SO14..........52 C7
GOSPORT..........52 C7
Gosport Discovery Ctr*
  PO12..........52 D5
Gosport Sh Prec [6] PO12..........52 D5
Gosport St SO41..........48 F4
Gosport War Meml Hospl
  PO12..........52 A5
Gotten La PO38..........40 B3
Grace Rd [6] PO33..........11 E5
Grace Woodford Dr PO32..........9 D8
Graeme Rd PO41..........15 A6
Grafton Cl PO12..........52 C8

Grafton Gdns SO41....48 C3
Grafton La PO36....35 F5
Grafton St
　Portsmouth PO2....53 D7
　Sandown PO36....35 F5
Graham Ho 4 SO14....51 C6
Graham Rd
　Gosport PO12....52 A8
　Portsmouth PO4....53 E3
　Southampton SO14....51 B6
Graham St SO14....51 C6
Granada Rd PO4....53 E1
Granary CI PO33....11 F5
Grand Par PO1....53 A3
Grange Ave PO33....12 A4
Grange Ct
　Shanklin PO37....43 C7
　Ventnor PO38....47 C6
Grange Dr PO30....20 D8
Grange Gdns PO35....25 C4
Grange Rd
　East Cowes PO32....3 D3
　Sandown PO36....35 E4
　Shanklin PO37....43 C7
Grangeside PO38....47 D6
Grange The
　Bembridge PO35....25 C4
　Newport PO30....20 D8
Grantham Ct PO31....3 A6
Grantham Rd SO19....51 F6
Granville Ct SO15....50 E7
Granville Rd
　....PO31....3 A4
　Totland PO39....14 C1
Granville Rise 3 PO39....14 D1
Granville Road Bridge 4
　....PO31....3 A4
Granville St SO14....51 B4
Grasmere Ave PO33....12 F4
Gravel Pit Rd PO33....10 D4
Grays Ct PO1....53 A4
Grayshott Rd PO4....53 F3
Graswood CI PO36....35 F6
Great Appleford Barns
　....PO38....40 E5
Great Preston Rd PO33....12 D3
Great Southsea St PO5....54 B1
GREAT THORNESS....7 E6
Green Cnr PO34....13 C2
Greenfield Ct PO33....12 E4
Greenfields Rd PO30....20 F8
Greenfinch CI PO30....20 A6
Greengate Ind Est PO31....3 B4
Greengates PO37....35 C1
Greenham Dr PO34....13 D2
Greenidge Ct 8 SO15....50 E8
Green La
　Cowes PO31....9 A8
　Freshwater PO40....27 B6
　Gosport, Alverstoke PO12....52 A5
　Gosport, Elson PO12....52 C9
　Ryde PO33....23 D6
　Shanklin PO37....43 C6
Green Land CI PO30....32 B4
Greenlands PO30....32 B4
Greenlands Rd PO32....3 D2
Greenlydd CI PO38....45 B3
Greenmount Com Prim Sch
　....PO33....12 C5
Green Mount Prim Sch
　....PO33....12 A5
Green Rd
　Gosport PO12....52 A5
　Portsmouth PO5....54 B2
Green St
　Newport PO30....20 F7
　Ryde PO33....12 C5
Green The
　Cowes PO31....2 F5
　Shanklin PO37....43 A8
　Shorwell PO30....31 B3
Greenway PO33....11 E4
Greenway CI
　Lymington SO41....48 C3
　Newport PO30....20 E8
Greenway Rd PO12....52 B7
Greenways
　Cowes PO31....8 F8
　Newport PO30....21 A7
　Totland PO39....26 G8
Greenways CI PO31....8 F8
Greenway The PO38....45 B4
Greenwich The 24 SO14....51 A3
Greenwood La PO30....34 F8
Greenwood Wlk PO30....20 F8
Greetham St PO5....54 B3
Gregory Ave PO33....13 B3
Gregory CI PO33....13 B3
Grenville CI PO30....3 D2
Grenville Dr PO33....12 A3
Grenville Ho 32 PO1....53 A5
Grenville Rd PO4....54 D1
Greville Rd SO15....50 D7
Greycliff PO38....47 D7
Greyfriars Ct PO5....54 B1
Greystone La PO33....23 A4
Greystones La PO40....27 D6
Griffin Ct SO17....51 C8
Griffin Ho PO31....3 A5
Grosvenor Ho
　4 Portsmouth PO5....54 B2
　8 Southampton SO15....50 F6
Grosvenor Mews
　5 Gosport PO12....52 C6
　Lymington SO41....48 D5

Grosvenor Sq SO15....50 F6
Grosvenor St PO5....54 B2
Grove Ave PO12....52 C6
Grove Bldgs 7 PO12....52 C5
Grove CI PO30....20 F6
Grove Cotts PO30....17 E7
Grove Ho PO5....54 B1
Grove Pastures SO41....48 E3
Grove PI SO41....48 E3
Grove Rd
　Cowes PO31....3 A3
　Gosport PO12....52 B8
　Lymington SO41....48 F3
　Ryde PO33....12 A3
　Sandown PO36....35 F6
　Southampton SO15....50 C7
　Ventnor PO38....47 A6
　Wroxall PO38....42 C4
Grove Road N PO5....54 B1
Grove Road S PO5....54 B1
Groves CI PO40....14 E2
Grove St SO14....51 B4
Grove The
　Bembridge PO35....25 C6
　Cowes PO31....3 A5
　Ventnor PO38....47 A6
Guadeloupe Rd PO36....35 F5
Guardhouse Rd PO1....53 B7
Guildford Park Camp
　....PO33....24 F7
Guildford Rd
　Portsmouth PO1....53 E6
　St Helens PO33....25 A7
Guildford St 1 SO14....51 C5
Guildhall Sq SO14....51 B3
Guildhall Wlk PO1....54 A3
Guild Ho 3 SO14....51 A3
Gully Rd PO34....13 D2
Gunville Cres PO30....20 A6
Gunville Rd PO30....20 A6
Gunville W PO30....19 F6
Gunwharf Quays PO1....52 F6
Gunwharf Quays (Sh Ctr)
　....PO1....53 A4
Gunwharf Rd PO1....53 A4
Guppy CI PO31....2 E4
GURNARD....2 E4
Gurnard Prim Sch
　....PO31....2 E4
Gurnard Hts PO31....2 D4
Gurney Rd SO15....50 C8
Gustar Gr PO32....9 D1
Gusters Shute PO30....18 B2
Guyers Rd PO40....27 C7
Gwen-Rhian Ct 4 SO15....50 F7
Gwessin Terr 6 PO12....52 C5
Gwydir CI PO33....12 A5

H

Hadrians Way PO36....24 A1
Haglane Copse SO41....48 C2
Haig CI PO33....35 D3
Halberry Ho PO30....20 F8
Halberry La PO30....20 F8
HALE COMMON....34 B5
Hale Ct PO1....54 C4
Halesowen Ho 4 PO5....54 A2
Hale Street N PO1....54 C4
Hale Street S PO1....54 C4
Half Moon St 8 PO1....53 A5
Halford CI PO36....35 F7
Halfpenny La PO31....53 A3
Halletts Shute PO41....15 A5
Halliday CI PO12....52 B6
Hall of Aviation (Mus)*
　SO14....51 B3
Hambledon Rd PO5....54 B4
Hambrook Rd 11 PO12....52 A7
Hambrook St PO5....54 A1
Hambrough La PO39....26 G7
Hambrough Rd PO38....47 A5
Hamilton Ct 16 PO5....53 C2
Hamilton Ho PO1....54 C4
Hamilton Mews SO41....48 F4
Hamilton PI SO41....48 D3
Hamilton Rd
　Portsmouth PO5....53 D2
　Ryde PO33....11 F4
Hamlet CI PO31....3 A6
Hammond CI PO41....15 A5
Hammond Ho 9 PO12....52 E5
Hampshire Cres 3 PO30....9 A1
Hampshire St PO1....53 E7
Hampshire Terr PO1....54 A2
HAMSTEAD....1 C1
Hamstead Dr PO41....6 A2
Hamstead Rd PO41....17 B8
Hamtun St 3 SO14....50 F3
Hamwic Ho 3 SO14....51 A6
Handel Rd SO15....50 F5
Handel Terr SO15....50 E6
Handford PI 2 SO15....50 F6
Handsworth Ho PO1....54 B4
Hanley Rd SO15....50 D8
Hannah Ho PO30....20 D8
Hanover Bldgs SO14....51 A4
Hanover Ct 7 PO21....53 A4
Hanover Ho 7 SO14....51 A4
Hanover St SO14....51 A5
Hanway Rd PO1, PO2....53 E7
Harborough Rd SO15....50 D8
Harbors Lake La PO36....34 D6
Harbour CI SO40....50 C2
Harbour Par PO1....54 F4
Harbour Rd PO1....52 E6
Harbour Strand PO35....25 C6

Harbour Twr 10 PO12....52 E5
Harbour Way PO31....2 F3
Harcourt Rd
　Gosport PO12....52 A6
　Portsmouth PO1....53 E7
　Southampton SO18....51 E8
Harding Rd PO33....12 D4
Harding Shute PO33....23 F6
Hard The PO1....53 A5
HARDWAY....52 A8
Hardy CI PO33....50 B6
Harford CI SO41....48 C1
Harley Wlk PO1....54 C4
Harness La PO31....2 C1
Harold Rd
　Portsmouth PO4....53 E3
　Southampton SO15....50 C7
Harrison's Cut SO14....51 A4
Harris Rd PO30....9 A2
Harrow Rd PO5....54 D2
Harry Cheek Gdns PO31....8 E8
Harry Law Hall PO1....54 B3
Hart CI SO19....51 F3
Hartford Ho PO33....54 A1
Hartington Rd SO14....51 B6
Hartley Ct 5 SO17....51 A8
Harts La PO38....32 F3
Harvester Way SO41....48 D6
Harvey CI PO32....3 D1
Harvey Rd PO30....20 F8
Haselworth Dr PO12....52 B2
Haselworth Prim Sch
　....PO12....52 B4
Haskell Rd PO30....9 A2
Haslar Marina PO12....52 E4
Haslar Rd
　Gosport, Clayhall PO12....52 D3
　Gosport, Newtown PO12....52 E5
Haslar Terr PO12....52 E5
Haslegrave Ho 2 PO2....53 D8
Haslemere Rd PO4....53 F3
Hatherley Mans 4 SO15....50 C7
Hatherton Rd PO37....43 C7
Havant St PO1....53 A5
Havelock Rd
　Portsmouth PO5....54 C2
　Southampton SO14....50 F5
Haven Close PO32....3 D1
Haven Crest PO36....24 B2
HAVENSTREET....11 C1
Havenstreet Main Rd
　....PO33....11 C1
Havenstreet Sta* PO33....22 D8
Haven The
　Gosport PO12....52 B3
　Southampton SO19....51 E4
Havisham Rd PO1....53 C7
Hawke St PO1....53 A5
Hawkeswood Rd SO18....51 C7
Hawk Ho 18 PO33....12 C6
Hawkins PO31....2 C2
Hawkins CI PO36....24 A3
Hawthorn CI
　Newport PO30....20 C7
　Ryde PO33....11 F5
Hawthorns The SO40....50 A1
Hawthorns Urban Wildlife
　Ctr* SO15....50 F8
Haydens CI SO41....48 F4
HAYLANDS....12 A3
Haylands Prim Sch
　....PO33....12 B3
Hayling CI PO12....52 C9
Hayloft The PO33....12 A2
Hayward Ave PO33....12 E3
Haywards Ct 11 PO1....53 A4
Hazel CI PO38....46 E7
Hazel Ct PO4....53 F3
Hazeleigh Ave SO19....51 E2
Hazel Green Village PO33....10 F4
Hazelmount Paddock
　....PO33....11 E6
Hazel Rd
　Lymington SO41....48 D5
　Southampton SO19....51 D3
Hazelwood CI PO33....12 B4
Hazely Combe PO30....34 A8
Hazlemere Ave PO33....11 E4
Hearn St PO31....20 D7
Hearts of Oak Mews
　....SO41....48 D4
Heasley La PO30....34 B8
Heath CI PO30....20 E6
Heatherley Ct PO5....54 C1
Heatherwood Park Rd
　....PO39....26 G8
Heathfield CI
　Bembridge PO35....25 C4
　Freshwater PO40....14 F2
　Newport PO30....21 A7
Heathfield Ho PO37....43 C7
Heathfield Mdws PO40....14 E2
Heathfield Rd
　Bembridge PO35....25 C4
　Freshwater PO40....14 F2
Heath Gdns PO36....35 D3
Heath Mdw PO36....14 E2
Heath Rd PO36....35 D3
Heath Villas PO36....14 E2
Heaton Rd PO12....52 A8
Hedley Ct PO37....43 A7
Hefford Rd PO22....53 D8
Heidelberg Rd PO4....53 F4
Heights Leisure Ctr PO36....35 E4
Helena Rd PO5....53 F2
Hendy CI PO5....54 B1

Hendy Rd PO32....3 D4
Henery St 10 PO12....52 C5
Henley Rd PO4....53 F3
Henry Player Ave PO12....52 D7
Henry Rd SO15....50 C7
Henry St SO15....50 F6
Henstead Ct 9 SO15....50 F6
Henstead Rd SO15....50 F6
Henty Rd SO16....50 B7
Herbert Rd PO4....53 E2
Herbert St PO1....53 C7
Herbert Walker Ave SO15....50 C4
Hercules St PO2....53 D8
Hereford Ct PO5....54 C1
Hereford Rd PO5....54 C1
Heritage Way, Priddy's Hard
　....PO12....52 C9
Hermes Ct 10 PO12....52 C9
Heron Ho 8 PO5....53 C2
Heron Rd PO38....33 A4
Heron Sq PO12....9 E5
Hersey Rise PO34....13 D2
Hertford PI PO1....53 D7
Hesketh Ho 4 SO15....50 C6
Heverswood PO33....12 E4
Hewitt CI PO12....52 A8
Hewitt Cres PO30....9 A2
Hewitt's Rd SO15....50 D5
Heysham Rd SO15....50 B7
Heyshott Rd PO4....53 E3
Heytesbury Ct PO41....15 D5
Heytesbury Rd
　Newport PO30....20 D8
　Yarmouth PO41....15 D5
Heyward Rd PO4....53 E4
Highbury Ct PO35....25 E4
Highbury St 8 PO1....53 A4
Highcliff Ave SO41....51 A8
Highcliffe Lodge PO36....35 D2
Highdown La PO39....26 G6
Highfield SO41....48 D3
Highfield Ave SO41....48 C3
Highfield CI PO33....12 E4
Highfield Rd
　Cowes PO31....2 F2
　Lymington SO41....48 C3
　Newport PO30....20 E7
　Portsmouth PO1....54 C3
　Shanklin PO37....43 B7
Highgate Rd PO4....53 F3
Highgrove Cvan Site PO33....24 F7
High Point SO18....51 E8
High Rd PO30....8 F1
High Salterns PO34....13 D3
High St
　Bembridge PO35....25 C4
　Brading PO36....24 B3
　Carisbrooke PO30....20 B5
　Cowes....3 B5
　Freshwater PO40....14 F1
　Godshill PO38....41 D8
　Gosport PO12....52 D5
　Lymington SO41....48 E4
　Newchurch PO36....34 E7
　Newport PO30....20 D7
　Niton PO38....45 B4
　Portsmouth PO1....53 A3
　Rhyde, Oakfield PO33....12 D4
　Ryde PO33....12 C6
　Sandown PO36....35 F6
　Seaview PO34....13 D4
　Shanklin PO37....43 C7
　16 Southampton SO14....51 A3
　Ventnor PO38....47 B6
　Whitwell PO38....45 E7
　Wootton PO33....10 E5
　Wroxall PO38....42 C4
　Yarmouth PO41....15 D6
Hightrees SO41....48 D1
Highview PO40....14 F1
High View Way SO18....51 F8
Highway The PO37....43 C4
Highwood La PO30, PO38....32 E6
Hilbre Rd PO33....24 F6
Hilda Ct 1 SO15....50 F7
Hilda PI 3 SO14....51 C5
Hildyards Cres PO41....35 D2
Hillborough Ct PO5....54 C1
Hillborough Ct 11 PO5....54 C1
Hillcrest Rd PO38....32 F4
Hillcroft CI SO41....48 E4
Hilldtch SO41....48 D6
Hill Farm Rd SO15....50 E6
Hillgrove Cvan Site PO33....24 F7
Hill Ho PO39....26 H8
Hillis Cnr PO31....8 C7
HILLISGATE....8 D5
Hillis Gate Rd PO30, PO31....8 C6
Hill La PO40....14 F3
Hill Place La PO41....16 C7
Hillrise Ave PO33....11 F4
Hills Ct 2 PO33....12 C6
Hillside
　Chillerton PO30....32 A4
　Newport PO30....20 E8
Hillside Rd SO41....48 E4
Hills La PO38....39 B4
Hill St
　Ryde PO33....12 B5
　Sandown PO36....35 E5
　Southampton SO19....51 D1
Hill Top
　Ryde PO30....34 F7
Hill Top Cotts PO40....14 F3
HILLWAY....25 B2
Hillway Rd PO35....25 C2
Hilton Rd
　Gosport PO12....52 C4

Hilton PO31 *continued*
　Gurnard PO31....2 D3
Hinton Rd PO30....20 B6
Hives Way SO41....48 D6
HMS Victory* PO1....52 F7
HMS Warrior* PO1....52 F6
Hobbs Ct 2 PO12....52 E5
Hogan CI PO30....9 A3
Hogan Rd PO30....9 A3
Holben Lodge SO41....49 B3
Holbrookes Cotts PO41....16 D7
Holbrook Rd PO1....54 C3
Holford Rd PO33....10 D6
Holgate La PO34....13 D2
Holland Rd
　Portsmouth PO4....54 D2
　Southampton SO19....51 D2
Hollies The PO33....11 D4
Hollingbourne CI SO18....51 D8
Hollis Dr PO30....30 B3
Hollow Glade PO38....41 D8
Hollow La
　Chillerton PO30....32 B4
　Godshill PO38....41 D8
Hollowood Rd PO30....35 A7
Hollows The PO30....19 F7
Holly Brooke CI PO37....35 B1
Holly Ct SO41....48 D7
Holly Ho SO19....51 E2
Holly Rd PO12....52 C5
Holly Tree CI PO33....12 D5
Hollywood Ct SO41....48 D5
Hollywood La SO41....48 D5
Holmbush Ct PO5....54 B1
Holmes Ct 3 PO41....15 D6
Homewood CI PO33....12 A2
Holmfield Ave PO41....16 D6
Holm Oaks SO41....48 C2
Holmsley CI SO41....48 B2
Holmwood CI PO35....25 E4
Holt Rd SO15....50 F6
Holy Cross RC Prim Sch
　....PO32....3 D4
Holy Rood Est SO14....51 A3
Holyrood Ho 9 SO14....51 A3
Holy Rood PI 6 SO14....51 A3
Holyrood St PO30....20 D7
Home Farm Ct PO30....32 C3
Homefort Ho 2 PO12....52 B5
Homegrove Ho PO5....54 C1
Homeheights 8 PO5....53 C2
Homelands PO30....7 D3
Home Meade PO30....20 F6
Homemerose Ho PO5....54 B2
Homesea Ho PO5....54 B2
Homewood Ho SO41....48 C2
Hooke CI PO40....15 A1
Hooke Hill PO40....15 A1
Hookes Way PO30....20 D8
Hope Lodge Sch SO18....51 E7
Hope Mead PO36....34 D8
Hope Rd
　....PO33....12 E4
　Shanklin PO37....43 D8
Hope Road App PO37....43 D8
Hope St PO1....54 B4
Hopkins Wlk PO30....22 A1
Horestone Dr PO34....13 D1
Horestone Rise PO34....13 D1
Hornbeam CI PO30....20 C8
Hornbeam Sq
　Ryde PO33....12 F2
　Ryde PO33....12 F2
Horndean Ho 6 PO1....54 C4
Hornet CI PO12....52 C4
HORRINGFORD....34 A7
Horsebridge Hill PO30....9 A3
Horseshoe Bridge SO14....51 C8
Horseshoe CI PO31....8 F7
Hoskins Ho PO1....53 B3
Hospital Rd PO32....3 C3
Houndwell PI SO14....51 A4
Howard CI
　Newport PO30....20 F8
　Niton PO38....45 B4
Howard Lo 20 PO5....53 C2
Howard Rd
　Shanklin PO37....35 D1
　Southampton SO15....50 D6
Howard's Gr SO15....50 C8
Howards Mead SO41....48 B2
Howell CI SO41....51 C5
Howgate CI PO35....25 E4
Howgate Rd PO35....25 D3
Howlett CI SO41....48 C2
Hoxall La PO30....29 D3
Hoy CI PO38....44 A7
Hudson Rd PO5....54 C2
Hulse Lodge 5 SO15....50 F8
Hulse Rd SO15....50 F8
Hulton CI SO19....51 D1
HULVERSTONE....29 B5
Hulverstone La PO30....29 B4
Hundred La SO41....49 A7
Hungerberry CI PO37....43 A7
Hunnycross Way PO30....20 D7
HUNNY HILL....20 C8
Hunny Hill
　Brighstone PO30....29 F3
　Newport PO30....20 D8
Hunnyhill Prim Sch PO30....20 C8
Hunter Rd PO4....53 F3
Huntly Way SO18....51 F7
Hunts Rd PO38....46 A3
Hurstake Rd PO30....20 D8
Hurst Castle* SO41....14 B6
Hurst Hill PO39....26 G7
Hurst Point View PO39....14 D1

Hurst View PO39 . . . . .26 G8
Hutchinson Dr PO33 . . . . . . .13 B3
Hutfield Ct **1** PO12 . . . . . . .52 B6
Huxford PO30 . . . . .34 A8
Hyde Park Ho PO5 . . . . .54 B3
Hyde Park Rd PO5 . . . . .54 B3
Hyde Rd PO37 . . . . .43 B8
Hyde St PO5 . . . . .54 B2
Hynes Ct **1** SO17 . . . . .51 B8

I

Idsworth Ho PO1 . . . . .54 B4
Imperial Appartments **8**
  SO14 . . . . .51 B3
Imperial Ave SO15 . . . . .50 B7
Imperial Pk SO14 . . . . .51 B7
Imperial Rd SO14 . . . . .51 B7
Imperial Way SO15 . . . . .50 C5
Ingledene Cl PO12 . . . . .52 C8
Inglewood Pk PO38 . . . . .46 C4
Ingle Rd PO5 . . . . .54 D1
Ingram Cl SO17 . . . . .51 C8
Inkerman Rd SO19 . . . . .51 D3
Institute Hill PO38 . . . . .45 B4
Inverness Rd
  Gosport PO12 . . . . .52 A7
  Portsmouth PO1 . . . . .53 E7
Irequois Ct SO14 . . . . .51 A4
Ironside Ct **7** SO14 . . . . . . .50 F3
Irwin Hts PO12 . . . . .52 A9
Isambard Brunel Rd PO1 . . .54 B3
Isenhurst Ct PO35 . . . . .25 D4
Island Free Sch The
  PO38 . . . . .42 C1
Island Learning Ctr
  PO30 . . . . .20 C8
Island VI Form
  PO30 . . . . .20 D6
Island Planetarium*
  PO41 . . . . .14 F6
Island Point SO41 . . . . .48 F4
Isle of Wight Airport
  PO36 . . . . .35 B5
Isle of Wight Bus Mus*
  PO33 . . . . .12 D5
Isle of Wight Coll PO30 . . .20 D8
Isle of Wight Donkey
  Sanctuary* PO38 . . . . .42 B7
·Isle of Wight Lavender*
  PO33 . . . . .21 C6
Isle of Wight Owl & Falconry
  Ctr* PO38 . . . . .42 A4
Isle of Wight Pearl*
  PO30 . . . . .29 E1
Isle of Wight Shipwreck Ctr
  & Maritime Mus* PO30 . .21 E2
Isle of Wight Steam
  Railway* PO33 . . . . .22 E8
Isle of Wight Studio Glass*
  PO30 . . . . .21 F2
ITCHEN 51 F4
Ivy Cl PO38 . . . . .45 B4
Ivy Ho **2** PO12 . . . . .52 C5
Ivy La PO1 . . . . .53 A6
Ivylands Cl PO39 . . . . .14 D1
Ivy Rd SO17 . . . . .51 C8

J

Jack Cockerill Way **8**
  PO5 . . . . .53 D1
Jackmans Cl SO19 . . . . .51 D3
Jacob's St PO1 . . . . .54 B4
Jago Rd PO2 . . . . .52 F7
Jamaica Pl PO12 . . . . .52 C5
Jamaica Rd PO12 . . . . .52 D6
James Ave PO36 . . . . .35 D3
James Butcher Ct **11** PO5 .53 D1
James Mews PO36 . . . . .35 D2
Jameson Gdns PO39 . . . . . . .14 E1
Jameson Rd SO19 . . . . .51 D1
James St SO14 . . . . .51 B4
Janaway Gdns SO17 . . . . . . .51 D8
Janson Rd SO15 . . . . .50 D8
Jarndyce Wlk PO2 . . . . .53 D7
Jasmine Ct
  Lymington SO41 . . . . .48 C4
  1 Southampton SO15 . . .50 F8
Jeal's La PO36 . . . . .35 F7
Jellicoe Cl PO33 . . . . .12 A3
Jellicoe Ho **8** PO1 . . . . . . .54 C4
Jellicoe Rd PO33 . . . . .12 A5
Jennifer Way PO32 . . . . .3 E2
Jennings Ct PO40 . . . . .27 C7
Jenny Streets La PO35 . . . . . .25 C2
Jensen Ct SO15 . . . . .50 F7
Jersey Rd PO2 . . . . .53 E8
Jervis Dr PO12 . . . . .52 B7
Jessie Rd
  Gosport PO12 . . . . .52 A5
  Portsmouth PO4 . . . . .53 E4
Jessie Terr **23** SO14 . . . . . .51 A3
Jireh Pl **3** PO1 . . . . .15 C6
Jo Benson Ct **3** PO4 . . . . .53 F2
Jocelyn Ct PO36 . . . . .36 A5
John Nash Ave PO32 . . . . . . .3 D3
John Rd PO30 . . . . .9 A2
Johnson St **4** SO14 . . . . . .51 A4
John's Rd SO19 . . . . .51 D1
John St
  Newport PO30 . . . . .20 E7
  Ryde PO33 . . . . .12 C5
  Southampton SO14 . . . . . . .51 A3
John Thornycroft Rd
  SO19 . . . . .51 C2

Joiners Mews SO19 . . . . .51 D2
Jonas Nichols Sq SO14 . . . . .51 B4
Jonathan Cl SO41 . . . . .48 E5
Jordan Cl PO31 . . . . .2 D4
Jordan Ho SO15 . . . . .50 C5
Jordans La SO41 . . . . .49 B8
Joseph Nye Ct **1** PO1 . . . .53 A5
Joseph St **9** PO12 . . . . . . .52 C5
Josephs Way PO37 . . . . .43 B8
Josian Wlk SO14 . . . . .51 B5
Joys La SO41 . . . . .49 E8
Jubilee Cl
  Freshwater PO40 . . . . .27 C8
  Godshill PO38 . . . . .41 C8
Jubilee Pl PO33 . . . . .12 D5
Jubilee Rd
  Gosport PO12 . . . . .52 B6
  Portsmouth PO4 . . . . .53 F3
Jubilee Terr PO5 . . . . .54 A1
Juniper Cl
  Carisbrooke PO30 . . . . .20 B7
  Lymington SO41 . . . . .48 B2
Juniper Ct **5** SO18 . . . . . . .51 F7
Juniper Rd SO18 . . . . .51 F7
Jupiter Ct PO1 . . . . .53 A4
Jurds Lake Way SO19 . . . . . .51 E1
Justin Cl PO12 . . . . .52 D7

K

Kealy Rd PO12 . . . . .52 A7
Keats Mews PO37 . . . . .43 C7
Keats Retreat PO37 . . . . .43 C7
Keats Vale PO30 . . . . .20 D1
Keelan Ct PO5 . . . . .53 D2
Keel Gdns **6** SO41 . . . . . . .48 E4
Keith Ct PO12 . . . . .52 B7
Keith Ho **24** PO12 . . . . . . .53 A5
Kellett Rd SO15 . . . . .50 E8
Kelly Ct **1** SO18 . . . . .51 E8
Kelsey Ct PO32 . . . . .3 E3
Kelston Cl SO15 . . . . .50 A7
Kemming Rd PO38 . . . . .45 D6
Kemmin La PO38 . . . . .45 F7
Kempfelt Ho **20** PO1 . . . . .53 A5
Kemps Quay Ind Pk SO18 .51 D7
Kendal Rd PO30 . . . . .26 H8
Kenilworth Ho **11** SO14 . .51 C6
Kenilworth Rd
  Portsmouth PO5 . . . . .53 D1
  Southampton SO15 . . . . . . .50 F6
Kennedy Cl PO33 . . . . .10 E4
KENNERLEY HEATH 33 B4
Kennet Cl PO12 . . . . .52 B2
Kensington Ct **14** PO12 . . .52 C8
Kensington Rd PO12 . . . . .52 C4
Kent Ave PO32 . . . . .3 A1
Kent Ho **4** SO14 . . . . .51 C5
Kentish Rd SO15 . . . . .50 C7
Kent Rd
  Portsmouth PO5 . . . . .54 B1
  Ventnor PO38 . . . . .47 B6
Kent St
  Portsmouth PO1 . . . . .53 A5
  Ryde PO33 . . . . .12 D4
  Southampton SO14 . . . . . . .51 C6
Kerrigan Ct SO17 . . . . .51 A7
Kerry Cl SO41 . . . . .48 C3
Kerry Fields PO34 . . . . .13 D1
Kestrel Cl PO36 . . . . .35 C2
Kestrel Way PO30 . . . . .20 A6
Keswick Rd SO19 . . . . .51 D2
Kettering Terr PO2 . . . . .53 C8
Keyes Ct **4** PO5 . . . . .53 D2
Key Haven Ct **1** PO39 . . . .14 D1
Kidson Ct PO2 . . . . .53 D8
Kilbride Path **5** PO2 . . . . .53 D8
Kilmiston Ct PO1 . . . . .53 E7
Kilpatrick Cl **6** PO2 . . . . . .53 D8
Kimberley Ct SO19 . . . . .51 E2
Kinchington Rd PO30 . . . . . .20 B6
King Albert Ct PO1 . . . . .54 C4
King Albert St PO1 . . . . .54 C4
King Arthur Cl PO33 . . . . . . .12 B5
Kingates La PO38 . . . . .45 C6
King Charles 1st Ct PO38 .47 A6
King Charles St **9** PO1 . . .53 A4
Kingcome Ho PO1 . . . . .54 A3
King Edward Ave SO16 . . . . .50 A8
King Edwards Cl PO37 . . . . .43 C8
King Edward VI Sch SO15 .50 E8
Kingfisher Cl PO30 . . . . .20 A6
King George V Cl PO33 . . . .12 E4
King Henry 1 St PO1 . . . . . . .54 A3
King James Cl PO31 . . . . .2 F4
King James Terr **2** PO1 . . .53 A2
King Richard 1 Rd PO1 . . . . .54 A3
Kings Bay Rd PO38 . . . . .47 C6
Kings Bench Alley **19** PO1 .53 A5
Kingsbury Rd SO14 . . . . .51 B7
Kings Cl
  Bembridge PO35 . . . . .25 C6
  Lymington SO41 . . . . .48 D4
Kingsclere SO19 . . . . .51 F1
Kings Cote Villas **3** PO5 .53 F1
Kings Cres SO41 . . . . .48 D4
Kingsdown Pl PO1 . . . . .54 D3
Kingsfield SO41 . . . . .49 A2
King's Ho **6** SO14 . . . . .51 A3
Kings Huts SO41 . . . . .48 A3
Kingsland Ct **3** SO14 . . . . .51 A4
Kingsland Ho **4** SO14 . . . . .51 A4
Kingsland Mkt SO14 . . . . . . .51 A4
KINGSLAND PLACE 51 A5
Kingsland Sq **5** SO14 . . . . .51 A4
Kingslea PO31 . . . . .3 A4
Kingslea Pk PO32 . . . . .3 D1

Kingsley Rd SO15 . . . . .50 B7
Kings Manor Rd PO40 . . . . . .15 B2
Kingsmere **1** PO31 . . . . . . .3 A4
Kings Mews SO15 . . . . .53 D2
Kings Park Rd SO15 . . . . .51 A6
Kings Rd
  East Cowes PO32 . . . . .3 C3
  Gosport PO12 . . . . .52 B6
  Lymington SO41 . . . . .48 D4
King's Rd
  Bembridge PO35 . . . . .25 C6
  Portsmouth PO5 . . . . .54 B1
  Ryde PO33 . . . . .11 E5
King's Saltern Rd SO41 . . . . .49 A2
King St
  Gosport PO12 . . . . .52 D6
  Portsmouth PO5 . . . . .54 B2
  Southampton SO14 . . . . . . .51 A3
King's Terr PO1, PO5 . . . . . . .54 A1
KINGSTON
  40 A7
  Portsmouth 53 F7
Kingston Cres PO2 . . . . .53 D8
Kingston Cross PO2 . . . . .53 D8
Kingston Pk SO41 . . . . .48 D2
Kingston Rd
  East Cowes PO32 . . . . .3 C2
  Portsmouth PO1, PO2 . . . . .53 E8
  Southampton SO15 . . . . . . .50 D6
Kingsway
  Cowes PO31 . . . . .3 A4
  Southampton SO14 . . . . . . .51 A5
Kingswell Path PO1 . . . . .54 B4
Kingswell St PO1 . . . . .54 B3
Kingswood
  3 Cowes PO31 . . . . .3 A4
  Marchwood SO40 . . . . .50 A1
King William St PO1 . . . . . . .53 A6
Kinterbury Ct **10** SO17 . . .51 A8
Kipling Cl SO19 . . . . .51 F1
Kirkstall Rd PO4 . . . . .53 F1
Kitbridge Rd PO30 . . . . .20 C7
Kite Hill PO33 . . . . .11 A5
KNIGHTON 22 E2
Knighton Rd SO19 . . . . .51 F4
Knighton Shute PO30 . . . . . .22 F3
Knight's Cross PO33 . . . . . . .21 F8
Knights Ct PO38 . . . . .47 B6
Kyngs Cl PO36 . . . . .24 A3
Kynon Cl **2** PO12 . . . . .52 C9

L

Laburnum Cl PO30 . . . . .20 E5
Laburnum Ct SO19 . . . . .51 D3
Lacey's La PO38 . . . . .45 B4
Lacon Cl SO18 . . . . .51 F8
Ladywood Ho PO5 . . . . .54 B2
Lake Common Rd PO36 . . . .35 D4
Lake Green Rd PO36 . . . . . . .35 D4
Lake Hill PO36 . . . . .35 E4
Lake Rd SO15 . . . . .50 C6
Lake Industrial Way PO36 .35 B3
Lakelands Dr SO15 . . . . .50 C6
Lake Rd
  Portsmouth PO1 . . . . .54 C4
  Southampton SO19 . . . . . . .51 D2
Laker Ho SO41 . . . . .50 F7
Lakeside Ct PO4 . . . . .53 F2
Lake Sta PO36 . . . . .35 E3
Lammas Cl PO31 . . . . .2 E5
Lamorbey Rd PO36 . . . . .35 D3
Lamorbey Terr PO36 . . . . . . .35 D3
Lamward Mans **1** SO14 . . .51 A7
Lance's Hill SO19 . . . . .51 F7
Landguard Manor Rd
  PO37 . . . . .35 C1
Landguard Rd
  Shanklin SO37 . . . . .43 C8
  Southampton SO15 . . . . . . .50 D6
Landon Ct PO12 . . . . .52 A3
LANDPORT 53 C7
Landport St
  Portsmouth PO1 . . . . .54 C4
  Portsmouth, Southsea PO5 .54 A2
Landport Terr PO1 . . . . .54 A2
Landport View PO1 . . . . .54 B4
Landscape La PO37 . . . . .21 B7
Landsdowne St PO5 . . . . .54 A2
Lane End Cl PO35 . . . . .25 E4
Lane End Cl PO35 . . . . .25 E4
Lane End Rd PO35 . . . . .25 E4
Lanes End PO12 . . . . .14 C1
Lanesend Prim Sch PO31 . .3 A2
Lane The
  Gosport PO12 . . . . .52 A2
  Portsmouth PO4 . . . . .53 F2
  Sandown PO36 . . . . .36 A4
Langbar Cl SO19 . . . . .51 E6
Langdon Mews **5** PO33 . . .12 C5
Langford Rd PO1 . . . . .53 F7
Langley Ct PO30 . . . . .20 E7
Langley Rd
  5 Cowes PO31 . . . . .3 B4
  Portsmouth PO2 . . . . .53 E8
  Southampton SO15 . . . . . . .50 A6
Langton Farm Gdns PO33 . .53 E7
Langtry Pl PO31 . . . . .3 A5
LANSDOWNE HILL 50 F4
Lansdowne Hill **4** SO14 . .50 F4
Lansdowne Ho **8** PO12 . . .52 A7
Lansdowne Rd SO15 . . . . . . .50 A7
Lansdown Gdns PO30 . . . . . .32 B4
Lanterns The PO35 . . . . .25 C5
Lanyards Lea PO33 . . . . .3 A3
Lapwing Ct PO12 . . . . .52 B8
Larch Ct PO1 . . . . .54 C4

Lark Rise
  Carisbrooke PO30 . . . . .20 A5
  Shanklin SO37 . . . . .35 C2
Lasham Ho **5** SO16 . . . . . .50 B8
Latham Ct SO15 . . . . .50 B7
Latimer Gate **22** SO14 . . .51 A3
Latimer Ho **1** SO15 . . . . . .50 F5
Latimer Rd PO33 . . . . .25 A6
Latimer St SO14 . . . . .51 A3
Launceston Cl **3** PO12 . . . .52 C8
Laundry La PO30 . . . . .20 C6
Laurel Cl
  8 Gosport PO12 . . . . . . .52 C8
  Southampton SO19 . . . . . . .51 D3
Laurel Est PO31 . . . . .3 B3
Laurel Ho **8** PO30 . . . . . . .20 D6
Lavender Cl SO19 . . . . .51 F5
Lavender Glade PO33 . . . . . .12 E3
Lavender Way PO33 . . . . .21 A6
Lavinia Rd
  Gosport PO12 . . . . .52 B5
  Gosport PO12 . . . . .52 B6
Lawn Ct SO17 . . . . .51 A7
Lawn Rd
  Lymington SO41 . . . . .48 B3
  Southampton SO17 . . . . . . .51 B8
Lawnside Rd SO15 . . . . .50 A8
Lawns The 9 D2
Lawrence Ct SO19 . . . . .51 F2
Lawrence Gr SO19 . . . . .51 F2
Lawrence Mans PO5 . . . . .54 D1
Lawrence Sq **8** PO12 . . . . .52 C5
Lawson Rd PO5 . . . . .54 D2
Lea Ct PO36 . . . . .35 D4
Leamington Ho **9** PO5 . . . .54 B2
Leander Dr **7** PO12 . . . . . .52 C8
Lea Rd SO19 . . . . .35 D4
Lear Rd PO12 . . . . .52 B6
Ledwell Ct PO12 . . . . .52 D7
Ledge St PO36 . . . . .35 F5
Lee Lands SO41 . . . . .48 D1
Leep La PO12 . . . . .52 B3
Lee Rd PO12 . . . . .52 A7
Lees La PO12 . . . . .52 B6
Leesland CE Inf Sch PO12 .52 A5
Leesland CE Jun Sch
  PO12 . . . . .52 B5
Leesland Rd PO12 . . . . .52 A6
Lees Lane N **8** PO12 . . . . . .52 B6
Leeson Rd PO38 . . . . .47 D7
Leigh Pk SO41 . . . . .48 C3
Leighton Ave SO41 . . . . .50 B8
Leighton Mount PO37 . . . . . .43 A7
Leighton Rd SO19 . . . . .51 F3
Leighwood Cl PO33 . . . . .12 B3
Lemon Rd SO15 . . . . .50 B7
Lennox Cl PO12 . . . . .52 C2
Lennox Ct **8** PO5 . . . . .53 D2
Lennox Mans PO5 . . . . .53 D1
Lennox Road N PO5 . . . . . . .53 D2
Lennox Road S PO5 . . . . .53 D2
Lentune Way SO14 . . . . .48 D2
Len Williams Terr PO2 . . . . . .53 E7
Leonard Rd PO12 . . . . .52 C6
Leopold St PO4 . . . . .53 F3
Leroux Cl SO15 . . . . .50 F5
Leslie Loader Ho SO17 . . . . .51 E5
Lessland La PO38, PO36 . . . .34 B2
Le Tissier Ct **6** SO15 . . . . .50 E6
Leventhorpe Ct PO12 . . . . . . .52 C5
Leveret Cl PO12 . . . . .52 C9
Lewis Ho **1** SO14 . . . . .51 A5
Leyland Cl PO12 . . . . .52 B4
Leyton Rd SO14 . . . . .51 C6
Lichfield Dr PO12 . . . . .52 C8
Lifeboat La PO12 . . . . .52 C8
Lift Rd PO37 . . . . .43 D7
Lighthouse The **10** PO5 . . .53 A4
Lilliput Doll & Toy
  Mus* PO36 . . . . .24 B3
Lime Kiln Shute PO36 . . . . . .34 D5
LIMERSTONE 30 E2
Limerstone Rd PO30 . . . . . . .30 D2
Lime St SO14 . . . . .51 A3
Limes The
  Marchwood SO40 . . . . .50 A1
  Newport PO30 . . . . .20 C7
  Shanklin PO37 . . . . .43 C6
Lime Tree Ct PO40 . . . . .27 B8
Lime Tree Ho **1** SO41 . . . .48 E4
Lincoln Cl PO35 . . . . .25 D3
Lincoln Rd PO1 . . . . .53 E5
Lincoln Way PO35 . . . . .25 D3
Linden Gr PO12 . . . . .52 B4
Linden Rd PO30 . . . . .20 C5
Linden Terr PO36 . . . . .24 B2
Linden Way SO41 . . . . .48 C4
Lind Hill **10** PO33 . . . . . . .12 C6
Lindon Ct PO4 . . . . .53 F4
Lind Pl PO33 . . . . .12 A6
Lind Rd PO12 . . . . .52 C2
Lindsay Ho **8** PO5 . . . . . . .53 D2
Lind St PO33 . . . . .12 C6
Liners Ind Est SO15 . . . . .50 C6
Lingdale Pl **3** SO17 . . . . . .51 A8
Lingfield Ct **2** PO1 . . . . . . .53 B3
Linington St **11** PO30 . . . . .20 D6
Linklater Path PO1 . . . . .53 D7
Link Rd **3** PO12 . . . . .52 D7
Linkside PO36 . . . . .35 D5
Linnet Cl PO30 . . . . .20 A6
Linnet Rise PO36 . . . . .35 C3
Linstone Dr PO41 . . . . .15 A5
Lion Brewery The **1** PO2 .53 D8
Lion Rd PO1 . . . . .52 F8
Lion St PO1 . . . . .53 B5
Lion Terr PO1 . . . . .53 B5

Lisbon Rd SO15 . . . . .50 D6
Lisle Cl SO41 . . . . .48 D3
LISLE COURT 49 C3
Lisle Court Rd SO41 . . . . .49 C3
Liss Rd PO4 . . . . .53 F4
Little Anglesey PO12 . . . . . . .52 B3
Little Anglesey Rd PO12 . . .52 A3
Little Arthur St PO2 . . . . .53 E7
LITTLE ATHERFIELD 39 C4
Little Coburg St PO1 . . . . . . .54 C3
Little Dene Copse SO41 . . . .48 B2
Little George St PO1 . . . . . . .53 E7
Little Green Orch PO12 . . . . .52 A3
Little Hambrook St **6**
  PO5 . . . . .54 A1
Little La PO12 . . . . .52 A3
Little Lance's Hill SO19 . . . . .51 F8
Little London PO30 . . . . .20 E8
Little Preston Rd PO33 . . . . . .12 A3
Little Princelett Cross
  PO36 . . . . .34 E2
Little Southsea St PO5 . . . . . .54 A1
Littlestairs Rd PO37 . . . . .35 F5
Littleton Cl PO38 . . . . .46 F6
Littletown La PO33 . . . . .10 D2
LITTLE WHITEHOUSE 7 F5
Little Whitehouse Rd PO30,
  PO31 . . . . .7 F5
Liverpool Rd PO1 . . . . .53 E5
Liverpool St PO1 . . . . .51 A7
Livesay Gdns PO1 . . . . .53 F6
Livingstone Rd
  Portsmouth PO5 . . . . .54 C1
  Southampton SO14 . . . . . . .51 A8
Loane Rd SO19 . . . . .51 F3
Lockerley Cl SO41 . . . . .48 E2
LOCKSGREEN 7 C2
LOCKSLEY 27 B7
Locksley Cl PO40 . . . . .27 B7
Locksley St SO15 . . . . .50 F7
Locksley Mews **7** PO40 . . .15 D3
Lodge Arts Ctr The* PO1 . .54 B3
Lodge Cl PO30 . . . . .30 A2
Lodge Gdns PO12 . . . . .52 A4
Lodge Rd
  Lymington SO41 . . . . .48 B3
  Southampton SO14 . . . . . . .51 A7
Lodgeside PO32 . . . . .3 D2
Lodge The SO15 . . . . .50 F7
Lodsworth Ho PO1 . . . . .54 C4
Lombard Ct **8** PO1 . . . . . . .53 A4
Lombard St PO1 . . . . .53 A3
Lomond Cl PO2 . . . . .53 D8
Londesborough Pl SO41 . . . .48 D2
Londesborough Rd PO5 . . . .53 E3
London Rd SO15 . . . . .51 A6
Long Acre Ct PO1 . . . . .53 E7
Longbeach PO40 . . . . .14 D2
LONGBRIDGE 34 D8
Longbridge Ho **8** PO5 . . . .54 B2
Longbridge Ind Pk SO14 . . .51 C3
Long Cl SO41 . . . . .48 A3
Long Curtain Rd PO5 . . . . . . .53 A2
Longford Pl SO41 . . . . .48 D1
Long La
  Downend PO30 . . . . .21 E4
  Newport PO30 . . . . .21 B6
Longlands La PO36 . . . . .34 C6
Longlands Shute PO35 . . . . . .24 E2
Long Lane Shute PO30 . . . . .21 D5
Longman Ct **22** PO35 . . . .53 C2
Longmead Rd PO33 . . . . .12 C4
Longmore Ave SO14 . . . . . . .51 D2
Longmore Cres SO19 . . . . . .51 D2
Long Orch PO33 . . . . .12 E3
Longs Wlk PO1 . . . . .53 D7
Long Water Dr PO12 . . . . . . .52 C2
Lonsdale Ave PO30 . . . . .9 A2
Lord Montgomery Way **1**
  PO1 . . . . .54 A2
Lords Ct PO1 . . . . .54 D3
Lords St PO1 . . . . .54 C4
Lorne Rd PO5 . . . . .54 D1
Louis Flagg Ho **2** PO5 . . .54 B2
Louis Rd PO36 . . . . .35 D4
Love La
  Bembridge PO35 . . . . .25 D6
  Cowes PO31 . . . . .3 A3
  Ventnor PO38 . . . . .46 E4
Lovett Way PO37 . . . . .35 C2
Lowcay Rd PO5 . . . . .53 E2
Lower Adgestone Rd
  PO36 . . . . .23 F1
Lower Alfred St **1** SO14 . .51 B6
Lower Banister St **7**
  SO15 . . . . .50 F6
Lower Bettesworth Rd
  PO33 . . . . .12 B3
Lower Brookfield Rd PO1 .53 E6
LOWER BUCKLAND 48 E5
Lower Buckland Rd SO41 .48 D5
Lower Canal Wlk SO14 . . . . .51 A3
Lower Church Path PO1 . . . .54 B3
Lower Church Rd PO31 . . . . .2 D3
Lower Fields PO38 . . . . .45 C4
Lower Forbury Rd PO5 . . . . .54 D2
Lower Furlongs PO36 . . . . . .24 B3
Lower Green Rd PO33 . . . . . .24 F7
LOWER HAMSTEAD 6 B2
Lower Highland Rd PO33 . .12 D4
Lower Horn Hill PO31 . . . . . .2 C3
LOWER HYDE 43 B8
Lower Hyde Est PO37 . . . . . .43 B8
Lower Mortimer Rd SO19 .51 D3

Lower Rd PO36 . . . . .35 D8
Lower Vicarage Rd SO19 . .51 D3
Lower William St SO14 . . . .51 D6
Lower Wingfield St PO1 . . .54 C4
Lower Woodside Rd PO33 10 E8
Lower York St SO14 . . . . .51 D6
LOWTHERVILLE 46 E6
Lowtherville Rd PO38 . . . . .46 F7
Luccombe Ct PO37 . . . . .43 C6
Luccombe Rd PO37 . . . . . . .43 C5
LUCCOMBE VILLAGE 43 C4
Lucerne Rd PO37 . . . . .43 C8
Lucerne Villa PO37 . . . . .43 C8
Lucia Foster Welch Coll
   Student Village **7** SO14 . .51 B3
Lucknow St PO1 . . . . .54 D3
Ludbrook Way PO38 . . . . . . .45 E7
Ludlow Inf Sch SO19 . . . . . .51 E4
Ludlow Jun Sch SO19 . . . . .51 E4
Ludlow Rd SO19 . . . . .51 E4
Lugley St PO30 . . . . .20 D7
Lukely Ct PO30 . . . . .20 C6
Lukely Gdns PO30 . . . . .20 C6
Lumsden Ave SO15 . . . . .50 D7
Lumsden Mans **3** SO15 . . .50 D7
Lushington Hill PO33 . . . . . .10 C4
LYMINGTON 48 C5
Lymington CE Inf Sch
   SO41 .48 D4
Lymington Jun Sch SO41 . .48 D4
Lymington New Forest Hospl
   SO41 .48 D4
Lymington Pier Sta SO41 . .49 A3
Lymington Rehabilitation
   Unit SO41 . . . . .48 E4
Lymington Town Sta
   SO41 .48 F4
Lynchens Cl PO35 . . . . .25 C4
Lynch La
   Brighstone PO30 . . . . .30 A5
   Calbourne PO30 . . . . .30 A7
Lyndhurst Rd PO12 . . . . .52 A5
Lyndock Cl SO19 . . . . .51 E2
Lyndock Pl SO19 . . . . .51 E2
Lynn Rd PO2 . . . . .53 F8
Lynwood Ct SO41 . . . . .48 D3
Lyon St SO14 . . . . .51 A6
Lysander Ct **21** PO1 . . . . . . .53 A4
Lyteltane Rd SO41 . . . . .48 D2

M

Mabey Cl PO12 . . . . .52 C3
Machin Cl PO30 . . . . .20 B6
Macketts La PO30 . . . . .34 B5
Macnaghten Rd SO18 . . . . .51 D8
Macnamara Almshouses
   PO31 . . . . .3 A2
Macrocarpa Rd PO38 . . . . . .47 A6
Maddison St **3** SO14 . . . . .50 F4
Madeira Ct PO38 . . . . .47 C6
Madeira La PO40 . . . . .14 C2
Madeira Rd
   Seaview PO34 . . . . .13 D3
   Totland PO39 . . . . .14 C1
   Ventnor PO38 . . . . .47 C6
Madeira Vale PO38 . . . . .47 C6
Madrisa Ct SO41 . . . . .48 E4
Mafeking Rd PO4 . . . . .53 F3
Magazine La SO40 . . . . .50 A3
Magdalen Cres PO31 . . . . . . .2 F4
Magnolia Dr PO33 . . . . .12 A3
Magnolia Rd SO19 . . . . .51 F5
Magnum Hall PO17 . . . . .35 D1
Maida Vale Rd PO37 . . . . . . .35 D1
Maiden La SO41 . . . . .48 F1
Main Rd
   Brighstone PO30 . . . . .30 B2
   Newport PO30 . . . . .7 D3
   Porchfield PO30 . . . . .7 D7
   Portmore SO41 . . . . .49 B7
   Rookley PO30 . . . . .33 A4
   Wellow PO41 . . . . .17 D4
Maitland St SO41 . . . . .48 D3
Maitland St PO1 . . . . .53 C1
Major Ct PO12 . . . . .52 B8
Makings Cl PO4 . . . . .27 C7
Malcolm Dyer Ct **8** PO30 .20 D4
Malcroft Mews SO40 . . . . . .50 A1
Maldon Rd SO19 . . . . .51 E4
Malins Rd PO2 . . . . .53 D8
Malins Road Apts **18** PO2 .53 D7
Mallard Point PO11 . . . . .9 B8
Mallfield Terr PO36 . . . . .24 B2
Mall Marlands (Sh Ctr) The
   SO14 .50 F4
Mall The
   Brading PO36 . . . . .24 B2
   Ryde PO33 . . . . .11 E4
   Sandown PO36 . . . . .35 E4
   Totland PO39 . . . . .14 D1
Malmesbury Pl SO15 . . . . . .50 D7
Malmesbury Rd SO15 . . . . .50 D7
Malta Rd PO2 . . . . .53 E8
Malthouse Cl **2** PO30 . . . . .20 D7
Malthouse Gn PO41 . . . . . . .17 E4
Malthouse Rd PO2 . . . . .53 D8
Malvern Rd PO5 . . . . .53 D1
Manchester Rd PO1 . . . . . . .53 E5
Mandela Way SO15 . . . . .50 E5
Manna Rd PO35 . . . . .25 C4
Manners La PO4 . . . . .53 E4
Manners Rd PO4 . . . . .53 E4
Manners View PO30 . . . . .9 B1

Manor Cres
   Newport PO30 . . . . .20 F7
   Rookley PO38 . . . . .32 F4
Manor Ct PO36 . . . . .35 D4
Manor Gn PO30 . . . . .17 E7
Manor Inf Sch PO1 . . . . .53 E7
Manor Park Ho **1** SO18 . . .51 E7
Manor Quay SO18 . . . . .51 D7
Manor Rd
   Freshwater Bay PO40 . . . . .27 E7
   Portsmouth PO1 . . . . .53 E7
   Sandown PO36 . . . . .35 D4
   Shanklin PO37 . . . . .43 B6
   Wroxall PO38 . . . . .42 D3
Manor Road N SO19 . . . . . . .51 E4
Manor Road S SO19 . . . . . . .51 E3
Manor Villas **4** PO39 . . . . .14 D1
Manor Wharf SO18 . . . . .51 C7
Mansion Ct **6** PO4 . . . . . . .53 E1
Mansion Rd
   Bembridge PO35 . . . . .25 D5
   Sandown PO36 . . . . .35 D3
   Whitwell PO38 . . . . .45 E7
Maple Ct
   Lymington SO41 . . . . .48 B2
   Southampton, Woolston
   SO19 .51 E2
Maple Dr PO30 . . . . .20 C7
Maple Leaf Ave PO33 . . . . . .12 E3
Maple Rd
   Portsmouth PO5 . . . . .53 E7
   Southampton SO18 . . . . . .51 E7
Maples Dr PO38 . . . . .47 C7
Maples The PO36 . . . . .35 D2
Marchwood Ind Pk SO40 . .50 A3
Marchwood Rd SO15 . . . . . .50 B6
Maresfield Rd PO32 . . . . .3 C4
Margam Ave SO19 . . . . .51 F5
Margaret Rule Hall **5**
   PO1 . . . . .54 B3
Margate Rd PO4 . . . . .54 C2
Margery's Ct **31** PO1 . . . . .53 A5
Marina Ave PO33 . . . . .12 F5
Marina Bldgs **3** PO12 . . . .52 B5
Marina Cl PO22 . . . . .3 C2
Marine Cotts **7** PO12 . . . . .52 B6
Marine Cross Rd PO37 . . . . .43 C8
Marine Ct PO38 . . . . .47 A5
Marine Dr PO41 . . . . .16 C8
Marine Par
   Southampton SO14 . . . . . .51 B4
   Ventnor PO38 . . . . .47 A5
Mariners Ct SO41 . . . . .48 F3
Mariners Way
   Cowes PO31 . . . . .3 A2
   Gosport PO12 . . . . .52 D4
Marine View PO32 . . . . .3 C3
Marine View Cl PO31 . . . . . . .2 F6
Marion Rd PO4 . . . . .53 F2
Maritime Archaeology Trust*
   SO14 .51 B2
Maritime Ave SO40 . . . . .50 A3
Maritime Chambers SO14 .51 B2
Maritime Way SO14 . . . . .51 A2
Maritime Wlk SO14 . . . . .51 B2
Mark Cl SO15 . . . . .50 A7
Market Hill PO31 . . . . .3 B5
Market Pl **11** SO14 . . . . .51 A3
Market Sq **1** PO41 . . . . . . .15 C6
Market St
   Ryde PO33 . . . . .12 C6
   Ventnor PO38 . . . . .47 A6
Marketway PO1 . . . . .54 B4
MARK'S CORNER 8 C5
Marlborough Cl PO33 . . . . . .12 E3
Marlborough Ct **8** PO12 .52 C9
Marlborough Rd PO12 . . . . .52 C9
Marlborough Pl SO41 . . . . . .48 D5
Marlborough Rd
   Carisbrooke PO30 . . . . .20 B6
   Ryde PO33 . . . . .11 F4
   Ventnor PO38 . . . . .47 A6
Marlborough Row PO1 . . . . .53 A6
Marlow Ct SO19 . . . . .51 F1
Marmion Ave PO5 . . . . .53 D2
Marmion Rd PO5 . . . . .53 D2
Marram Cl SO41 . . . . .48 E5
Marshall Ct **10** SO15 . . . . .50 F8
Marshall Sq SO15 . . . . .50 F8
Marsh Cl
   Freshwater Bay PO40 . . . . .27 C7
   Sandown PO36 . . . . .36 A4
Marsh Gn PO30 . . . . .30 B1
Marsh Ho **6** SO14 . . . . . . .51 A3
Marsh La
   Lymington SO41 . . . . .48 E5
   Southampton SO14 . . . . . .51 B3
Marsh Rd
   4 East Cowes PO32 . . . . .3 C4
   Gurnard PO31 . . . . .2 C3
Martine Ct PO40 . . . . .14 D2
Maryfield PO30 . . . . .20 D7
Maryfield SO41 . . . . .51 B4
Marymead Cl PO33 . . . . .12 D6
Mary Rose* PO1 . . . . .52 F7
Mary Rose Ave PO33 . . . . . . .10 E4
Mary Rose St PO1 . . . . .54 B3
Mary Rose The PO1 . . . . .54 B3
Matthews Way PO34 . . . . . . .13 D2
Maturin Cl SO41 . . . . .48 C1
Mauretania Ho **16** SO14 . .51 C4
Maxstoke Cl PO5 . . . . .54 C3
Maxted Cl PO11 . . . . .3 A3
May Ave SO41 . . . . .48 D5
Maybrick Rd PO33 . . . . .12 A5
May Cl PO38 . . . . .33 C1
Maycroft Ct SO41 . . . . .50 F8
Mayfair Gdns SO15 . . . . .50 F7
Mayfield Dr PO30 . . . . .21 A7

Mayfield Rd
   East Cowes PO32 . . . . .3 D2
   Gosport PO12 . . . . .52 C4
   Ryde PO33 . . . . .12 A5
Mayflower Cl SO41 . . . . .49 A2
Mayflower Ct
   Cowes PO31 . . . . .3 B4
   7 Southampton, Banister's Park
   SO15 .50 F7
   10 Southampton SO16 . .50 B8
Mayflower Rd SO15 . . . . .50 B8
Mayo Cl PO1 . . . . .53 D7
May Rd SO15 . . . . .50 C7
Maythorne Way PO37 . . . . . .43 C4
Maytree Inf Sch SO14 . . . . .51 B6
Mayville High Sch PO5 . . . . .53 D2
Meaders Rd PO33 . . . . .12 D4
Meadow Barn Cl PO39 . . . . .26 H8
Meadowbrook PO33 . . . . . . .11 F5
Meadow Cl
   Bembridge PO35 . . . . .25 D5
   Brighstone PO30 . . . . .30 B1
   Whitwell PO38 . . . . .45 F4
Meadow End PO35 . . . . .25 D5
Meadow Glade PO40 . . . . . .27 C8
Meadow Gn PO30 . . . . .20 D5
Meadowlands SO41 . . . . . . .48 B4
Meadowmead Ave SO15 . .50 A7
Meadow Rd
   East Cowes PO32 . . . . .3 D2
   Lymington SO41 . . . . .48 C2
Meadow St PO5 . . . . .54 A2
Meadow View Cl PO33 . . . . .12 B3
Meadow Way PO36 . . . . .36 C5
Meadow Wlk PO1 . . . . .54 B4
Mead Rd SO41 . . . . .48 B2
Medeway PO36 . . . . .36 A5
Medham Farm La PO31 . . . . .9 A8
Medina Ave PO30 . . . . .20 E6
Medina Breeze Wk PO32 . . . .9 E4
Medina Coll SO19 . . . . .9 D1
Medina Court Ind Est PO31 .3 B2
Medina House Sch PO30 . .20 F7
Medina L Ctr PO30 . . . . .9 D1
Medina Pk PO30 . . . . .9 E6
Medina Rd PO31 . . . . .3 B4
Medina View PO32 . . . . .3 C2
Medina Village Ind Est
   PO31 . . . . .3 B4
Medina Way PO30 . . . . .20 D8
Medley Pl SO15 . . . . .50 A7
Melbourne Ho PO1 . . . . .54 B3
Melbourne Pl
   Cowes PO31 . . . . .3 A6
   Portsmouth PO5 . . . . .54 B2
Melbourne St
   Newport PO30 . . . . .20 C6
   Southampton SO14 . . . . . .51 B4
Melbury Cl SO41 . . . . .48 D3
Melcombe Ho PO31 . . . . .2 F6
Melton Hall PO33 . . . . .12 D5
Melville Gdns PO36 . . . . . . .35 F5
Melville Rd PO12 . . . . .52 B8
Melville St
   Ryde PO33 . . . . .12 C6
   Sandown PO36 . . . . .35 E5
Merchants Row **6** PO1 . . .54 A3
Merchants Wlk **16** SO14 . .53 F3
Meredith Inf Sch PO2 . . . . . .53 E8
Merganser Cl PO12 . . . . .52 B8
Meriden Rd PO5 . . . . .54 A2
Merlin Lodge SO19 . . . . .51 D3
Mermaid Way SO14 . . . . .51 A3
Merridale Rd SO19 . . . . .51 E5
Merrie Gdns PO36 . . . . .35 C3
Merryl La PO38 . . . . .41 C7
MERRY OAK 51 F5
Merryoak Gn SO19 . . . . .51 F5
Merryoak Rd SO19 . . . . .51 F5
MERSTONE 33 D6
Merstone La PO30, PO38 . . .33 D6
Merton Cl **3** PO5 . . . . .54 C1
Merton Rd PO5 . . . . .54 C1
Methuen St SO14 . . . . .51 A7
Mews La
   Newport, Fairlee PO30 . . . . .9 D1
   Newport, Staplers PO30 . . .21 B8
Mews The
   2 Gosport PO12 . . . . .52 E5
   Newport PO30 . . . . .20 D7
Micawber Ho **22** PO1 . . . .53 D7
Midanbury Cl **3** SO18 . . . .51 E8
Midanbury Wlk **3** SO18 . .51 F8
Middle Barn La PO38 . . . . . .42 E3
Middle Common Rd SO41 .48 A3
Middle Ct PO1 . . . . .53 E7
Middle Rd SO41 . . . . .48 D3
Middle St
   Portsmouth PO5 . . . . .54 B2
   Southampton SO14 . . . . . .51 A7
MIDDLETON 27 A7
Middleton Terr PO31 . . . . .3 B5
Midhurst Ho PO1 . . . . .54 C4
Mile End Rd PO2 . . . . .53 C7
Milestone Cres PO36 . . . . . .34 E7
Milford Rd
   Lymington SO41 . . . . .48 C1
   Portsmouth PO1 . . . . .54 C3
   Shanklin PO37 . . . . .43 C8
Military Rd
   Brighstone PO30 . . . . .38 F7
   Brook PO30 . . . . .28 D6
   Chale PO38 . . . . .39 C2
   Gosport, Alverstoke PO12 .52 A2
   Gosport, Clayhall PO12 . . .52 C2
   Portsmouth, Landport PO1 .53 B7

Millais Rd SO19 . . . . .51 E3
MILLBANK 51 C5
Millbank Ho **14** SO14 . . . .51 C6
Millbank St SO14 . . . . .51 C5
Millbrook Point Rd SO15 . .50 A6
Millbrook Road E SO15 . . . .50 D5
Millbrook Road W SO15 . . .50 A6
Millbrook Sta SO15 . . . . .50 A6
Millennium Way PO36 . . . . .35 D4
Miller Cl PO30 . . . . .9 A3
Millers Ct PO37 . . . . .35 C2
Millers' La PO30 . . . . .20 A4
Miller's Pond Gdns SO19 . .51 F3
Millfield Ave PO22 . . . . .3 D4
Millfield Rd PO30 . . . . .20 B6
Mill Gate Ho **30** PO1 . . . . .53 A5
Mill Hill Rd PO31 . . . . .3 A3
Milligan Ho PO33 . . . . .12 B4
Milligan Rd PO33 . . . . .12 B4
Mill La
   Bembridge PO35 . . . . .30 B1
   Brighstone PO30 . . . . .30 B1
   Lymington SO41 . . . . .48 F4
   Newport PO30 . . . . .9 E4
   Portsmouth, Landport PO1 .53 C7
   South Baddesley SO41 . . . .49 F4
Mill Pond Rd PO12 . . . . .52 B7
Mill Rd
   Bembridge PO35 . . . . .25 C4
   Gosport PO12 . . . . .52 A7
   Shalfleet PO30 . . . . .17 E7
   St Helens PO33 . . . . .25 A6
   Yarmouth PO41 . . . . .15 D5
Mill Sq PO33 . . . . .10 F4
Mill St PO30 . . . . .20 D7
Millstream Ct PO30 . . . . .20 C7
Millward Pl PO33 . . . . .12 C4
Millward Rd PO33 . . . . .12 C4
Millways PO40 . . . . .14 F2
Milne Ct PO30 . . . . .20 D8
Milner Cl SO15 . . . . .50 C8
Milne Way SO19 . . . . .20 E5
Milton Rd
   Cowes PO31 . . . . .3 B2
   Southampton SO15 . . . . . .50 F6
Milverton Ho PO5 . . . . .54 B2
Mimosa Cl PO30 . . . . .20 C7
Mimosa Ct PO37 . . . . .43 C8
Minerva Cres **20** PO1 . . . .53 A4
Minerva Ct **2** PO4 . . . . . . .53 E1
Minerva Dr **9** PO12 . . . . . .52 C8
Minerva Rd PO12 . . . . .52 C8
Minnitt Rd PO12 . . . . .52 E5
Minstead Ct **4** SO17 . . . . .51 A8
Minster Cl **8** SO10 . . . . . . .50 C6
Mirabella Cl SO19 . . . . .51 D2
Mistral **1** SO14 . . . . .51 B3
Mitchell Ave PO38 . . . . .47 A6
Mitchell Cl SO19 . . . . .51 E2
Mitchell's Rd PO33 . . . . .12 A3
Mitten Rd PO35 . . . . .25 D4
Moira Ho PO31 . . . . .3 B5
Molesworth Rd PO12 . . . . . .52 C4
Monastery Rd SO18 . . . . . . .51 E7
Monckton Rd PO12 . . . . .52 B2
Monks Brook PO30 . . . . .9 B2
Monks Ct **4** SO41 . . . . .48 F2
Monks La PO40 . . . . .14 E4
Monkton St PO30 . . . . .12 D5
Monmouth Ct SO41 . . . . . . .48 E3
Montagu Cl PO12 . . . . .52 C9
Montague Wallis Ct **40**
   PO1 . . . . .53 A5
Monterey Rd PO33 . . . . .12 A3
Montgomerie Rd PO5 . . . . .54 C2
Monument Ct SO14 . . . . . . .51 A2
Monument La SO41 . . . . . . .49 A5
Moon Cl PO32 . . . . .3 D3
Moons Hill PO39, PO40 . . . .26 H6
Moorgreen Rd PO31 . . . . .3 A4
Moorhead Ct SO14 . . . . .51 C2
Moorings The PO31 . . . . .3 A3
Moorland Rd PO1 . . . . .54 B4
MOORTOWN 30 B3
Moortown La PO30 . . . . .30 A3
Moor View PO38 . . . . .33 D1
Moraunt Cl **1** PO12 . . . . . .52 C9
Mordaunt Rd SO14 . . . . .51 A7
Morecombe Ct **4** PO5 . . . .54 C2
Moreland Rd PO12 . . . . .52 B6
Morey Ct PO33 . . . . .12 B5
Morley Cl SO19 . . . . .51 F6
Mornington Rd PO31 . . . . . . .2 F6
Morris Rd SO15 . . . . .50 E5
Mortimer Rd SO19 . . . . .51 E4
MORTON 24 B1
Mortonbrook PO36 . . . . .35 F7
Morton Comm PO36 . . . . . .36 A5
Morton Lodge PO36 . . . . . . .24 A1
Morton Manor* PO36 . . . . . .24 A1
Morton Rd PO36 . . . . .24 A1
Morton Mews PO36 . . . . . . .24 A1
Morton Old Rd PO36 . . . . . .24 A1
Morton Rd PO36 . . . . .24 A1
Mosbach Pl **5** SO41 . . . . .48 E4
Moselle Ct SO15 . . . . .50 C5
Mottisfont Cl **1** SO15 . . . .50 A6
MOTTISTONE 29 C2
Mottistone Gdns & Est (NT)*
   PO30 .29 D4
Moulin Ave PO5 . . . . .54 A1
Mound Cl PO12 . . . . .52 A4
Mountbatten Ave PO31 . . . . .2 F5
Mountbatten Bsns Ctr
   SO15 .50 E5

Mountbatten Dr
   Carisbrooke PO30 . . . . .20 B7
   Ryde PO33 . . . . .12 A4
Mountbatten Way
   Portsmouth PO1 . . . . .53 B7
   Southampton SO15 . . . . . .50 C5
Mountfield **8** PO40 . . . . . .15 D6
Mountfield Rd PO38 . . . . . . .42 B3
Mountjoy Ct **4** PO1 . . . . . . .53 A5
Mount Pleasant Ho PO30 . .20 E6
Mount Pleasant Ind Pk
   SO14 .51 A8
Mount Pleasant Jun Sch
   SO14 .51 B7
Mount Pleasant La SO41 . .48 A7
Mount Pleasant Rd
   Gosport PO12 . . . . .52 B4
   Newport PO30 . . . . .20 D6
   Southampton SO14 . . . . . .51 B6
Mount Rd
   East Cowes PO32 . . . . .4 A1
   Wootton PO32 . . . . .10 A8
Mount St PO12 . . . . .12 C5
Mount The PO41 . . . . .15 D6
Mousehole La SO18 . . . . . . .51 F8
Muggleton La PO30 . . . . . . .30 E1
Muira Est SO14 . . . . .51 C5
Mulberry Cl
   Gosport PO33 . . . . .52 B5
   Newport PO30 . . . . .20 C7
Mulberry Way PO33 . . . . . . .12 F2
Mulberry Wlk SO15 . . . . .50 C8
Mullen Cl SO19 . . . . .51 E4
Mumby Rd PO12 . . . . .52 D6
Murefield Rd PO1 . . . . .54 C3
Murray's La PO1 . . . . .52 F7
Museum Rd PO1 . . . . .53 H2
Mus of Archaeology*
   SO14 .51 A2
Mus of Island History*
   PO30 .20 E7

N

Nancy Rd PO1 . . . . .54 D3
Nansen Cl PO35 . . . . .25 D3
Napier Rd PO5 . . . . .53 D2
Napier The PO37 . . . . .43 D7
Napoleons Landing PO36 . .35 F4
Nat Gonella Sq **4** PO12 .52 D5
Nat Mus of the Royal Navy*
   PO1 . . . . .52 F6
Nat Oceanography Centre*
   SO14 .51 B2
Naval Terr PO32 . . . . .3 D1
Needlemakers **3** PO14 . . .19 E1
Needles Old Battery (NT) The*
   PO39 .26 D5
Needles Pk The* PO39 . . . . .26 D5
Nelson Cl PO32 . . . . .3 D3
Nelson Cres PO33 . . . . .11 F4
Nelson Ct
   Cowes PO31 . . . . .3 B2
   8 Portsmouth PO1 . . . . . .53 D7
Nelson Ho **3** PO12 . . . . . . .52 E5
Nelson La PO33 . . . . .12 D6
Nelson Pl
   Lymington SO41 . . . . .48 F3
   Ryde PO33 . . . . .12 C6
Nelson Rd
   Gosport PO12 . . . . .52 B5
   Newport PO30 . . . . .20 C6
   Portsmouth, Landport PO1 .53 D7
   Portsmouth PO5 . . . . .54 C1
   Southampton SO15 . . . . . .50 C6
Nelson's Quay PO33 . . . . . . .24 F6
Nelson St
   Ryde PO33 . . . . .12 C6
   12 Southampton SO14 . .51 B3
Nepean Cl PO12 . . . . .52 B2
Neptune Cl **1** PO1 . . . . . . .53 A4
Neptune Ho SO14 . . . . .51 B2
Neptune Way SO14 . . . . .51 B2
Nessus St PO2 . . . . .53 D8
Netley Ct **8** PO12 . . . . .52 C9
Netley Mans **10** PO5 . . . . .53 C2
Netley Rd **13** PO5 . . . . .53 C2
Netley Terr **14** PO5 . . . . . . .53 C2
NETTLECOMBE 41 D1
Nettlecombe Ave PO4 . . . . .53 E1
Nettlecombe La PO38 . . . . .45 E7
NETTLESTONE 13 D3
Nettlestone Gn PO34 . . . . . .13 C3
Nettlestone Hill PO33,
   PO34 .13 D3
Nettlestone Prim Sch
   PO34 .13 C2
Neva Rd SO18 . . . . .51 F8
NEW BARN 3 E4
New Barn Bsns Pk PO30 . . .31 C3
New Barn La PO30 . . . . .31 C3
New Barn Rd PO32 . . . . .3 E3
NEWBRIDGE 17 D3
Newbridge Jun Sch PO2 . .53 F7
Newbridge Way SO41 . . . . .48 C1
NEWCHURCH 34 D7
Newchurch Prim Sch
   PO36 .34 E7
New Cliff Ho SO19 . . . . .51 E1
Newcombe Rd SO15 . . . . . . .50 E6
Newcomen Rd PO4 . . . . .53 E1
Newcome Rd PO1 . . . . .53 E6
NEWENDEN 48 E2
New Horizons Prim Sch
   PO2 . . . . .53 E8

Newland Ave PO12 . . . . 52 A5
Newlands
 Merstone PO30 . . . . 33 D5
 St Helens PO33 . . . . 25 A6
Newlands Ave SO15 . . . . 50 D7
Newman La PO38 . . . . 40 A3
Newman St SO16 . . . . 50 B8
Newnham La PO33 . . . . 11 C3
Newnham Rd PO33 . . . . 11 E3
NEWPORT 20 B7
Newport CE Prim Sch
 PO30 . . . . 20 C7
Newport Rd
 Cowes PO31 . . . . 8 F8
 Freshwater Bay PO40 . . . . . 27 E7
 Godshill PO38 . . . . 33 C1
 Niton PO38 . . . . 45 B4
 Sandown PO36 . . . . 35 C3
 Ventnor PO38 . . . . 44 F6
Newport Roman Villa★
 PO30 . . . . 20 C7
Newport St PO33 . . . . 12 C5
New Rd
 Brading PO36 . . . . 24 B2
 Brighstone PO30 . . . . 30 A1
 Porchfield PO30 . . . . 7 D2
 Portsmouth PO2 . . . . 53 F7
 Sandown PO36 . . . . 35 D4
 Southampton SO14 . . . . . . 51 A5
 Wootton PO33 . . . . 10 F5
 Yalford PO30 . . . . 39 A7
New Road E PO2 . . . . 53 F8
New St
 Lymington SO41 . . . . 48 E4
 Newport PO30 . . . . 20 D6
 Sandown PO36 . . . . 35 E4
New Street Mews SO41 . . . . 48 E4
New Theatre Royal★ PO1 . . 54 A3
NEWTOWN
 Gosport 52 D5
 Newport 6 E2
 Southampton 51 B6
Newtown CE Prim Sch
 PO12 . . . . 52 C6
*Newtown Harbour National
 Nature Reserve★ PO30 . . 6 D2*
*Newtown Marshes Nature
 Reserve★ PO30 . . . . 6 E2*
Newtown Old Town Hall★
 PO30 . . . . 6 E2
NEW VILLAGE 27 C8
Nicholas Cl PO36 . . . . 24 A1
Nicholson Gdns [1] PO1 . . . 54 C3
Nicholson Rd PO33 . . . . 12 D3
Nicholson St PO30 . . . . 9 A3
Nichols Rd SO14 . . . . 51 B5
Nickel St [5] PO5 . . . . 54 A1
Nickleby Ho [4] PO1 . . . . . . 54 C3
Nightingale Cl PO35 . . . . . . 25 D5
Nightingale Gr SO15 . . . . . 50 C7
Nightingale Rd
 Carisbrooke PO30 . . . . 20 A6
 Portsmouth PO5 . . . . 53 B2
 Southampton SO15 . . . . . . 50 C7
Nightingdale Ct [3] SO15 . . 50 C6
Nine Acres Prim Sch
 PO30 . . . . 20 D6
NINGWOOD 17 C6
Ningwood Hill PO41 . . . . . . 17 A7
Ninham Cl PO37 . . . . 35 C2
Nippert Ct [2] PO30 . . . . . . 20 D6
Nirvana Mans [12] PO5 . . . . 53 D1
NITON 45 B3
Niton Prim Sch PO38 . . . . . 45 B4
Niton Rd SO19 . . . . 51 E3
Niton Shute PO38 . . . . 45 A4
Nobbs La PO1 . . . . 53 A4
Node Cl PO33 . . . . 12 B3
Nodes Rd PO31 . . . . 8 F8
Nodgham La PO30 . . . . 20 A5
Noke Common Rd PO30 . . . . 8 E4
Norcliffe Rd SO17 . . . . 51 A8
Norcott Dr PO35 . . . . 25 D4
Norfolk Rd SO15 . . . . 50 D7
Norfolk St PO5 . . . . 54 B2
Norland Rd PO4 . . . . 54 D1
NORLEYWOOD 49 F8
Norleywood Rd SO41 . . . . . . 49 E8
Norman Ct
 Camp Hill PO30 . . . . 8 F1
 [4] Portsmouth PO4 . . . . . 53 E2
Normandy La SO41 . . . . 49 A1
Normandy Way SO40 . . . . . 50 A1
Norman Ho [16] SO31 . . . . 51 C6
Norman Rd
 Gosport PO12 . . . . 52 A4
 Portsmouth PO4 . . . . 53 E2
 Southampton SO15 . . . . . . 50 D5
Norman Way PO33 . . . . 10 E6
Norrish Cn PO2 . . . . 53 E7
NORTHAM 51 C6
Northam Bsns Ctr [3]
 SO14 . . . . 51 C6
Northam Mews PO1 . . . . . . 54 C3
Northam Rd SO14 . . . . 51 B5
Northam St PO1 . . . . 54 C3
Northbourne Ave PO37 . . . . 43 B8
Northbrook Cl PO37 . . . . . . 53 D7
Northbrook Rd SO14 . . . . . . 51 B5
North Cl SO41 . . . . 49 C2
Northcliff Bsns PO37 . . . . . 35 D1
Northcliff Hts PO37 . . . . . . 35 D1
Northclose Rd PO35 . . . . . . 25 D5
Northcote Rd PO4 . . . . 53 E3
North Court Cl PO30 . . . . . . 31 B2
North Cross St PO12 . . . . . . 52 D5
North Ct PO1 . . . . 53 E7

Northern Anchorage
 SO19 . . . . 51 D3
Northern Way PO1 . . . . 52 F8
Northesk Ho PO1 . . . . 54 C4
North Fairlee Rd PO30 . . . . . 9 E3
Northgate Ave PO2 . . . . 53 F8
North Greenlands SO41 . . . 48 E2
Northlands Gdns SO15 . . . . 50 E7
Northlands Rd SO15 . . . . . . 50 E8
Northover Rd SO41 . . . . . . 48 A4
North Rd
 Shanklin PO37 . . . . 43 C8
 Southampton SO17 . . . . . . 51 C8
North St
 Brighstone PO30 . . . . 30 B2
 Gosport PO12 . . . . 52 D6
 Lymington SO41 . . . . 48 C2
 Portsmouth PO1 . . . . 54 C4
 Portsmouth, Portsea PO1 . . 53 A5
 Sandown PO36 . . . . 36 A4
 Ventnor PO38 . . . . 47 D6
Northumberland Rd
 Newport PO30 . . . . 9 A1
 Portsmouth PO5 . . . . 54 D3
 Southampton SO14 . . . . . . 51 B6
North View
 Newchurch PO36 . . . . 34 D6
 Thorley PO41 . . . . 16 D6
North Wlk PO33 . . . . 12 E6
NORTHWOOD 8 E8
Northwood Bus Pk PO31 . . . . 9 A8
Northwood Dr PO33 . . . . . . 12 B6
Northwood Prim Sch PO31 . . 8 E7
NORTON 15 A5
Norton Cl SO19 . . . . 51 E3
Norton Grange Village
 PO41 . . . . 15 A6
NORTON GREEN 15 A3
Norton Green Ind Pk
 PO40 . . . . 14 F3
Nostalgia Toy Mus★
 PO38 . . . . 41 D8
Nubia Cl PO33 . . . . 2 F5
Nunnery La PO30 . . . . 20 C4
Nunwell House & Gdns★
 PO36 . . . . 23 F3
Nunwell St PO36 . . . . 35 E5
Nurseries The PO40 . . . . . 14 F1
Nursery Gdns PO32 . . . . 3 C3
Nursery La PO33 . . . . 12 A5
Nutfield Pl PO1 . . . . 54 C4
Nyria Way PO12 . . . . 52 D5

O

Oakbank Rd SO19 . . . . 51 D3
Oak Ct SO41 . . . . 48 C2
Oakfield CE Prim Sch
 PO33 . . . . 12 E4
Oakfield Ct PO33 . . . . 12 D4
Oakfield Rd PO33 . . . . 12 D4
Oakhill Rd PO33, PO34 . . . . 13 B4
Oak Hills PO37 . . . . 43 A7
Oaklands SO41 . . . . 48 F2
Oaklands Cl PO33 . . . . 11 B5
Oakleigh Ct PO33 . . . . 12 E5
Oakley Ct [11] SO41 . . . . . 48 E4
Oakley Ho
 Portsmouth PO5 . . . . 54 B1
 [3] Southampton, Banister's Pk
 SO15 . . . . 50 F7
 [12] Southampton SO15 . . 50 A8
Oakley Rd SO16 . . . . 50 A8
OAKFIELD 12 D4
Oaklyn Gdns PO37 . . . . 35 C1
Oak Rd
 Newport PO30 . . . . 20 F8
 Southampton SO19 . . . . . . 51 E2
Oaks Cl PO32 . . . . 3 E4
Oakside Gdns PO35 . . . . . . 25 C4
Oak St PO12 . . . . 52 C5
Oaks The SO19 . . . . 51 F5
Oaktree Cl PO36 . . . . 35 D3
Oak Tree Way PO32 . . . . 3 D4
Oak Vale PO33 . . . . 12 D4
Oakville Mans [11] SO15 . . 50 F6
Oakwood Cl PO33 . . . . 12 B3
Oakwood Ct PO30 . . . . 20 C7
Oakwood Rd PO33 . . . . 12 B3
Oasis Mayfield SO19 . . . . . . 51 F2
Obelisk Ct SO19 . . . . 51 D2
Obelisk Rd SO19 . . . . 51 E2
Oberland Ct SO41 . . . . 48 D4
Oceana Ho SO15 . . . . 50 E5
Oceanic Way SO40 . . . . 50 B3
Ocean Rd SO14 . . . . 51 A1
Ocean View Rd PO38 . . . . . 46 F6
Ocean Way SO14 . . . . 51 B2
Ochiltree Ho PO37 . . . . 43 B7
Ockendon Cl PO5 . . . . 54 B2
Officers' Quarters The
 PO12 . . . . 52 D6
Ogle Rd SO14 . . . . 50 F4
Old Auction Ho [13] PO12 . 52 E5
Old Bembridge Rd PO35 . . . 25 C6
Old Blackgang Rd PO38 . . . 44 F2
Old Bridge Rd PO4 . . . . 53 E2
Oldbury Ho PO37 . . . . 43 B7
Old Coastguard Cotts
 PO40 . . . . 27 C6
Old Commercial Rd PO1 . . . 53 C7
Old Cricket Mews SO15 . . . 50 F8
Old Farmhouse Mews
 SO41 . . . . 48 E5
Old Farm Wlk SO41 . . . . . . 48 E5
Old Forge Cl The PO33 . . . . 11 F5
Old Forge Ct SO41 . . . . 48 D2

Old Infirmary Ho [13] PO1 . 53 A4
Old Maltings The SO41 . . . . 48 D3
Old Oak View PO30 . . . . 8 F1
Old Orchards SO41 . . . . . . 48 E2
Old Park Rd PO38 . . . . 46 A3
OLD PORTSMOUTH 53 A3
Old Rd
 East Cowes PO32 . . . . 3 D4
 Gosport PO12 . . . . 52 C4
 Southampton SO14 . . . . . . 51 B2
Old Reservoir La PO36 . . . . 35 E4
Old Salterns Gate PO34 . . . 13 D4
Old School Ct PO38 . . . . . . 42 B5
Old School La PO30 . . . . . . 22 D1
Old Seaview La PO34 . . . . . 13 D3
Old Smithy & Gdns The★
 PO38 . . . . 41 D8
Old Star Pl [2] PO1 . . . . . . 53 A5
Old Station Rd PO38 . . . . . . 47 A6
Old Town Ct PO31 . . . . 3 B5
Old Town Hall Ct PO38 . . . . 47 B6
Old Vicarage La PO30 . . . . . 7 A1
Old Westminster La [1]
 PO30 . . . . 20 D7
Olinda St SO19 . . . . 51 E6
Oliver Rd SO41 . . . . 48 C3
Olivers Ct PO2 . . . . 53 E8
Olivia Ct [3] PO30 . . . . 20 D7
Omega Ho PO5 . . . . 54 C3
Omega St PO5 . . . . 54 C3
Ommaney Rd [1] PO41 . . . . 15 D6
Onslow Rd
 [4] Portsmouth PO5 . . . . . 53 D1
 Southampton SO14 . . . . . . 51 A6
Orchard Cl
 Freshwater PO40 . . . . 15 A1
 Wroxall PO38 . . . . 42 B5
Orchard Ct PO37 . . . . 35 C1
Orchard Ho [4] SO14 . . . . . 51 A3
Orchard La SO14 . . . . 51 A3
Orchardleigh Rd PO37 . . . . 43 C7
Orchard Mews PO36 . . . . . . 35 E6
Orchard Pl
 Cowes PO31 . . . . 3 A4
 Southampton SO14 . . . . . . 51 A3
Orchard Rd
 East Cowes PO32 . . . . 3 D3
 Portsmouth PO4 . . . . 53 E4
 Seaview PO34 . . . . 13 C4
 Shanklin PO37 . . . . 43 B7
Orchard St PO30 . . . . 20 D6
Orchards Way PO30 . . . . . . 31 B2
Orchard The PO30 . . . . 30 B2
Orchid Lodge PO37 . . . . . . 35 D1
Ordnance Rd
 Gosport PO12 . . . . 52 D5
 Southampton SO15 . . . . . . 51 A6
Ordnance Way SO40 . . . . . . 50 A3
Orion Ave PO12 . . . . 52 C8
Ormsby Rd PO5 . . . . 54 B1
Orwell Cl PO12 . . . . 52 C8
Osborne Chase PO31 . . . . . 3 A3
Osborne Cl PO33 . . . . 12 C4
Osborne Ct PO31 . . . . 3 A5
Osborne Ho★ PO32 . . . . . . 3 F2
Osborne Hts PO32 . . . . 3 E4
Osborne Rd
 East Cowes PO32 . . . . 3 C3
 Gosport PO12 . . . . 52 D6
 Portsmouth PO5 . . . . 53 C2
 Ryde PO33 . . . . 12 B4
 Shanklin PO37 . . . . 43 C7
Osborne Road S SO41 . . . . 51 C8
Osterley Rd SO19 . . . . 51 E4
Oswald Rd SO19 . . . . 51 D2
Our Lady & St Joseph RC
 Prim Sch SO41 . . . . 48 A4
Outram Rd PO5 . . . . 54 C1
Overdell Ct [8] SO15 . . . . . 50 E7
Oxford Ave SO14 . . . . 51 B6
Oxford Rd
 Portsmouth PO5 . . . . 54 D1
 Southampton SO14 . . . . . . 51 A7
Oxford St
 Cowes PO31 . . . . 8 F7
 Southampton SO14 . . . . . . 51 A3
Oyster Mews [7] PO1 . . . . . 53 A3
Oyster St PO1 . . . . 53 A3

P

Pacific Cl SO14 . . . . 51 C2
Packsfield La PO33 . . . . . . 10 C3
Paddock Cl
 Godshill PO38 . . . . 41 D8
 Shorwell PO30 . . . . 31 B2
Paddock Dr PO35 . . . . 25 F4
Paddock Gdns PO33 . . . . . . 48 D5
Paddock Rd PO37 . . . . 43 B7
Paddock The
 Gosport PO12 . . . . 52 A4
 Winford PO36 . . . . 34 F4
Padwell Rd SO14 . . . . 51 A7
Paget Rd PO12 . . . . 52 A3
Paget St SO14 . . . . 51 B4
Pagham Pl PO38 . . . . 33 B4
Pain's Rd PO5 . . . . 54 C2
PALLANCEGATE 8 D5
Pallance La PO31 . . . . 7 F5
Pallance Rd PO31 . . . . 8 B5
Palm Ct [17] PO5 . . . . 53 C2
Palmer's La PO36 . . . . 34 E7
Palmers Rd PO33 . . . . 10 D6
Palmerston Rd [26] PO5 . . . 53 C2
Palmerston Mans [3] PO5 . 53 C2

Palmerston Rd
 Portsmouth PO5 . . . . 53 C2
 Shanklin PO37 . . . . 43 C7
 Southampton SO14 . . . . . . 51 A4
Palmerston Road Prec [4]
 PO5 . . . . 53 C2
Palmyra Rd PO12 . . . . 52 A8
Pamplyn Cl SO41 . . . . 48 C4
Pan Cl PO30 . . . . 20 E6
Pan La
 Newport PO30 . . . . 20 F6
 Niton PO38 . . . . 45 B4
Pannall Rd PO12 . . . . 52 A8
Pan St PO1 . . . . 54 B4
Parade The
 Cowes PO31 . . . . 3 B5
 Portsmouth PO1 . . . . 53 A6
Paradise Cotts PO38 . . . . . 45 D8
Paradise St PO1 . . . . 54 B4
Parham Rd PO12 . . . . 52 C7
Parish Ct SO41 . . . . 48 E4
Park Ave
 Lymington SO41 . . . . 48 D4
 Ventnor PO38 . . . . 46 F5
Park Cl PO30 . . . . 19 F7
Park Court Flats [7] SO15 . 50 C6
Park Ct
 Cowes PO31 . . . . 3 A5
 Portsmouth PO5 . . . . 54 B1
Parkers Hill PO40 . . . . 14 F1
Park Gate PO32 . . . . 3 E2
Park Ho [9] PO5 . . . . 53 C2
Parkhouse Rd PO30 . . . . 9 A3
PARKHURST 9 A2
Parkhurst Rd PO30 . . . . 9 A2
Park La
 Nettlestone PO34 . . . . 13 C1
 Shorwell PO30 . . . . 39 B8
 [1] Southampton SO15 . . . 50 F5
Parkland Pl [8] SO17 . . . . . 51 A8
Parklands Ave PO31 . . . . . . 2 F4
Parklands Cl PO12 . . . . 52 B7
Parkmead Ct PO33 . . . . . . 12 D5
Park Mews PO36 . . . . 35 E6
Park Rd
 Brading PO36 . . . . 24 A3
 Cowes PO31 . . . . 2 F3
 Gosport PO12 . . . . 52 B4
 Lymington SO41 . . . . 48 D4
 Seaview PO34 . . . . 13 C4
 Ryde PO33 . . . . 12 D5
 Shanklin PO37 . . . . 43 D8
 Wootton Bridge PO33 . . . . 10 B3
Park Rise PO33 . . . . 35 E5
Parkside The SO16 . . . . . . 50 A8
Park St
 Gosport PO12 . . . . 52 B6
 Portsmouth PO5 . . . . 54 A2
 Southampton SO15, SO16 . 50 B8
Parkstone Ave PO4 . . . . . . 53 E2
Park Terrs [11] PO12 . . . . . 52 C5
Park View PO33 . . . . 10 C3
Park View Cl PO38 . . . . 42 B5
Parkwater Farm Ind Est
 PO30 . . . . 19 B7
Parkway
 Freshwater PO40 . . . . 15 A2
 Ryde PO33 . . . . 11 E4
Park Way PO36 . . . . 34 F4
Park Wlk SO14 . . . . 51 A5
Parsonage Rd
 Sandown PO36 . . . . 35 F7
 Southampton SO14 . . . . . . 51 C6
Partlands Ave PO33 . . . . . . 12 B4
Partlands Cl PO33 . . . . 12 B4
Partnership Park The
 PO4 . . . . 53 F5
Partridge Rd PO12 . . . . 9 A2
Paulsgrove Rd PO2 . . . . . . 53 F8
Pavilion Ct [4] SO15 . . . . . 50 E7
Pavilion Rise PO33 . . . . . . 12 E5
Pavilion Way PO12 . . . . . . 52 D6
Payne's Rd SO15 . . . . 50 D7
Peacock Cl PO37 . . . . 43 A7
Peacock Hill PO35 . . . . 25 A1
Peacock La PO1 . . . . 53 A3
Pearce Ct PO12 . . . . 52 C6
Pearmain Dr [6] SO41 . . . . 48 E2
Pearman Ct SO41 . . . . 48 C2
Peartree Ave SO19 . . . . . . 51 E5
Peartree Cl SO19 . . . . 51 D4
Pear Tree Cl PO33 . . . . 12 A3
Peartree Ct
 [7] Lymington SO41 . . . . . 48 E2
 Southampton SO19 . . . . . 51 E4
PEARTREE GREEN 51 D4
Peartree Rd SO19 . . . . 51 D4
Peel Pl PO5 . . . . 54 B2
Peel Rd PO12 . . . . 52 C5
Peel St SO14 . . . . 51 C5
Peggotty Ho [22] PO13 . . . 53 D7
Pelham Cl PO33 . . . . 10 F5
PELHAMFIELD 12 B6
Pelham Rd
 Cowes PO31 . . . . 3 B3
 Gosport PO12 . . . . 52 B6
 Portsmouth PO5 . . . . 53 C2
 Ventnor PO38 . . . . 46 D5
Pellhurst Rd PO33 . . . . 12 B4
Pell La PO33 . . . . 2 A4
Pelvieve Cl PO33 . . . . 11 F4
Pemberley Ct PO36 . . . . . . 35 D4
Pembroke Cl PO1 . . . . 53 A3
Pembroke Rd PO1 . . . . 53 A3
Penhale Inf Sch PO1 . . . . . 53 E5
Penhale Rd PO1 . . . . 53 E5
PENNINGTON 48 B1
Pennington Cl SO41 . . . . . . 48 C2

New–Por 63

Pennington Cross SO41 . . . 48 D2
Pennington Inf Sch SO41 . . 48 C2
Pennington CE Jun Sch
 SO41 . . . . 48 C3
Pennington Oval SO41 . . . . 48 B2
Pennycress Dr PO30 . . . . . 21 A6
Penny Ct [2] PO12 . . . . 52 C6
Penny St PO1 . . . . 53 A3
Pepys Cl
 Gosport PO12 . . . . 52 B2
 Portsmouth PO4 . . . . 53 F3
Percival Rd PO2 . . . . 53 F8
Percy Chandler St PO1 . . . . 54 C4
Percy Rd
 Gosport PO12 . . . . 52 C5
 Portsmouth PO4 . . . . 53 E4
 Sandown PO36 . . . . 35 D4
 Southampton SO16 . . . . . . 50 B8
Perkins Ho [8] PO1 . . . . . . 53 B5
Perowne Way PO36 . . . . . . 35 E7
Perseus Terr [18] PO1 . . . . 53 A4
Perth Ho PO1 . . . . 54 C3
Peterborough Rd SO14 . . . . 51 A7
Petersfield Ho PO1 . . . . . . 54 C4
Petersham Ho [5] PO5 . . . . 53 D1
Petticoat La PO30 . . . . 20 D7
Pettinger Gdns SO17 . . . . . 51 B8
Peveril Rd SO19 . . . . 51 E4
Phoenix Flats PO32 . . . . 3 C3
Pickwick Ho [16] PO1 . . . . 53 D7
Picton Ho [10] PO5 . . . . . . 54 B2
Pierhead Rd PO2 . . . . 53 A8
Pier Rd
 East Cowes PO32 . . . . 3 F3
 Portsmouth PO1 . . . . 53 B3
 Sandown PO36 . . . . 13 E3
Pierrellen Gdns PO37 . . . . 35 C1
Pier St
 Sandown PO36 . . . . 35 F5
 Ventnor PO38 . . . . 47 A6
 Yarmouth PO41 . . . . 15 C6
Pilgrim Pl SO41 . . . . 48 E3
Pinegrove Rd SO19 . . . . . . 51 F4
Pine Ridge Ct PO39 . . . . . . 14 C1
Pinetree Cl PO30 . . . . 48 B3
Pine Tree Ct PO31 . . . . 2 E5
Pineview Dr PO30 . . . . 19 F6
Pink Rd PO2 . . . . 53 E8
Pipit Cl PO12 . . . . 52 B8
Pippin Cl [8] SO41 . . . . . . 48 E2
Pippins Cl PO30 . . . . 30 A2
Pippins The PO31 . . . . 3 A3
Pirelli St SO14 . . . . 50 F4
Pitt Place La PO30 . . . . 29 F3
Pitt Rd SO15 . . . . 50 C6
Pitts La PO33 . . . . 11 F6
Pitt St PO1 . . . . 54 C4
Pitts The PO38 . . . . 47 D7
Pixley Hill PO40 . . . . 15 A4
Place Rd PO31 . . . . 2 F2
Place Side PO31 . . . . 2 F2
Plaish La PO30 . . . . 19 E3
Planet Ice PO33 . . . . 12 E4
Plantation Ct SO41 . . . . . . 48 D4
Platform Rd SO14 . . . . 51 A2
Player St PO33 . . . . 12 C5
Playfair Rd PO5 . . . . 54 C2
Play La PO33 . . . . 12 A4
Playstreet La PO33 . . . . . . 12 A4
Plover Cl PO36 . . . . 35 E6
Plymouth St PO5 . . . . 54 B2
Polecat Rise PO30 . . . . 21 A5
Poleclose La PO30 . . . . 19 E7
Poles La SO41 . . . . 48 E1
POLYGON 50 E6
Polygon Ct SO15 . . . . 50 E6
Polygon Sch SO15 . . . . 50 E5
Polygon The SO15 . . . . 50 E6
Pomona Rd PO37 . . . . 43 C7
Pompey Ctr PO4 . . . . 53 F5
Pondcast La PO33 . . . . 11 C1
Pond La SO14 . . . . 13 C3
PONDWELL 13 A3
Pondwell Cl PO33 . . . . 13 B3
Pondwell Hill PO33 . . . . . . 13 B3
Ponsonby Ho PO5 . . . . 54 B2
Poole Ave PO30 . . . . 9 A3
Poole Rd SO19 . . . . 51 E4
Popham Rd PO37 . . . . 43 C6
Poplar Cl PO35 . . . . 25 F4
Poplar Rd SO19 . . . . 51 F6
Poplars The
 Bembridge PO35 . . . . 25 D4
 Fishbourne PO33 . . . . 11 B6
Porchester Rd SO19 . . . . . 51 E3
PORCHFIELD 7 D3
Porchfield Bsns Pk PO30 . . . 7 E3
Porchfield Rd PO30 . . . . 7 B1
Porchester Rd PO2 . . . . . . 53 E8
Porter Ave PO36 . . . . 35 D3
Porter Cl PO36 . . . . 35 D3
Porter's La SO14 . . . . 50 F3
Portland Ho [7] PO12 . . . . 52 C5
Portland Rd PO5 . . . . 53 C2
Portland St
 Newport PO30 . . . . 20 D6
 Southampton SO14 . . . . . . 50 F4
Portland Terr
 [2] Portsmouth PO5 . . . . . 53 C2
 Southampton SO14 . . . . . . 50 F4
Port La Salle PO41 . . . . . . 15 B5
PORTMORE 49 A7
Port Royal St PO5 . . . . 54 C4

PORTSEA 53 B6
PORTSEA ISLAND 53 F6
Portside Cl SO40 ....50 A3
PORTSMOUTH 54 A4
Portsmouth Acad The PO1.53 E6
Portsmouth City Mus &
  Gallery* PO1 ....53 B3
Portsmouth Gram Jun Sch 1
  PO1 ....53 B4
Portsmouth Gram Sch 6
  PO1 ....53 B3
Portsmouth Harbour Sta
  PO1 ....52 F6
Portsmouth High Sch
  27 Portsmouth PO5.......54 A1
  Portsmouth PO5 ....54 A1
Portsmouth & Southsea Sta
  PO1 ....51 B8
Portswood Ave SO17.......51 B8
PORTSWOOD PARK 51 B8
Portswood Pk SO17........51 B8
Postern Ct 9 SO14 ....50 F3
Postern Rd PO30 ....8 F1
POUND GREEN 27 B8
Pound La
  Calbourne PO30...........18 B5
  Shorwell PO30 ....31 A1
  Ventnor PO38 ....47 A6
Pound Mead PO33 ....12 A4
Pound Rd SO41 ....48 B2
Pounds Terr PO1 ....53 A6
Pound Tree Rd SO14 ....51 A4
Powell Cl PO30 ....21 B7
Powell Ho PO30 ....20 E7
Powell Sq 8 PO1 ....53 A5
Power Rd PO1 ....53 E6
Powerscourt Rd PO2 ....53 E8
Powlett Rd SO41 ....48 E3
Poynings Pl PO1 ....53 A3
Presidents Ct 12 PO12 ....52 C9
Preston Cl PO33 ....12 D3
Preston Rd
  Bembridge PO35 ....25 D4
  Portsmouth PO2 ....53 F8
Pretoria Rd PO4 ....53 F3
PRIDDY'S HARD 52 C8
Priestlands La SO41.........48 C3
Priestlands Pl SO41.........48 C3
Priestlands Rd SO41........48 C3
Priestlands Sch SO41.......48 D2
Prince Alfred St PO12......52 B4
Prince George St PO1.......53 A5
Princelett Shute PO36......34 D3
Prince of Wales Ave SO15 50 A8
Prince of Wales Entrance
  PO32 ....3 E2
Prince of Wales Rd 3
  PO12 ....52 C5
Prince Regent Ct PO5......54 B2
Princes Cl PO39 ....14 E1
Princes Ct 2 SO14 ....51 C6
Princes Ct 1 PO1...........53 D7
Prince's Espl PO31...........2 D5
Princes Ho
  Portsmouth PO5 ....54 A1
  3 Southampton SO14.....51 C6
Prince's Pl 1 PO1 ....53 D7
Princes Rd
  Freshwater PO40..........14 E1
  Southampton SO15 ....50 D6
Princess Cl PO32 ....3 D3
Princess Royal Cl SO41 ...48 D4
Princess St PO1 ....3 A4
Prince's St
  Portsmouth PO1 ....53 D7
  Southampton SO14 ....51 C6
Prince St PO33 ....12 C5
Princes Way PO37 ....35 C2
Prior Cres PO30 ....9 A3
Priors Wlk PO30 ....20 B7
Priory Cl
  Portsmouth PO5 ....54 D2
  Ventnor PO38 ....46 F6
Priory Dr PO34 ....13 D1
Priory Farm La PO30.......20 B5
Priory Ho 6 SO14 ....51 A5
Priory Rd
  Carisbrooke PO30 ....20 A5
  Gosport PO12 ....52 B9
  Gosport PO12 ....52 C9
  Shanklin PO37 ....43 C6
  Southampton, St Denys
    SO17......................51 C8
Priory Sch
  Portsmouth PO4 ....52 D2
  Whippingham PO32.........3 F7
Priory Wlk PO38 ....45 C4
Pritchetts Way PO38 ......33 A5
Private Rd SO41 ....48 E5
Privett Ho PO1 ....53 A6
Proctor La PO1 ....53 F5
Prospect Rd
  Cowes PO31 ....3 A6
  Newport PO30 ....20 E6
  Portsmouth PO1 ....53 C7
  Shanklin PO37 ....43 C7
Providence Ct 2 PO1......53 C7
Puckaster La PO38...........45 B2
Puckpool Cl PO33 ....13 A4
Puckpool Hill PO33, PO34..13 A4
Puckwell La PO38............45 B4
Pump House La PO32 ....3 D2
Pump La SO15...............25 C6
Purbrook Rd PO1............53 E5

Purdy Rd PO30 ....20 B6
Pursley Cl PO36 ....35 C2
Pycroft Cl SO19..............51 F5
Pye St PO1 ....54 B4
PYLE 44 C7
Pyle Shute PO38.............39 F2
Pyle St PO30 ....20 D7
Pylewell Park Gdns*
  SO41 ....49 E4
Pyramids L Ctr PO5.........53 D1
Pyrford Gdns 3 SO41......48 E2
Pyrford Mews SO41.........48 E2

Q

Quarr Abbey* PO33.........11 C5
Quarr Cl PO33 ....11 E5
Quarr Hill PO33...............11 D5
Quarr Pl PO33 ....11 E5
Quarr Rd PO33 ....11 B6
Quarry La PO30 ....17 F4
Quarry Rd PO33 ....12 C6
Quarryside PO30 ....20 D5
Quarry Stone Cl PO33.....11 F5
Quarry View PO30 ....8 F1
Quarry View Ct PO30 ....8 F1
Quarterdeck The PO1 ......52 E6
Quay 2000 SO14............51 C8
Quay Arts Ctr* PO30......20 E7
Quay Hill SO41 ....48 F4
Quay La PO36................48 F4
Quay La SO41 ....48 F4
Quays 'Eddie Read'
  Swimming & Diving
  Complex The SO15........50 F3
Quayside Rd SO18 ....51 D7
Quay St
  Lymington SO41............48 F4
  Newport PO30.............20 E7
  5 Yarmouth PO41..........15 C6
Queen Elizabeth Ave
  SO41 ....48 D4
Queen Katherine Rd SO41 48 F3
QUEEN'S BOWER 34 F6
Queens Cl PO40 ....27 B8
Queen's Cres PO5 ....54 B1
Queen's Ct
  East Cowes PO32 ....3 D2
  Southampton SO15........50 E5
Queens Dr PO36 ....24 A3
Queens Gate
  East Cowes PO32 ....3 D3
  Portsmouth PO1 ....53 B2
Queensgate Foundation Prim
  Sch PO32 ....3 E1
Queen's Gr PO5 ....54 B1
Queens Ho 2 SO14........51 A3
Queens Keep
  22 Portsmouth PO5........53 C2
  4 Southampton SO15.....50 F5
QUEENSLAND 51 B5
Queen's Pl PO5 ....54 B1
Queens Rd
  Freshwater PO40...........27 B8
  Newport PO30 ....20 E5
Queen's Rd
  Bembridge PO35 ....25 D5
  Cowes PO31 ....3 A6
  Gosport PO12 ....52 C5
  Portsmouth, Buckland PO2 .53 B8
  Portsmouth PO1 ....52 F7
  Ryde PO33..................12 B5
  Sandown PO36 ....35 F6
  Shanklin PO37 ....43 C7
Queen St
  Lymington SO41............48 D3
  Portsmouth PO1 ....53 A5
Queen's Terr
  Portsmouth PO5 ....54 B1
  Southampton SO14 ....51 A3
Queenstown Rd SO15 .....50 D6
Queensway SO14 ....51 A3
Queen's Way PO5...........54 B1
Queens Wlk PO33...........12 F4
Quinton Cl PO5 ....54 C2

R

Racecourse PO32............10 A4
Radcliffe Ct SO14...........51 B5
Radcliffe Rd SO14 ....51 B6
Radnor St PO5...............54 B2
Radstock Rd SO19 ....51 E3
Radway Cres SO15..........50 D8
Raglan Ct PO12..............52 A5
Raglan St PO5................54 C3
Railway Flats PO1...........53 E5
Railway View 4 PO33......12 B5
Railway View Rd SO17.....51 C8
Rainbow Pl SO15............50 C6
Raleigh Ho PO1..............53 A5
Ramillies Ho 18 PO12.....52 C5
Ramley Rd SO41.............48 B3
Rampart Rd SO18...........51 D7
Rampart Row PO12.........52 E4
Rampart The SO41..........48 D5
Ranalagh Dr PO33 ....11 D6
Randolph St SO15 ....50 C7
Ranelagh Ct 9 SO17........51 A8
Ranelagh Gdns SO15.......50 E7
Ranelagh Rd PO36..........35 C5
Ranger Ct SO14 ....51 B2
Rashley Mews SO41.........48 E3
Ratcliffe Ave PO4 ....53 E3
Raven Croft PO5.............54 B1
Raven Rd SO14 ....51 B6

Ravenscourt Rd SO41......48 D2
Ravenswood Gdns 12
  PO5 ....53 D2
Rawlinson Terr PO1.........53 A6
Raymond Rd SO15..........50 D7
Rayners PO38.................46 E7
Rebecca Ct 8 PO30 ....20 C6
Recreation Ground Rd
  PO30 ....20 C6
Rectory Cl
  Gosport PO12 ....52 A3
  Wootton PO33 ....10 E5
Rectory Dr PO33 ....10 E5
Rectory La
  Brighstone PO30 ....30 B2
  Gatcombe PO30...........32 C8
  Niton PO38 ....45 B4
Rectory Rd
  Niton PO38 ....45 B4
  Shanklin PO37 ....43 C6
Redan The PO12.............52 C2
Redcliff Cl PO36.............36 C5
Red Fox Sq PO30 ....20 F6
Redhill Ho PO1...............54 C4
Redhill La PO38..............42 A6
Red House Mews SO41....48 E3
Redlake Rd PO40 ....15 B2
Redlands Dr SO19 ....51 F6
Redmoor Cl SO19 ....51 F6
Rednal Ho PO5 ....54 C3
Red Rd PO33 ....10 F5
Redshank Way PO30 ....9 E4
Redstart Cl PO30 ....20 A6
Redstone Bsns Ctr PO30..36 A4
Redver Gdns PO30 ....20 D8
Redvers Cl SO41 ....48 D2
Redwing Cl PO30 ....20 B6
Redwing Quay PO35 ....25 C5
Redwood Cl
  Carisbrooke PO30 ....20 B7
  Lymington SO41...........48 D5
Reed's Pl PO12 ....52 B7
Reeds Rd PO12 ....52 B8
Reed St PO33 ....12 C4
Reeth Flats PO38 ....45 B2
Regency Ct 12 PO1.........53 A4
Regent Ct PO1 ....53 D7
Regent Pl PO5................54 A1
Regent's Gr 8 SO16........50 B8
Regent's Gr 6 SO16........50 B8
Regents Park Com Coll 3
  SO16 ....50 A8
Regent's Park Gdns SO15 50 B7
Regent's Park Rd SO15....50 A7
Regents Pl PO12 ....52 D7
Regent St
  Portsmouth PO1 ....53 C7
  Shanklin PO37 ....43 C8
  Southampton SO14 ....50 F4
Regina Rd PO40 ....15 A1
Reigate Ho PO1..............54 C4
Reldas The 9 PO1...........53 A3
Renny Rd PO1 ....53 F5
Renouf Cl SO41..............48 C3
Renown Ho 15 PO12........52 C5
Resolution Ho 18 PO12....52 C5
Retreat The PO5 ....54 B1
Revenge Ho 16 PO12.......52 C5
Rew Cl PO38..................46 E6
Rew Down Nature Reserve*
  PO38 ....46 D7
Rew La PO38..................46 D7
Rew St
  Cowes PO31 ....2 D2
  Gurnard PO31...............2 C2
REW STREET 2 C1
Rew Valley Sp Ctr PO38 ..46 E7
Reynolds Ct PO31............2 F4
Reynolds Rd
  Gosport PO12 ....52 C3
  Southampton SO15 ....50 C8
Rhododendron Wlk PO32...4 B2
Riboleau St PO33 ....12 C5
Ricardo Way SO41..........48 C3
Richmond Ho 11 SO15....50 C6
Richmond Meade PO40....14 E1
Richmond Pl
  Portsmouth, Portsea PO1..53 B5
  Portsmouth, Southsea PO5..53 C2
Richmond Rd
  Gosport PO12 ....52 A5
  Portsmouth PO5 ....53 D2
  Southampton SO15 ....50 C6
Richmond St SO14 ....51 B3
Richmond Terr 17 PO5.....53 C2
Richville Rd SO16 ....50 A8
Ridge The PO31..............9 B8
Ridget La PO30 ....29 C3
Ridgeway La SO41..........48 D1
Ridgeway The PO36.........35 F7
Rigby Rd SO17...............51 B8
Ringbury SO41................48 D6
Ringwood Rd PO33 ....11 F5
Rink Rd PO33.................12 D5
Rink Rd Ind Est PO33......12 E5
Ripplewood SO40 ....50 A1
Riverbourne Ct SO18.......51 D8
River Ct SO41.................48 F4
Riverdene Pl SO18 ....51 D8
River Rd PO41................15 C6
Riverside Bsns Pk SO41...48 F4
Riverside Ct
  Southampton, Bitterne Manor
    SO18......................51 C7
  Southampton, Bitterne
    SO18......................51 E5
Rivers Reach SO41..........48 F3
River's St PO5................54 C2

River View PO32 ....9 F8
River View Ho SO19 ....51 D3
Riverview Pk PO30............9 C3
River Way PO30..............20 D8
RN Submarine Mus & HMS
  Alliance* PO12 ....52 E4
Road View PO2 ....53 C8
Robere Ho SO19 ....51 D3
Robert Mack Ct 39 PO1...53 A5
Roberts Rd PO1..............53 C5
Robin Ct SO15................50 E5
Robin Hill Countryside
  Adventure Pk* PO30.....21 F4
Robin Hood St PO30 ....20 F7
Rochester Rd PO4...........53 F3
Rochester St SO14 ....51 C5
ROCK 30 A4
Rockstone Ct 2 SO14......51 A6
Rockstone La SO14 ....51 A6
Rockstone Pl SO15..........50 F6
Rodney Ho 10 PO12........52 D5
Roebuck Dr PO12............52 C8
Rogate Ho 8 PO1 ....54 C4
Rogers Cl PO12 ....52 B7
Rogerson Ct PO31 ....2 F2
Rogers The PO37 ....35 C2
Rolfs Cl PO35.................25 E4
Rolla Ct 3 PO30 ....20 D6
Rollesbrook Gdns SO15....50 E6
Rolls Hill PO31 ....48 E4
Roman Ho SO18 ....51 C7
Romsey Cl SO15.............50 D6
Ronsons Cl PO31.............3 A3
Ronstan Gdns PO40.........15 B2
Rooke Ho PO12..............53 A5
Rookes La SO41 ....48 E2
Rooke St SO30...............51 A4
ROOKLEY 32 F5
Rookley Ctry Pk* PO38....33 A4
ROOKLEY GREEN 34 C7
Rope Quays PO12...........52 D6
Rope Walk 4 PO31 ....3 B4
Rope Wlk PO41...............13 D4
Rosalind Ct PO33 ....12 C3
Roseberry Ct PO36..........35 E5
Rosebrook Ct 4 SO18......51 E7
Rose Cl PO36 ....24 A3
Rose Ct PO36.................35 E5
Rosemary La
  22 Portsmouth PO1.......53 A5
  Ryde PO33..................12 C3
Rosemary Vineyard*
  PO33 ....12 C2
Rosemead PO36..............35 D3
Rosemount PO36 ....35 E4
Rose Rd SO14 ....51 A8
Rose The PO12 ....52 B2
Rosetta Dr PO12..............3 C3
Roseway PO36................35 D5
Rosewood Gdns SO40......50 A1
Rosida Gdns SO15 ....50 E6
ROSLIN 32 C1
Roslyn Ho PO5 ....54 B1
Rosoman Ct SO19 ....51 F4
Rosoman Ho SO19 ....51 F4
Rosoman Rd SO19 ....51 F4
Rossington Ave SO18 ......51 F8
Rossington Way SO18......51 F7
Rostrevor La 8 PO4........53 E1
Rostrevor Mans 8 PO4 ....53 E1
Rosyth Rd SO19 ....51 F3
Rotary Ct PO33 ....12 B3
Rotary Ho SO15..............50 D8
Rothesay Rd PO12 ....52 A8
Rothschild Cl SO19 ....51 E1
ROUD 41 B5
Roud La PO38 ....41 B5
Rougemont PO33 ....12 C3
Roundhouse Ct SO41.......48 D3
Rowan C
  Portsmouth PO4 ....53 F4
  Southampton SO19 ....51 F3
Rowan Gdns PO30 ....20 C7
Rowans Pk SO41.............48 D3
Rowans The PO33...........12 D4
Rowantree Dr PO34 ....13 D2
Rowborough La PO36......24 B4
Rowborough Rd SO18......51 F8
Rowena Ct PO5...............54 B2
Rowlands Cross PO33......11 D2
Rowlands La PO33 ....22 E6
Rowridge La PO30 ....19 A2
Roxan Ct 5 SO17............50 F7
Royal Cl PO17................35 C2
Royal Cres PO36.............35 F5
Royal Crescent Rd 10
  SO14 ....51 B3
Royal Entrance PO32 ....3 E3
Royal Exchange PO30......20 F7
Royal Mews 18 PO5.........53 C2
Royal South Hants Hospl
  SO14 ....51 A6
Royal St SO16................35 F5
Royal Wlk PO33..............12 C3
Rudd Way 18 SO14.........51 A3
Rudmore Rd PO2 ....53 C8
Rudmore Sq PO2 ....53 C8
Rufflers Way PO33 ....11 F5
Rugby Rd PO5 ....54 C1
Rush Ct PO38.................43 A2
Ruskins The PO35...........25 C5
Ruskins The PO35...........25 C5
Russell Ho PO30 ....20 E8
Russell Rd PO30 ....20 B6
Russell St
  Gosport PO12 ....52 A7
  11 Southampton SO14...51 A3
Russet Cl 3 SO41...........48 F2
Rustington Ho 3 PO1......53 B3

Rychris Ct PO37..............43 C7
Rydal Rd PO12...............52 A9
RYDE 12 E6
Ryde Academy PO33.......12 A4
Ryde Bsns Pk PO33.........12 A3
Ryde Cl 3 PO33..............12 C6
Ryde Esplanade Sta PO33 12 C6
Ryde House Dr PO33 ....12 A4
Ryde Pier Head Sta PO33 12 C6
Ryde Rd PO34................13 D4
Ryde Sch with Upper Chine
  PO33 ....12 B5
Ryde Terr SO14 ....51 B3

S

Sackville St PO5 ....54 B2
Sadlers Cl PO33 ....12 E4
Sainsbury Lodge PO1......54 D3
St Agathas Way PO1.......54 B4
St Alban's Gdns PO38......46 F6
St Albans Rd PO4 ....53 F3
St Alban's Rd
  Southampton SO14 ....51 B5
  Ventnor PO38 ....46 F6
St Andrews Ho 3 SO17...51 A3
St Andrews Rd SO14.......51 A5
St Andrew's Rd
  Gosport PO12 ....52 B5
  Portsmouth PO5 ....54 C2
St Andrew's St 7 PO31....3 B4
St Andrews Way PO40.....14 F2
St Annes Gdns SO41.......48 D3
St Anne's Gdns SO15......50 E3
St Annes Mews 18 SO14..51 A8
St Anne's RC Sch SO15...50 F6
St Anne's Rd SO19 ....51 E2
St Ann's Cres PO12 ....52 A7
St Ann's Ct PO4 ....53 F3
St Augustine Rd PO4.......53 F3
St Augustines Rd PO30....20 B7
St Barbara PO40.............14 E3
St Barbe Mus & Art Gall*
  SO41 ....48 E4
St Bartholomew's Gdns
  PO5 ....54 C1
St Bernard Ho 3 SO14....51 A3
St Boniface Cliff Rd PO37..35 D1
St Boniface Gdns PO38...42 B6
St Boniface Rd PO38.......47 B6
St Boniface Terr PO38.....47 B6
St Catherine's Lighthouse*
  PO38 ....44 F1
St Catherine's Oratory*
  PO38 ....44 E5
St Catherines Pl PO38.....47 B6
St Catherines Rd SO18....51 E8
St Catherine's Rd PO38...47 A6
St Catherine's Sch PO38..47 A6
St Catherine St
  Portsmouth PO5 ....53 D1
  Ventnor PO38 ....47 B6
St Catherines View
  Godshill PO38.............41 C8
  Ventnor PO38 ....47 B6
St Christopher Ct 1 PO5..53 E1
St Cross Bsns Pk PO30.....9 B2
St Cross Ct 1 PO30 ....20 D7
St Cross La PO30 ....20 D7
St Cyres Memorial Cotts
  SO41 ....48 F5
St David's Rd
  East Cowes PO32 ....3 C3
  Portsmouth PO5 ....54 C2
St Denys PO17 ....51 C8
St Denys' Sta SO17 ....51 C8
St Edmunds PO38...........40 A4
St Edmund's Rd SO16......50 B8
St Edmunds Wlk PO33.....10 E5
St Edward's Rd
  Gosport PO12 ....52 B5
  Portsmouth PO5 ....54 B1
St Edward's Terr 6 PO12..52 A7
St Faith's Cl PO12 ....52 A6
St Faith's Rd
  Cowes PO31 ....3 A3
St Francis Cath & CE
  Prim Sch PO38 ....42 C1
St Francis Rd PO12 ....52 C2
St George's App PO30.....20 E6
St George's Beneficial CE
  Prim Sch 45 PO1 ....53 A5
St George's Cl PO33 ....12 C6
St George's Ct 7 PO5......54 A1
St George's Ho 4 SO17...51 B8
St George's La PO30.......20 F4
St George's Rd
  Portsmouth, Old Portsmouth
    PO1.......................53 A4
  Ryde PO33..................12 B6
  Shanklin PO37 ....43 C8
St Georges St PO1 ....53 A5
St Georges St SO14 ....51 A4
St George's Way PO1......53 A5
St George's Way PO1......53 A5
St Georges Wlk PO12......52 D6
ST HELENS 24 F6
St Helens Ho PO4...........53 F2
St Helen's Mans 7 PO4...53 E1
St Helen's Par PO4.........53 E1
St Helen's Prim Sch PO33 24 F7

St Helier Rd PO12 . . . . .52 C9
St James Cl
  East Cowes PO32 . . . . .3 D4
  Yarmouth PO41 . . . . .15 C6
St James Ct ⁴ PO30 . . . . . . .20 D7
St James Ho 14 SO14 . . . . .51 A3
St James's Sq ⁶ PO30 . . . . .20 D7
St James's Sq ² PO41 . . . . .15 C6
St James's Rd
  Portsmouth PO5 . . . . .54 B2
  Southampton SO15 . . . . . . .50 D8
St James's St
  Newport PO30 . . . . .20 D7
  Portsmouth PO1 . . . . .53 B5
St James's St
  Newport PO30 . . . . .20 D6
  ⁸ Ryde PO33 . . . . .12 C6
  Yarmouth PO41 . . . . .15 C6
St John's Ave PO33 . . . . . . .12 D4
St Johns Cathedral RC
  Prim Sch PO1 . . . . .54 C3
St John's CE Prim Sch
  PO12 . . . . .52 B8
St John's Cl PO30 . . . . .20 D7
St John's Cl PO12 . . . . .52 B6
St John's Coll PO5 . . . . . . .54 C1
St John's Cres PO36 . . . . . . .36 A4
St John's Hill PO33 . . . . . . .12 D4
St Johns Prim Sch & Nursery
  18 SO14 . . . . .50 F3
St Johns Mews PO5 . . . . . .54 C1
ST JOHN'S PARK 12 E4
St John's Pl 14 PO30 . . . . . .20 D6
St John's RC Cath* PO1 . .54 A4
St John's Rd
  Newport PO30 . . . . .20 D6
  Ryde PO33 . . . . .12 C5
  Sandown PO36 . . . . .35 F5
  Shanklin PO37 . . . . .43 C7
  Wroxall PO38 . . . . .42 B5
St John's Road Sta PO33 . .12 D4
St John's Sq 6 PO12 . . . . . .52 B6
St John's Wood Rd PO33 . .12 D5
St Joseph's Cl PO32 . . . . . . .3 E2
St Josephs Mews PO5 . . . .54 C1
St Jude's CE (Controlled)
  Prim Sch PO1 . . . . .53 B3
St Judes Cl PO5 . . . . .54 C3
St Julien's Hospl
  (Almhouses) SO14 . . . . . .51 A2
ST LAWRENCE 46 A3
St Lawrence Rd ² SO41 . .51 B3
St Lawrence Shute PO38 . .46 B4

St Lukes Dr PO35 . . . . .25 D4
St Luke's Rd PO12 . . . . . . .52 A7
St Margarets PO38 . . . . . . .46 F7
St Margarets CE Prim Sch
  PO38 . . . . .46 E7
St Margarets Glade PO38. .46 E7
St Mark's CE Prim Sch
  SO15 . . . . .50 D7
St Mark's Cl PO12 . . . . .52 B2
St Marks Ct 1 PO12 . . . . . .52 A6
St Mark's Pl PO12 . . . . .52 B3
St Marks Rd
  Lymington SO41 . . . . .48 B3
  Southampton SO14 . . . . . . .51 B5
St Mark's Rd PO12 . . . . . . .52 A3
St Martin's Ave PO37 . . . . .35 D1
St Martin's Ho 1 PO5 . . . .53 D1
St Martins Rd PO38 . . . . . . .42 C4
St Mary's Ave PO12 . . . . . .52 A6
St Mary's CE Prim Sch
  SO14 . . . . .51 B4
St Mary's Cl PO33. . . . . . . .12 B3
St Mary's Coll SO18 . . . . . .51 F8
St Mary's Ct PO36 . . . . . . .24 B3
St Mary's Ho PO1 . . . . .53 F6
St Mary's Hospl (Newport)
  PO30 . . . . .9 A1
St Mary's Hospl
  (Portsmouth) PO1 . . . . . .53 F6
St Mary's L Ctr SO14 . . . . .51 A6
St Mary's Pas 8 PO33 . . . .12 C5
St Mary's Pl SO14 . . . . .51 A4
St Mary's RC Prim Sch
  Gosport PO12 . . . . .52 A6
  Ryde PO33 . . . . .12 E5
St Mary's Rd
  Brading PO36. . . . . .24 A3
  Cowes PO31 . . . . .3 A4
  Portsmouth PO1 . . . . .53 F6
  Southampton SO14 . . . . . . .51 A6
St Mary's Stadium
  (Southampton FC) SO14 .51 B4
St Mary St SO14 . . . . .51 B4
St Matthews Cl ² SO14 . .51 A5
St Matthews Ct PO12 . . . . .52 B6
St Michael's Ave PO33 . . . .12 B3
St Michaels Cl PO30 . . . . . .17 F7
St Michaels Rd PO33 . . . . . .24 F6
St Michael's Rd PO1 . . . . . .54 A2
St Michael's Sq 8 SO14 . .50 F3
St Michael's St 13 SO14 . .50 F3
St Nicholas Cl PO30. . . . . . .20 D5
St Nicholas St PO1 . . . . . . .53 A3
St Patrick's RC Prim Sch
  SO19 . . . . .51 E3
St Paul's Ave PO37. . . . . . . .43 C8
St Paul's Cres PO37 . . . . . . .43 C8
St Paul's Rd PO5 . . . . .54 A2
St Paul's Sq PO5. . . . . .54 A2
St Paul's View Rd PO30 . .20 E8
St Peters Ct PO33. . . . . .11 C1
St Peter's Gr PO5 . . . . .54 C1
St Pete Way PO36. . . . . .35 F6
St Ronan's Ave PO4 . . . . . . .53 E2

St Ronan's Rd PO4. . . . . . . .53 E2
St Saviors RC Prim Sch
  PO39 . . . . .26 H7
St Saviour's Rd PO39 . . . . . .26 H8
St Simons Rd PO5 . . . . .53 D2
St Stephens Rd PO2 . . . . . .53 E8
St Swithins Cres PO41 . . . . .15 F6
St Swithuns Ct 8 SO14 . .51 A6
St Swithun's RC Prim Sch 19
  PO5 . . . . .54 B1
St Thomas of Canterbury RC
  Prim Sch PO30 . . . . .20 B5
St Thomas Pk SO41 . . . . . . .48 D3
St Thomas Rd PO22 . . . . . . .3 D4
St Thomas's Ct 8 PO1 . . . .53 A4
St Thomas's Sq 12 PO33 . .12 C6
St Thomas's Rd PO12 . . . . .52 B9
St Thomas's Sq 6 PO30 . .20 D7
St Thomas's St
  Lymington SO41 . . . . .48 E3
  Portsmouth PO1 . . . . .53 A3
St Thomas' St PO33 . . . . . . .12 C6
St Urians PO30 . . . . .35 D4
St Ursula Gr PO5 . . . . .54 C1
St Valerie Rd PO12 . . . . . . .52 B4
St Vincent Coll PO12 . . . . . .52 B6
St Vincent Rd
  Gosport PO12 . . . . .52 B7
  Portsmouth PO5 . . . . .53 D2
St Vincents Cotts PO33 . . .12 A5
St Vincent's Rd PO33 . . . . .12 A5
St Vincent St PO5 . . . . .54 A2
St Wilfred Dr PO33 . . . . . . .12 C6
Salcombe Rd SO15. . . . . . . .50 C7
Salem Rd PO37 . . . . .43 C7

Salisbury Rd
  Portsmouth PO4 . . . . .53 F2
  Ryde PO33 . . . . .12 E3
Salisbury St 6 SO15. . . . . .50 F6
Salisbury Way PO30 . . . . . .35 F6
Salsette Ct PO31. . . . . .3 C6
Salterne Ho 8 SO41 . . . . .48 E2
Saltern's Rd PO34 . . . . .13 D4
Salter's Rd PO33 . . . . .12 A3
Saltmarsh Rd SO14 . . . . . . .51 B3
Samantha Ct PO37. . . . . . . .43 D8
Samber Cl SO41 . . . . .48 C4
Samber Hill PO30 . . . . .39 A8
Samphire Cl SO41 . . . . .48 E5
Sampson Rd PO1 . . . . .53 F7
Samuel Rd PO1. . . . . .53 F6
Sandcove Rise PO34 . . . . . .13 D3
Sandcroft Ave PO33. . . . . . .12 C4
SANDFORD 42 A8
Sandford Barns PO38 . . . . .41 F8
Sandford Cotts PO38 . . . . . .41 F8
Sandham Cl PO36. . . . . .35 C7
Sandham Gdns PO33. . . . . .35 C3
Sandhurst Rd SO15 . . . . . . .50 C6
Sandhurst Rd SO15 . . . . . . .50 E6
San Diego Rd PO12 . . . . . .52 B7
Sandlands PO34 . . . . .13 D2
Sandon Ct PO36 . . . . .35 F5
SANDOWN 35 E5
Sandown Rd
  Bembridge PO35 . . . . .25 B2
  Brading PO36. . . . . .24 D1
  Lake PO36 . . . . .35 D2
Sandown Sta PO36. . . . . . . .35 D1
Sandpath PO33 . . . . .11 E5
Sandpipers
  Bembridge PO35 . . . . .25 E4
  Seaview PO34 . . . . .13 D3
Sandringham Ct
  13 Gosport PO12. . . . . . . .52 C9
  5 Southampton, Millbrook
Sandringham La PO1 . . . . . .50 A6
Sandringham Rd PO1 . . . . . .54 D3
Sandrock Rd PO38 . . . . .45 A2
Sandy Cl PO30. . . . . .20 F1
Sandy La
  Blackwater PO30. . . . . .20 D1
  Shanklin PO37 . . . . .35 C1
Sandy Way PO30. . . . . .11 C1
Sapphire Cl 8 SO14 . . . . . .51 B4
Sapphire Ct 8 PO1 . . . . . .52 C8
Saracen Cl SO41 . . . . .48 C1
Savoy Ct
  Newport PO30 . . . . .20 E7
  Sandown PO36 . . . . .36 A3
  Shanklin PO37 . . . . .43 C7
Saxon Cl SO30 . . . . .21 A7
Saxon Ho 8 SO14 . . . . . . .51 C6
Saxon Pl SO41. . . . . .48 D6
Saxon Rd SO15 . . . . .50 D5
Saxon Wharf Ind Est SO19 .51 D6
Scarrots La PO30 . . . . .20 D7
School Cl PO30 . . . . .34 E7
School Cres PO38 . . . . .46 D6
SCHOOL GREEN 14 F1
School Green Rd PO40 . . . . .14 F1
School Hill Rd PO33 . . . . . . .3 C3
School La
  Arreton PO30 . . . . .21 F2
  Calbourne PO30 . . . . .18 A2
  Carisbrooke PO30 . . . . .20 A5
  Lymington SO41 . . . . .48 E4
  Lymington, Warborne SO41. .48 F7
  Newchurch PO36 . . . . .34 E7
  Newport PO30 . . . . .20 E7
  Niton PO38 . . . . .45 B4
  Wootton PO33 . . . . .10 F5

School Pl SO19 . . . . .51 E4
School Rd PO38 . . . . .41 D8
School St PO33 . . . . .12 D4
Scinde Cres PO37. . . . . .43 C8
Sconce Rd PO41 . . . . .15 A6
Scotchells Brook La PO36 .35 B4
Scotchell's Cl PO37 . . . . . . .35 C2
Scott Rd
  Portsmouth, Portsea Island
  PO1. . . . . .52 F7
  Southampton SO19 . . . . . . .51 F1
Scotts Cl PO30. . . . . .17 E7
Scullards La 1 SO14. . . . . .50 F4
Sea Breeze Cotts PO30. . . .29 F1
Sea Cl
  Ryde PO33. . . . . .12 B6
  Sandown PO36 . . . . .35 D2
SEAFIELD 52 D4
Seafield Rd PO34 . . . . .13 D4
Seafield Terr PO12 . . . . .52 C4
Seager's Ct PO1 . . . . .52 F4
Seagrove Dr PO36 . . . . .35 F6
Seagrove Farm Rd PO34 . .13 D3
Seagrove Manor PO34 . . . .13 D3
Seagrove Manor Rd PO34 .13 D3
Seahorse Wlk PO12. . . . . . .52 D6
Sealark Rd PO12 . . . . .52 B8
Sea Mill Gdns 15 PO1. . . . .53 A5
Sea Rd SO19. . . . . .51 D4
Searle Ct SO14 . . . . .12 D4
Seaton Cl SO41 . . . . .48 E5
SEAVIEW 13 C3
Seaview Cotts ² PO39. . . .14 E1
Seaview Ho PO34 . . . . .13 E3
Seaview La PO34 . . . . .13 D3
Seaview Rd PO31 . . . . .3 A3
Sea View Rd
  Cranmore PO41. . . . . .5 E2
  Totland PO40 . . . . .14 D2
Seaward Gdns SO19 . . . . . .51 E4
Seaward Rd SO19. . . . . .51 E4
Seaward Twr 11 PO12. . . . .52 E5
Sedgeley Gr PO12. . . . . .52 A8
Sedgley Cl PO5 . . . . .54 C2
Selborne Gdns PO12 . . . . . .52 A5
Selbourne Terr PO1 . . . . . . .54 D3
Seldon Ave PO33 . . . . .12 F4
Selhurst Ho PO1 . . . . .54 A4
Sellwood Rd PO40 . . . . .27 C7
Selma Ct 1 PO5. . . . . .53 D2
Selman Gdns PO31. . . . . .8 F8
Selsey Ave PO12 . . . . .52 A9
Selsey View PO37 . . . . .35 D1
Selwyn Ct PO33. . . . . .35 A6
Senator Ind Est PO36. . . . . .36 A5
Serpentine Rd 7 PO5. . . . .53 C2
Settle Cl 8 SO16 . . . . .50 B8
Settlers Ct PO1. . . . . .54 C4
Seven Sisters Cl PO38. . . . .46 A3
Seven Sisters Rd PO38 . . . .46 A4
Seymour Cl PO12 . . . . .53 D7
Seymour Ct 1 PO12 . . . . . . .3 C4
Seymour Pl PO35 . . . . .25 C6
Shaftesbury Rd
  Gosport PO12 . . . . .52 C4
  Portsmouth, Southsea PO5 .53 C2
Shaftsbury Rd PO12. . . . . . .52 C4
Shakespeare Ave SO17. . . . .51 B8
Shakespeare Rd PO1. . . . . . .53 E7
Shakespeare Terr 12 PO33 .53 A3
Shalbourne Rd PO12 . . . . . .52 A8
SHALCOMBE 29 A8
SHALFLEET 17 D7
Shalfleet CE Prim Sch
  PO41. . . . . .17 B7
Shallow La SO41. . . . . .48 E8
Shamblers Rd PO31 . . . . .3 B3
Shamrock Cl PO12 . . . . .52 D5
Shamrock Quay SO14 . . . . .51 D5
Shamrock Rd SO19 . . . . . . .51 D3
SHANKLIN 43 D7
Shanklin CE Prim Sch
  PO37 . . . . .43 B7
Shanklin Chine* PO37. . . .43 C7
Shanklin Rd
  Godshill PO38 . . . . .41 F8
  Portsmouth PO4 . . . . .53 E4
  Shanklin PO37 . . . . .42 F7
Shanklin Sta PO37 . . . . .43 D6
Shanklin Theatre* PO37 . .43 C7
Shanklin Twrs PO37 . . . . . . .43 C7
Shannon Ho 1 PO12 . . . . . .52 C9
Shannon Ho 9 SO14. . . . . .51 C5
Shaplands Mews 5 PO33 .12 C6
Sharon Ct
  Cowes PO31 . . . . .3 A6
  4 Gosport PO12. . . . . .52 C6
Sharon Orchard* PO33 . . .12 C2
Shearer Rd PO1 . . . . .54 D3
Sheat Farm Ind Est PO30 .32 C6
Sheffield Rd PO1 . . . . .54 D2
Sheilings The PO40 . . . . . . .14 E2
Shelley Ct SO15. . . . . .50 B8
Shepheard's Way PO12. . . .52 C3
Shepherd Mews ² PO33 . .12 C6
Shepherds' La PO30 . . . . . . .34 B8
Sherfield Ho 10 SO15 . . . . .50 E7
Sherwin Wlk PO12 . . . . .52 A4
Sherwood Rd
  Gosport PO12 . . . . .52 A5
  Newport PO30 . . . . .9 A1
Shide Chalk Pit Nature
  Reserve* PO30 . . . . .20 F5
Shide Cross PO30. . . . . .20 D5

Shide Ct PO30 . . . . .20 E5
Shide Rd PO30. . . . . .20 E5
Shide Villa PO30 . . . . .20 E5
Shiner Ct PO34 . . . . .13 C2
Shipbuilding Rd PO12 . . . . .52 F8
Ship Leopard St 17 PO12 . .53 A5
Shipyards Rd PO30 . . . . .30 A2
SHIRLEY 50 C8
Shirley Ave SO15. . . . . .50 C8
Shirley Bsns Pk SO15 . . . .50 C6
Shirley High St SO15,
  SO16 . . . . .50 B8
Shirley Park Rd SO16 . . . . .50 B8
Shirley Rd
  Portsmouth PO5 . . . . .53 E2
  Southampton SO15 . . . . . . .50 C7
Shirley Twrs SO15 . . . . .50 C8
Sholing Rd SO19 . . . . .51 E4
Sholing Sta SO19 . . . . .51 F2
Shooters Hill PO31. . . . . .3 B4
Shore Hill PO38 . . . . .47 A5
Shore Path PO31 . . . . .2 D4
Shore Rd
  Gurnard PO31 . . . . .2 D4
  Ventnor PO38 . . . . .47 D6
Short Row PO1 . . . . .53 A6
SHORWELL 31 B3
Shorwell Shute PO30 . . . . . .31 B4
Shotts La SO41. . . . . .49 C4
Shrewsbury Ct PO34 . . . . . .13 D3
Shrubbery Dr PO33 . . . . . . .11 E5
Shrubb's Ave PO41 . . . . . . .48 C3
Shute The PO30. . . . . .34 E8
Sibden Hill & Batts Copse
  Nature Reserve* PO37 . .43 A7
Sibden Mews PO37. . . . . . . .43 C7
Sibden Rd PO37 . . . . .43 B7
Sidings The PO31. . . . . .3 B3
Silcombe La PO40 . . . . .14 E1
Silver Birch Dr PO30 . . . . . .20 B7
Silverdale Ct 8 SO15. . . . . .50 F7
Silverdale Rd SO15 . . . . . . .50 E7
Silver St 1 PO5. . . . . .54 A1
Silver Trees PO37 . . . . .43 A7
Simeon St PO33 . . . . .12 D6
Simmonds Cl PO40 . . . . . . .27 C7
Simnel St 8 SO14 . . . . .50 F3
Sirenia Cl PO30 . . . . .20 A4
Sir George's Rd SO15 . . . . .50 D6
Sirius Cl PO34 . . . . .13 D2
Sirius Ct PO5. . . . . .54 B2
Sirius Ho 1 PO5 . . . . .53 D2
Sir Max Aitken Mus* PO31 .3 B5
Six Cotts PO32 . . . . .10 A7
Six Dials SO14. . . . . .51 A5
Skinner's Hill PO36 . . . . . . .34 F6
Skipper Cl SO40 . . . . .50 A3
Skipton Cl PO38 . . . . .12 D4
Slay La PO38 . . . . .45 D7
Slindon St PO1 . . . . .54 B3
Slingsby Cl PO1. . . . . .54 A1
Slipway The PO11 . . . . .2 F3
Sloane Stanley Ct PO12 . . .52 C5
Slocum Ho 18 PO12 . . . . . .52 C5
Sloop La PO33 . . . . .10 F5
Smallbrook Junction*
  PO33 . . . . .12 D2
Smallbrook La PO33 . . . . . .12 D2
Smallbrook Stadium
  PO33 . . . . .12 C1
Small Horse Fm Cl PO39. .14 D2
Smart's Cross PO38 . . . . . . .41 C4
Smithards La PO31. . . . . .3 B3
Smith St PO12 . . . . .52 E7
Snook's Hill PO30 . . . . .22 D8
Snooks La PO30 . . . . .49 B6
Snowberry Rd PO30 . . . . . . .20 C7
Snowdrop La PO30. . . . . . . .32 A8
Soberton Ho PO1. . . . . .54 C4
Solent Ave SO41 . . . . .49 A3
Solent Bsns Ctr SO15 . . . .50 B6
Solent Cl
  Lymington SO41. . . . . .48 F3
  Ryde PO33. . . . . .12 F5
Solent Ct
  28 Portsmouth PO5. . . . . . .53 C2
  Ryde PO33. . . . . .12 D6
  Southampton SO19 . . . . . . .51 E1
Solent Gate 12 PO5. . . . . . .53 E1
Solent Gdns
  Freshwater PO41. . . . . .14 E2
  Ryde PO33 . . . . .12 F5
Solent Ho PO40 . . . . .14 F3
Solent Ind Ctr SO15. . . . . . .50 C6
Solent Landing PO35. . . . . .25 C6
Solent Mead SO41 . . . . .48 E3
Solent Rd
  Cranmore PO41. . . . . .5 E1
  Southampton SO15 . . . . . . .50 E4
Solent View
  Bembridge PO35 . . . . .25 D5
  Totland PO40 . . . . .14 D2
  Walhampton SO41. . . . . . . .49 B3
Solent View Cl PO34 . . . . . .13 D3
Solent View Rd
  Gurnard PO31 . . . . .2 D3
  Seaview PO34 . . . . .13 D2
Solihull Ho PO5 . . . . .54 A2
Solway Ho 10 SO14 . . . . . .51 C6
Somborne Rd SO19 . . . . . . .51 F1
Somerset Cl 8 PO33 . . . . . .12 C2
Somerset Rd
  Portsmouth PO5 . . . . .53 D1
  Ryde PO33. . . . . .12 E3
  Seaview PO34 . . . . .13 D3
Somerset Terr SO15. . . . . . .50 C6
Somers Cl PO12. . . . . .52 C6
Somers Road N PO1 . . . . . .54 D3

Somerton Ind Est PO31. . . .3 A2
Somervell Cl PO12. . . . . . . .52 A3
Sommers Ct SO19 . . . . .51 C3
SOUTHAMPTON 51 D1
Southampton Central Sta
  SO15 . . . . .50 E5
Southampton City Art Gall*
  SO15 . . . . .50 F5
Southampton City Coll
  SO14 . . . . .51 B4
Southampton Maritime
  Mus* SO14 . . . . .50 F3
Southampton Rd SO41. . . .48 D5
Southampton Solent Marine
  Operations Ctr
  SO40 . . . . .50 A2
Southampton Solent Univ 10
  SO14 . . . . .51 A5
Southampton St 8 SO15. .50 F6
Southampton W Activity Ctr
  SO14 . . . . .51 C3
South Baddesley Rd SO41. .49 B4
SOUTH BADDESLEY 49 E6
South Baddesley CE Prim Sch
  SO41 . . . . .49 E6
South Bank Rd PO32. . . . . . .3 D2
Southbourne Rd SO41. . . . .48 D4
Southbrook Rd 8 SO15. . . .51 A6
Southcliffe Ho 1 SO14. . . .51 A6
Southcliff Rd SO14 . . . . .51 A7
South Cross St PO12. . . . . .52 D5
Southdown PO38 . . . . .39 E2
Southdown Mews PO40 . . .27 E7
Southdown Rd PO40 . . . . . .27 E7
Southern Rd
  Lymington SO41. . . . . .48 D3
  Southampton SO15 . . . . . . .50 E4
Southfield Gdns PO33. . . . .12 B3
SOUTHFORD 41 B2
Southford La PO38 . . . . .45 D8
South Front SO14 . . . . .51 A4
South Gr SO41 . . . . .48 F3
Southgrove Rd PO38 . . . . . .47 A6
Southgrove Terr PO38 . . . . .47 A6
Southlands SO41 . . . . .48 D3
Southlands Sch SO41. . . . . .48 F7
South Mill Rd SO15 . . . . . . .50 A7
South Normandy 4 PO1 . .53 A4
South Parade PO5 . . . . .53 D1
South Parade Pier* PO4. .53 E1
South Quay PO33 . . . . .25 A6
South Rd
  Cowes PO31 . . . . .3 B3
  Portsmouth, Portsea Island
  PO1. . . . . .51 C8
  Southampton SO17 . . . . . . .51 C8
SOUTHSEA 53 C1
Southsea Castle* PO5. . . .53 C1
Southsea Inf Sch 7 PO5. .53 E2
Southsea Model Village*
  PO4. . . . . .53 F1
Southsea Terr PO5 . . . . .54 A1
South St
  Gosport PO12 . . . . .52 D5
  Lymington SO41. . . . . .48 C2
  Newport PO30 . . . . .20 E7
  Portsmouth PO5 . . . . .54 A1
  11 Ryde PO33 . . . . .12 C5
  Ventnor PO38 . . . . .47 B6
  Yarmouth PO41 . . . . .15 D6
South Terr PO1 . . . . .53 A5
Southview 4 PO4 . . . . .53 F2
South View PO30 . . . . .20 D6
South View Cotts PO38 . . . .40 A4
South View Rd SO15 . . . . . .50 D8
Southwick Ho 6 PO1 . . . . .54 C4
PO36 . . . . .35 D5
Sovereign Ave PO12 . . . . . .52 C8
Sovereign Way PO33 . . . . . .12 B4
Spanners Cl PO38 . . . . .40 A4
Spartina Dr SO41 . . . . .48 E5
Spear Rd SO14 . . . . .51 B4
Speeds La PO33 . . . . .11 B1
Spencer Cl PO33. . . . . .12 C5
Spencer Ct ² PO5. . . . . . . .53 D2
Spencer Glade PO33 . . . . . .12 A6
Spencer Rd
  Portsmouth PO4 . . . . .53 F2
  Ryde PO33. . . . . .12 B6
Spenlow Cl PO33 . . . . .12 A4
Spice Quay 1 PO31 . . . . . .53 A3
Spicer Ho PO1. . . . . .53 C1
Spicer St PO1 . . . . .54 B4
Spindleberry Cl PO30 . . . . .20 C7
Spindlers Rd PO38 . . . . .46 A3
Spinnaker Cl PO31. . . . . . . .12 C2
Spinnaker Ct 8 PO1 . . . . . .53 A5
Spinnaker Quay PO1 . . . . . .52 F4
Spinnaker Twr* PO1 . . . . . .52 F5
Spitfire Ct SO19 . . . . .51 D3
Spithead Ave PO12 . . . . . . .52 C2
Spithead Bsns Ctr PO36 . .35 C3
Spithead Ct PO34 . . . . .53 C3
Spring Cl SO19 . . . . .51 F4
Spring Cres SO17 . . . . .51 B8
Spring Ct 1 SO15. . . . . .50 E5
Springfield Cl SO41 . . . . . . .49 A3
Springfield Ct SO19. . . . . . .51 F2
Spring Field Mews PO36 . . .35 F5
Spring Firs SO19 . . . . .51 E3
Spring Garden La PO12 . . .52 C6
Spring Gdns
  Portsmouth PO1 . . . . .54 A3
  Shanklin PO37 . . . . .43 C8

Spring continued
Ventnor PO38 . . . . .47 C6
Springhead PO38 . . . . .45 A4
SPRINGHILL 3 E4
Spring Hill PO38 . . . . .47 B6
Spring Hill Ct PO38 . . . . . .47 B6
Springhill RC Prim Sch
SO15 . . . . .50 E6
Spring La PO30 . . . . .20 B5
Spring Rd
Lymington SO41 . . . . .49 A2
Southampton, Itchen SO19 . .51 F4
Southampton, Merry Oak
SO19 . . . . .51 F6
Spring St PO1 . . . . .54 B3
SPRING VALE 13 B4
Springvale Rd PO34 . . . . . .13 B5
Spring Wlk
Newport PO30 . . . . .19 F6
Portsmouth PO1 . . . . .54 B4
Square The
Freshwater Bay PO40 . . . . . .27 C7
Gosport PO12 . . . . .52 C9
Lymington SO41 . . . . .48 C3
Squires Wlk SO19 . . . . .51 E1
Squirrel Cres SO19 . . . . . . .51 E1
Stacey Ct PO5 . . . . .53 C1
Stafford Rd
Portsmouth PO5 . . . . .54 C1
Southampton SO15 . . . . . . .50 D6
Stag La PO30 . . . . .9 B4
Stag Rd PO36 . . . . .35 E3
Stainers Cl PO33 . . . . .12 C5
Stamford St PO1 . . . . .54 D4
Standford St SO14 . . . . .51 B4
Stanford Gdns SO41 . . . . . .48 D2
Stanford Hill SO41 . . . . . . .48 D3
Stanford Rd SO41 . . . . .48 D3
Stanhope Dr PO31 . . . . .3 C2
Stanhope Gate ■ PO5 . . . .53 C2
Stanhope Lodge PO31 . . . . .2 F5
Stanhope Rd PO1 . . . . .54 B3
Stanley La PO5 . . . . .53 C2
Stanley Rd
Cowes PO31 . . . . .3 B3
Lymington SO41 . . . . .49 A2
Stanley St PO5 . . . . .53 C2
Stansted Rd PO5 . . . . .54 D2
Stanton Bldgs SO15 . . . . . .50 A7
Stanton Rd SO15 . . . . .50 A7
Stanton Rd Ind Est SO15 . .50 A7
STAPLERS 21 A7
Staplers Ct PO30 . . . . .20 F7
Staplers Rd PO30 . . . . .21 B7
Starkes Ho PO41 . . . . .17 A6
Starks Cl PO30 . . . . .31 B2
Star St PO33 . . . . .12 C5
Station App
25 Portsmouth PO1 . . . . . . .53 A5
Sandown PO36 . . . . .35 E5
Station Ave SO16 . . . . .35 E5
Station Gdns PO36 . . . . . . .24 B2
Station La PO36 . . . . .35 E5
Station Rd
Ashey PO33 . . . . .23 B7
Bembridge PO35 . . . . .25 C6
Brading PO36 . . . . .24 B3
Newbridge PO41 . . . . .17 C4
Newnorgal PO30, PO41 . . . .17 C4
Sandown PO36 . . . . .35 E5
Southampton, Sholing SO19 .51 F3
St Helens PO33 . . . . .24 F6
Wootton Bridge PO33 . . . . .10 D3
Wroxall PO38 . . . . .42 C4
Yarmouth PO41 . . . . .15 D5
Station St
Lymington SO41 . . . . .48 F4
Portsmouth PO1 . . . . .54 B3
Ryde PO33 . . . . .12 C5
Staunton St PO1 . . . . .54 B4
Steel St PO5 . . . . .54 A1
STEEPHILL 46 D5
Steephill Court Rd PO38 . .46 D5
Steephill Down Rd PO38 . .46 F6
Steephill Rd
Shanklin PO37 . . . . .43 C7
Ventnor PO38 . . . . .46 F6
Steerforth Cl PO2 . . . . .53 D8
Stenbury View PO38 . . . . . .42 C3
Stephen Lodge PO5 . . . . . .54 B1
Stephenson Cl PO12 . . . . . .52 A3
Stephenson Rd PO31 . . . . . . .3 A3
Steuart Rd SO18 . . . . .51 D7
Stewart Ct PO40 . . . . .15 A1
Stewart Pl PO11 . . . . .53 E7
Steyne Cross PO35 . . . . . . .25 C3
Steyne Rd
Bembridge PO35 . . . . .25 D4
Seaview PO34 . . . . .13 D3
Stickworth Hall PO30 . . . . .33 F7
Stirling St PO2 . . . . .53 D8
Stoddart Ave SO19 . . . . . . .51 F6
Stoke Gdns PO12 . . . . .52 C5
Stoke Rd PO12 . . . . .52 C5
Stokes Ct ■ SO15 . . . . .50 E6
Stokeway 4 PO12 . . . . .52 C5
Stonechat Cl PO30 . . . . .20 B6
Stoneham Cotts PO33 . . . . .11 E5
Stone La
Gosport PO12 . . . . .52 A4
5 Gosport PO12 . . . . .52 B5
Stonelands Orch PO33 . . . .11 F5
Stonelands Pk PO33 . . . . . .11 F5
Stonepitts Cl PO33 . . . . . . .12 A6
Stones Cl PO31 . . . . .3 A4

Stone St PO5 . . . . .54 A1
Stonewood Gate PO33 . . . .24 F7
Stony La PO1 . . . . .53 A6
Stower Pl PO36 . . . . .35 F7
Strand SO14 . . . . .51 A4
Strand The PO33 . . . . .12 D6
Stratford Ho PO5 . . . . .54 B2
Stratford Pl SO41 . . . . .48 D5
Strathmore Rd PO12 . . . . . .52 C5
Strathwell Cres PO38 . . . . .45 D6
Strawberry La PO30 . . . . . . .29 E5
Stroud Rd PO40 . . . . .27 C6
Stroud Wood Rd PO33 . . . .11 E2
Suffolk Ave SO15 . . . . .50 D7
Sultan Rd PO1, PO2 . . . . . . .53 D7
Summerfields Prim Sch
PO30 . . . . .20 F8
Summers Ct PO40 . . . . .27 A8
Summers La PO39 . . . . .26 H7
Summers St SO14 . . . . .51 C6
Sunbeam Way PO12 . . . . . .52 B4
Sun Ct PO5 . . . . .54 C2
Sundowner SO14 . . . . .51 B2
Sun Hill
Calbourne PO30 . . . . .18 B2
Cowes PO31 . . . . .3 B5
Sunningdale Rd PO30 . . . . .20 C6
Sunnyhill Cl PO36 . . . . .35 C3
Sunnyside Gdns PO36 . . . .35 E4
Sunnyvale PO37 . . . . .43 C8
Sunny Wlk PO1 . . . . .53 A6
Sun Pl PO33 . . . . .12 C5
Sunset Bgwls PO40 . . . . . . .14 D2
Sunset Cl PO40 . . . . .14 F1
Sunset Dr PO36 . . . . .35 F6
Sun St PO1 . . . . .53 A5
Surbiton Gr PO33 . . . . .12 D4
Surrey Ct SO15 . . . . .50 C6
Surrey Rd SO19 . . . . .51 D2
Surrey St
Portsmouth PO1 . . . . .54 B3
Ryde PO33 . . . . .12 C4
Sussex Ct
6 Gosport PO12 . . . . .52 C9
Portsmouth PO5 . . . . .54 B1
Sussex Pl
Portsmouth, Landport PO1 . .54 B4
Portsmouth PO5 . . . . .54 B1
SUSSEX PLACE 54 A4
Sussex Rd
Portsmouth PO5 . . . . .54 B1
Southampton SO14 . . . . . . .51 A4
Sussex Terr PO5 . . . . .54 B1
Sutherland Rd PO4 . . . . . . .53 E4
Sutton Cl PO33 . . . . .12 D3
Suvretta Ho PO37 . . . . .43 C7
Swains La PO35 . . . . .25 E5
Swains Rd PO35 . . . . .25 D5
Swallow Cl PO30 . . . . .20 A6
Swanage Cl SO19 . . . . .51 E3
SWANMORE 12 C3
Swanmore Rd PO33 . . . . . .12 B4
Swan Quay SO18 . . . . .51 D8
Swan St PO30 . . . . .20 F5
Swaylands Cl PO33 . . . . . . .12 F7
Sway Rd SO41 . . . . .48 B6
Swedish Hos SO41 . . . . .49 E8
Swift Gdns SO19 . . . . .51 D1
Swift Hollow SO19 . . . . . . .51 D1
Swift Rd SO19 . . . . .51 D1
Swiss Cottage Mus* PO32 . .4 B2
Swiss Cottage Rd PO32 . . . .4 A2
Sycamore Gdns PO30 . . . . .20 C7
Sycamores The PO33 . . . . . .12 D4
Sydenham Ct PO1 . . . . .54 D3
Sydenham Terr PO1 . . . . . . .54 D3
Sydney Cl PO30 . . . . .20 E5
Sydney Cotts PO36 . . . . . . .24 B3
Sydney Ho PO1 . . . . .54 B4
Sydney Rd PO12 . . . . .52 B5
Sylvan Ave PO32 . . . . .3 D3
Sylvan Dr
Carisbrooke PO30 . . . . .20 B7
Newport PO30 . . . . .20 C7
Synor Ho 12 SO15 . . . . .51 A6

T

Tadhurst Ho 4 PO1 . . . . . . .54 C3
Talbot Cl 2 SO14 . . . . .51 A3
Talbot Rd
Portsmouth PO4 . . . . .53 E4
Sandown PO36 . . . . .35 E4
Tamar Ct PO36 . . . . .35 F7
Tamarisk Gdns SO18 . . . . . .51 E8
Tamworth Ct 3 PO12 . . . . .52 B4
Tandy Cl PO33 . . . . .12 A4
Tanglewood SO40 . . . . .50 A1
Tankerville Rd SO19 . . . . . .51 D3
Tapnell Cotts PO41 . . . . . . .16 C1
Tasman Cl SO14 . . . . .51 B2
Tasman Ct SO14 . . . . .51 B2
Taswell Rd PO5 . . . . .53 D2
Tattels La PO41 . . . . .16 C6
Taylor Cl SO19 . . . . .51 D1
Taylor Rd PO12 . . . . .52 C5
Tebourba Dr PO12 . . . . .52 A4
Ted Bates Ct 7 SO15 . . . . .50 E6
Ted Bates Rd 8 SO14 . . . . .51 B3
Ted Kelly Ct 43 PO5 . . . . . .53 A5
Telephone Rd PO4 . . . . .53 E4
Temeraire 11 SO15 . . . . . . .50 F8
Templar Ct 2 SO15 . . . . . . .51 E2
Temple Gdns SO19 . . . . . . .51 F2
Temple La PO12 . . . . .52 A4
Temple St PO1 . . . . .54 B4

Tennyson Cl
Ryde PO33 . . . . .12 A5
Tennyson Mon PO1 . . . . . . .11 D6
Tennyson Ho 6 PO33 . . . . .12 C6
Tennyson Mon The*
PO39 . . . . .26 H5
Tennyson Rd
Cowes PO31 . . . . .3 B3
Freshwater PO40 . . . . .14 E1
Portsmouth PO2 . . . . .53 F8
Yarmouth PO41 . . . . .15 E6
Tennysons View PO40 . . . . .27 D6
Tennyson View PO30 . . . . . .18 A3
Terence Gdns PO4 . . . . .53 E2
Terminus Rd PO31 . . . . .3 A5
Terminus Terr SO14 . . . . . . .51 B3
Ternal Mead PO38 . . . . .33 D1
Terrace La PO40 . . . . .27 C6
Terrace Rd PO30 . . . . .20 D6
Terrace The PO38 . . . . .44 C5
Testcombe Rd PO12 . . . . . . .52 B4
Testwood Rd SO15 . . . . .50 B6
Teviot Ho 9 SO41 . . . . .51 C6
Tewkesbury Ave PO12 . . . . .52 B8
Thackeray Rd SO17 . . . . . . .51 B8
Thatchers La SO41 . . . . .49 F8
Theatre Mews 17 PO5 . . . . .53 D2
Thetis Rd PO1 . . . . .3 B4
Thicket The PO5 . . . . .54 C1
Thomas Grant Ave PO12 . . .52 D7
THORLEY 16 C6
Thorley Rd PO41 . . . . .15 E6
THORLEY STREET 16 D5
Thornbrake Rd PO12 . . . . . .52 C4
Thornbrough Cl PO33 . . . . .12 A5
Thornbury Ave SO15 . . . . . .50 E7
Thorncroft Rd PO1 . . . . .53 E5
THORNCROSS 38 F8
Thorncross La PO30 . . . . . . .38 G7
Thorners Ct 8 SO15 . . . . . .50 F6
Thorner's Homes, Centre Ct
15 SO15 . . . . .50 B8
Thorner's Homes, North Ct
14 SO15 . . . . .50 B8
Thorner's Homes, South Ct
16 SO15 . . . . .50 B8
Thorner's Homes, West Cl 18
SO15 . . . . .50 B8
Thorness La PO31 . . . . .7 E5
Thorngate St 5 PO12 . . . . .52 A7
Thorngate Way 6 PO12 . . .52 D5
Thornhill Flats PO33 . . . . . . .3 A5
Thornleigh Rd SO19 . . . . . .51 E2
Thornton Cl PO33 . . . . .12 F4
Thornton Manor Dr PO33 . .12 F4
Thornton Rd PO33 . . . . .12 F4
Thornycroft Ave SO19 . . . . .51 D2
Threefield La SO14 . . . . .51 B3
Three Gates Bus Pk PO33 . . .2 F2
Three Gates Rd PO31 . . . . . .2 F2
Three Tun Cl PO1 . . . . .53 A5
Thruxton Ct SO19 . . . . .51 E3
Ticonderoga Gdns SO19 . . .51 E1
Tides Reach
Cowes PO31 . . . . .3 B4
Southampton SO18 . . . . . . .51 D8
Yarmouth PO41 . . . . .15 D5
Tiger Rd PO1 . . . . .52 F8
Tilbrook Rd SO15 . . . . .50 A8
Tilbury Rd PO31 . . . . .2 D3
Timberley Ho 2 PO4 . . . . .54 C3
Timpson Ho PO4 . . . . .13 D3
Timpson Rd PO1 . . . . .54 C4
Timsbury Ct SO19 . . . . .51 F4
Tinkers Hill PO30 . . . . .20 F7
Tintern Gr 2 SO15 . . . . . . .50 E5
Tintern Rd PO12 . . . . .52 A5
Tipton Ho PO5 . . . . .54 B2
Tithe Barn SO41 . . . . .48 E5
Tivoli Ct PO4 . . . . .53 F8
Toby St PO1 . . . . .54 B4
Tolt Cottages PO30 . . . . . . .32 C5
Tonbridge St PO5 . . . . .53 C2
Torcross Cl SO19 . . . . .51 E2
Toronto Pl PO12 . . . . .52 B6
Toronto Rd PO2 . . . . .53 E7
Torquay Ave
Gosport PO12 . . . . .52 A9
Southampton SO15 . . . . . . .50 D8
TOTLAND 26 H8
Tottenham Rd PO1 . . . . .54 D4
Tower Ho SO19 . . . . .51 E1
Tower Rd PO4 . . . . .53 F3
Tower St PO1 . . . . .52 F4
Tower The 3 PO12 . . . . . . .52 B6
Town End PO38 . . . . .45 B4
Towngate Ret Pk PO30 . . . .20 D7
Town La
Chale Green PO38 . . . . .40 A5
Newport PO30 . . . . .20 E7
Newtown PO30 . . . . .6 E1
Sandown PO36 . . . . .35 F5
Town Mews PO36 . . . . .35 F5
Town Quay
Cowes PO31 . . . . .3 B5
Portsmouth PO1 . . . . .52 F4
Southampton SO15 . . . . . . .50 F2
Trafalgar Ct
Cowes PO31 . . . . .3 A5
12 Newport PO30 . . . . .20 D6
6 Portsmouth PO5 . . . . . . .53 D2
Trafalgar Dr PO33 . . . . .11 F4
Trafalgar Pl
Lymington SO41 . . . . .48 F4
Portsmouth PO1 . . . . .54 D4
Trafalgar Rd
Newport PO30 . . . . .20 D6

Trafalgar Rd continued
Southampton, Freemantle
SO15 . . . . .50 C6
Trafalgar Sq PO12 . . . . .52 B6
Tranby Rd SO19 . . . . .51 E4
Tranmere Cl SO41 . . . . .48 F2
Treefields PO33 . . . . .12 A5
Treeside Rd SO15 . . . . .50 C8
Tregantle Mews PO12 . . . . .52 A5
Trelawny Way PO35 . . . . . . .25 D5
Trent Ho 8 SO14 . . . . .51 C5
Trevanions Way PO39 . . . . .27 A8
Trevor Rd
Newport PO30 . . . . .20 C6
Portsmouth PO4 . . . . .53 E3
Tribe Rd PO12 . . . . .52 A6
Trimmer's Ct PO1 . . . . .52 F5
Trinity Church La PO31 . . . . .3 A6
Trinity Cl PO12 . . . . .52 C6
Trinity Ct
Ryde PO33 . . . . .12 D6
8 Southampton SO15 . . . . .50 C6
Trinity Gn PO12 . . . . .52 E5
Trinity St
Southampton SO14 . . . . . . .51 A5
Ventnor PO38 . . . . .47 B6
Trinity St PO33 . . . . .12 D5
Troubridge Ct 7 PO1 . . . . .53 D7
Troughton Cl PO36 . . . . . . .35 F5
Tudor Ct 8 PO5 . . . . .53 D1
Tulse Hill PO38 . . . . .47 A6
Tupman Ho 9 PO1 . . . . . . .53 D7
Turf Wlk PO39 . . . . .14 C1
Turner Rd PO1 . . . . .53 D7
Tuttons Hill PO31 . . . . .2 E3
Tweed La SO41 . . . . .48 D8
Twining Rd PO38 . . . . .46 B4
Twin Oaks SO19 . . . . .51 F3
Two Firs PO36 . . . . .34 D6
Twyford Ho SO15 . . . . .50 F7
Tylers Cl SO41 . . . . .48 E8
Tyne Wlk PO35 . . . . .25 D5
Tyseley Rd PO5 . . . . .54 B2

U

Uffa Fox Pl PO31 . . . . .3 B3
Ulster Cres PO30 . . . . .9 A1
Undercliff Dr PO38 . . . . . . .45 D3
Undercliff Gdns PO38 . . . . .46 E5
Undermount PO38 . . . . .44 D7
Undershore SO41 . . . . .48 E6
Undershore Rd SO41 . . . . . .49 A4
Unicorn Rd PO1 . . . . .54 B4
Unicorn Training Ctr The
PO1 . . . . .54 A4
Union Pl
7 Lymington SO41 . . . . . . .48 E4
Portsmouth PO1 . . . . .54 C4
Union Rd
Cowes PO31 . . . . .3 A5
Ryde PO33 . . . . .12 C6
Sandown PO36 . . . . .35 F5
Southampton SO14 . . . . . . .51 C6
Union St
Newport PO30 . . . . .20 D6
16 Portsmouth PO5 . . . . . .53 A5
Ryde PO33 . . . . .12 C6
University of Portsmouth
PO1 . . . . .54 B2
Univ of Portsmouth (Eldon
Bldg) PO1 . . . . .54 B2
Unwin Cl SO19 . . . . .51 D1
Uplands Rd
Cowes PO31 . . . . .8 F8
Totland PO39 . . . . .14 D1
Upper Adgestone Rd
PO36 . . . . .23 E1
Upper Arundel St PO1 . . . .54 B3
Upper Ash Dr PO38 . . . . . . .45 A6
Upper Banister St 1
SO15 . . . . .50 F6
UPPER BONCHURCH 47 D7
Upper Bugle St SO14 . . . . .50 F3
Upper Comm Rd SO41 . . . .48 A4
Upper Green Rd PO33 . . . . .24 F7
Upper Highland Rd PO33 . .12 D4
Upper Horn Hill PO31 . . . . .2 C3
Upper House La PO30 . . . . .20 D8
UPPER HYDE 42 F7
Upper Hyde Farm La
PO37 . . . . .43 A8
Upper Hyde La PO37 . . . . . .43 A8
Upper La PO30 . . . . .30 B2
Upper Moorgreen Rd PO31 . .2 F3
UPPER PENNINGTON 48 A3
Upper Rd PO36 . . . . .23 D1
Upper Woodside Rd PO33 10 F7
Upper Yarborough Rd
PO32 . . . . .3 D3
UPTON 51 D2
Upton Cl SO19 . . . . .51 D2
Upton Rd PO33 . . . . .12 A3

V

Vadne Gdns PO12 . . . . .52 B7
Vale Gr PO12 . . . . .52 A8
Vale The PO5 . . . . .53 C2
Valley Wlk PO32 . . . . .4 A3
Vancouver Wharf SO19 . . . .51 C4
Vanguard Rd 5 PO12 . . . . .52 C9
Varna Rd SO15 . . . . .50 B6
Varos Cl PO12 . . . . .52 A7
Vaughan Way PO37 . . . . . . .43 C6

Vectis Cotts PO30 . . . . .9 B4
Vectis Rd PO32 . . . . .3 D2
Velsheda Cl PO39 . . . . .14 D1
Velsheda View PO31 . . . . . . .2 F3
Venner Ave PO31 . . . . .2 F3
VENTNOR 47 B5
Ventnor Botanic Gdn*
PO38 . . . . .46 D4
Ventnor Heritage Mus*
PO38 . . . . .47 A6
Ventnor Rd
Portsmouth PO4 . . . . .53 E4
Shanklin PO36 . . . . .34 E2
Whitwell PO38 . . . . .45 E5
Vereker Dr PO33 . . . . .3 D4
Verlands Cl PO38 . . . . .45 B3
Vernon Cl PO12 . . . . .52 A6
Vernon Rd PO12 . . . . .52 A6
Vernon Sq PO33 . . . . .12 C5
Vernon Wlk 5 SO15 . . . . . .50 F6
Verulam Rd SO14 . . . . .51 B7
Verwood Dr PO33 . . . . .11 E4
Vespasian Cl SO18 . . . . .51 D7
Vespasian Rd SO18 . . . . . . .51 D7
Vicarage La PO36 . . . . .24 B4
Vicarage Wlk PO30 . . . . . . .20 D6
Victoria & Albert Almshouses
PO32 . . . . .9 E8
Victoria Ave
Portsmouth PO1 . . . . .53 B3
Shanklin PO37 . . . . .43 B7
Ventnor PO38 . . . . .12 E3
Victoria Cres PO33 . . . . .9 B4
Victoria Ct
East Cowes PO32 . . . . .3 D3
Freshwater Bay PO40 . . . . . .27 C7
Newport PO30 . . . . .20 D6
6 Portsmouth PO5 . . . . . . .53 D2
Shanklin PO37 . . . . .43 C7
Victoria Gr
Portsmouth PO5 . . . . .53 D2
Portsmouth PO5 . . . . .54 C1
Victoria Mews PO31 . . . . . . .3 A4
Victoria Pl
6 Gosport PO12 . . . . .52 B5
4 Lymington SO41 . . . . . . .48 E2
Ryde PO33 . . . . .12 C5
Victoria Rd
Bouldnor PO41 . . . . .16 C8
Cowes PO31 . . . . .3 A5
Freshwater Bay PO40 . . . . . .27 C7
Newport PO30 . . . . .20 E8
Portsmouth PO1 . . . . .53 A6
Sandown PO36 . . . . .36 A3
Southampton SO19 . . . . . . .51 D2
Yarmouth PO41 . . . . .15 D5
Victoria Road N PO5 . . . . . .54 C2
Victoria Road S PO5 . . . . . .53 D2
Victoria St
Gosport PO12 . . . . .52 C6
Portsmouth PO1 . . . . .53 D7
Ryde PO33 . . . . .12 C5
Southampton SO14 . . . . . . .51 C5
Ventnor PO38 . . . . .47 B6
Victor Rd PO1 . . . . .53 F7
Victory Cl PO33 . . . . .11 F4
Victory Cres SO15 . . . . .50 B6
Victory Rd
27 Portsmouth PO1 . . . . . .53 A5
Southampton SO15 . . . . . . .50 B6
Victory Ret Pk PO2 . . . . . . .53 C7
Victory Sq SO15 . . . . .50 B6
Village Rd PO12 . . . . .52 A3
Villiers Ct 18 PO5 . . . . .53 C2
Villiers Rd
Portsmouth PO5 . . . . .53 C2
Southampton SO15 . . . . . . .50 C8
Vincent Rd SO15 . . . . .50 C8
Vincent's Gr SO15 . . . . .50 C8
Vincent St SO15 . . . . .50 C8
Vincent's Wlk SO14 . . . . . . .51 A4
Vineyard Cl SO19 . . . . .51 D3
Viney Rd SO41 . . . . .48 F1
Vinings Gdns PO36 . . . . . . .35 F6
Vinings Rd PO36 . . . . .35 F6
Vinyard The PO41 . . . . .15 F6
Vitre Gdns SO41 . . . . .48 E2
Vittlefield Cross PO30 . . . . .19 C7
Vittlefields Ind Est PO30 . .19 B7
Vivash Rd PO1 . . . . .54 D3
Vosper Rd SO19 . . . . .51 D2
Vulcan The 19 PO1 . . . . . . .53 A4
Vyse La 18 SO14 . . . . .50 F3

W

WACKLAND 34 C7
Wackland La PO36 . . . . .34 D7
Wainsford Cl SO41 . . . . .48 B2
Wainsford Rd SO41 . . . . . . .48 A2
Wakefield Pl PO12 . . . . .52 A3
Waldegrave Cl SO19 . . . . . .51 D1
WALHAMPTON 49 A6
Walhampton Hill SO41 . . . .48 F5
Walhampton Sch SO41 . . . .49 A6
Walker's La PO30 . . . . .31 B2
Wallace Ct PO33 . . . . .10 F7
Wallace Rd
Portsmouth PO2 . . . . .53 F8
Southampton SO19 . . . . . . .51 F1
Wallis Cl PO38 . . . . .42 C4
Walls Rd PO35 . . . . .25 E4
Walmer Rd PO1 . . . . .53 E5
Walpole Rd PO12 . . . . .52 D5
Walpole Terr 2 PO12 . . . . .52 D5
Waltham St PO5 . . . . .54 A2
Walton Cl PO12 . . . . .52 A5
Walton Ct 10 PO1 . . . . .53 A4

Walton Lodge P033 . . . . 12 E5
Walton Rd P012 . . . . 52 A5
Waltzing Waters Aqua
 Theatre* P033 . . . . 12 F1
Warblington Ct 2 P01. . . 53 A4
Warblington St P01. . . . . 53 A4
WARBORNE 48 F8
Warborne La S041 . . . . . 48 F8
Ward Ave P032 . . . . 3 A5
Ward Cl P030. . . . . 20 B7
Warden Rd P039. . . . . 14 E1
Warders Ct 2 P012. . . . . . 52 B6
Ward Ho P01 . . . . 53 A6
Ward Rd P039 . . . . 14 C1
Wards Cotts P031. . . . . 3 B5
Warlands La P030 . . . . . . 17 D6
Warnes La P030 . . . . 30 B2
Warnford Cl P012 . . . . . 52 A5
Warnford Ct S015 . . . . . 50 D7
Warren Ct P036 . . . . 35 D4
Warren Point P031 . . . . . . 9 B8
Warren The P036 . . . . 35 F7
Warrior Ave P01 . . . . 53 A6
Warwick Cres P05 . . . . . 54 B2
Warwick Ho 10 S014. . . 51 C6
Warwick Pl 8 P012 . . . . . 12 C5
Warwick St P033 . . . . 12 C5
Washington Rd P02. . . . . 53 B8
WATERFORD 49 B1
Waterford Cl S041. . . . . . 48 F3
Waterford La S041. . . . . . 48 F2
Watergate 12 P012 . . . . . 52 C5
Watergate Rd P030 . . . . 20 D4
Waterhouse La S015. . . . 50 B7
Waterhouse Way S015 . . 50 B7
Water La 2 S015. . . . . . . 50 F5
Waterloo Cres P033 . . . . 11 F4
Waterloo Rd
 Gosport P012 . . . . 52 C2
 Lymington S041. . . . . . . 48 F4
 Southampton S015 . . . . 50 D6
Waterloo St P05. . . . . 54 B2
Waterloo Terr S015 . . . . 50 F6
Waterman Terr P05. . . . . 54 D1
Waters Edge P041. . . . . . 15 F6
Waterside Pool P033 . . . 12 D6
Watery La P036. . . . . 34 D5
Watts Rd P01. . . . . 53 D7
Wavecrest Cl S040. . . . . 50 A3
Waverley Cl P037. . . . . . . 43 D7
Waverley Dr P04. . . . . . . 53 E2
Waverley Rd
 Portsmouth P04 . . . . 53 E2
 Southampton S015 . . . . 50 D5
Wavesound Cl P035. . . . . 25 E4
Wayside Dr P030 . . . . . . 20 D8
Weavers Yd P035 . . . . . . 25 E4
Webbers Way P012 . . . . 52 C3
Webster Way P036. . . . . 35 A8
WEEKE 54 B8
Week La P038 . . . . 46 A6
WEEKS 12 C4
Weeks Rd
 Ryde, Swanmore P033 . . 12 C3
 Ryde, Weeks P033. . . . . . 12 C4
Weevil La P012 . . . . 52 D7
Welch Rd
 Gosport P012 . . . . 52 A8
 Portsmouth P04 . . . . 53 E2
Weller Ho 11 P01. . . . . . 53 D7
Wellesley Way P030. . . . 20 F7
Wellington Ct
 East Cowes P032 . . . . . . 3 E2
 11 Gosport P012. . . . . . 52 C9
 Ryde P033 . . . . 12 B6
 Southampton S015 . . . . 50 D6
Wellington Lodge P033 . . 12 B6
Wellington Rd
 Carisbrooke P030 . . . . . 20 B6
 Ryde P033 . . . . 11 F4
Wellington Sq P041. . . . . 15 D5
Wellington St P05 . . . . . . 54 D3
WELLOW 16 F5
Wellow Ct 10 S018. . . . . 51 E8
Wellow Top Rd P041 . . . 17 B4
Well Rd P012 . . . . 3 C4
Well St P033 . . . . 12 C4
Wellwood Ho P033 . . . . . 11 E5
Wellworthy Rd S041 . . . 48 D6
Wentworth Cl P037 . . . . 43 A7
Wesley Ct
 Portsmouth P01 . . . . 54 D3
 Ventnor P038 . . . . 46 F6
Wessex Ct 8 S017. . . . . 51 A8
Wessex Gate 2 S015 . . 50 E7
West Ashey Farm Cotts
 P033 . . . . 23 A5
West Ave P036 . . . . 35 D3
West Bargate 2 S014. . . 50 F4
West Bay Rd S015 . . . . . 50 C5
Westbourne Rd P02 . . . . 53 F8
Westbrook La P031 . . . . . 2 D4
West Cl
 Cranmore P041. . . . . 5 D2
 Lymington S041. . . . . . . 48 B2
Westcliff Mews S019. . . . 51 D3
Westcourt Cl P030. . . . . 31 B2
West Ct
 Portsmouth, Buckland
  P01 . . . . 53 E7
 Southampton S019 . . . . 51 F1
Western Ave S015 . . . . . 50 A6
Western District Cut
 S015 . . . . 50 D7
Western Esplande S014,
 S015 . . . . 50 F3
Western Par P05 . . . . 53 B2

Western Rd
 Lymington S041. . . . . . . 48 D4
 Shanklin S037 . . . . 43 C7
Western Way P01. . . . . . . 52 F8
Westfield Bglws P036. . . 47 C6
Westfield Ind Est P012. . 52 A5
Westfield Mans P038 . . . 47 C6
Westfield Pk P033 . . . . . 12 B6
Westfield Rd
 Lymington S041. . . . . . . 49 A2
 Southampton S015 . . . . 50 A7
 St Helens P033 . . . . 24 F7
Westgate St 14 S014. . . . 50 F3
West Gn P033 . . . . 24 F7
West Hayes S041 . . . . . . 48 F3
West Hill Cl S015 . . . . . . 50 E5
Westhill Dr P037 . . . . 43 B7
West Hill Gr 2 P031. . . . . 3 B4
Westhill La P041. . . . . . . 15 A6
Westhill Rd
 Cowes P031 . . . . 3 B4
 Shanklin S037 . . . . 43 B6
West Hill Rd P033 . . . . . 12 E5
West La P033, P036 . . . . 23 F5
Westlake Ave P036. . . . . 35 D2
Westland Gdns P012 . . . 52 A4
Westlands P039 . . . . 14 E1
West Marlands Rd S014. . 50 F5
Westmill Rd 20 C6
Westmill Rd P030 . . . . . . 20 C6
Westminster La P030 . . . 20 C7
Westminster Pl P01. . . . 53 D7
WESTON 51 F1
Weston Cl S019. . . . . 51 F1
Weston Com Sch P039 . . 26 G8
Weston Grove Rd S019 . . 51 D2
Weston La
 Southampton S019 . . . . 51 F1
 Totland P039 . . . . 26 G7
Weston Rd
 Cowes P031 . . . . 3 A4
 Totland P039 . . . . 26 G8
West Park Rd S015 . . . . 50 F5
West Pl P033 . . . . 12 B5
West Quay S014 . . . . 50 F4
West Quay Rd S015 . . . . 50 E4
West Rd S019 . . . . 51 E2
Westridge Cross P033 . . 12 E2
Westridge Cnr P033. . . . 12 F1
Westridge Rd S017 . . . . 51 B8
Westrow Gdns S015 . . . 50 F7
Westrow Rd S015 . . . . . 50 F7
West Side P036. . . . . 24 A3
Westside La P038. . . . . . 39 F2
West St
 Brading P036. . . . . 24 B3
 Godshill P038 . . . . 41 C8
 Newport P030 . . . . 20 C6
 Portsmouth P01 . . . . 52 F4
 Ryde P033. . . . . 12 B6
 Seaview P034 . . . . 13 D4
 Southampton S014 . . . . 50 F3
 Ventnor P038 . . . . 47 B6
West View P030. . . . . 20 D6
Westview Cotts P030. . . . 44 C7
West View P031. . . . . 2 C1
Westview Terr P033 . . . . 12 D5
Westway P031. . . . . 3 E8
West Way S041. . . . . 48 C2
West Wight Mid Sch
 P040 . . . . 27 B8
West Wight Sp Ctr P040 . 27 B8
Westwood Cl P031. . . . . . 2 F4
Westwood Ct 12 S017. . . 51 A8
Westwood Dr P033 . . . . 12 B5
Westwood Rd
 Ryde P033 . . . . 12 B5
 Southampton S017 . . . . 51 A8
Wharf Cl
 Portsmouth P02 . . . . 53 C8
 Southampton S019 . . . . 51 E2
Wharf Rd
 Portsmouth P02 . . . . 53 C8
 Southampton S019 . . . . 51 E2
Wharncliffe Ho S019. . . . 51 D3
Wharncliffe Rd S019. . . . 51 D3
Wheatear Cl P030 . . . . . . 20 A6
Wheatstone Rd P04 . . . . 53 F3
Wheeler Cl P012 . . . . 52 B7
Wheelers Bay Rd P038. . 47 B5
Wheeler Way P037 . . . . . 35 D2
Whinscot Cl P038. . . . . . 45 D7
WHIPPINGHAM 9 E8
Whippingham Cty Prim Sch
 P032 . . . . 9 F7
Whippingham Rd P032. . . 9 F7
Whitaker Cres S041. . . . 48 C3
Whitchurch Ct S019 . . . 51 F3
Whitcombe Cross P030. . 20 B3
Whitcombe Gdns P01. . . 53 F6
Whitcombe Rd P030 . . . 20 B3
Whiteacres Cl 4 P012. . . 52 B6
Whitecliff Ho P033 . . . . . 36 C5
White Cloud Pk P04. . . . 53 F3
White Cloud Pl P04. . . . 53 F3
Whitecroft Rd P030. . . . 20 D1
WHITECROSS 35 D3
Whitecross Ave P037. . . 35 C2
Whitecross Bsns Ctr
 P037 . . . . 35 C2
Whitecross Farm La P036 . 35 C2
Whitecross La
 Apse Heath P037 . . . . . . 34 F2
 Shanklin S036, S037. . . 35 C2
Whitefield Terr P033 . . . 12 D4
White Hart Ap
 4 Gosport P012. . . . . . 52 B5
 Portsmouth P01 . . . . 53 A6
Whitehead Cres P033. . . 10 E5
Whitehouse Gdns S015 . . 50 A6

Whitehouse Rd P030. . . . . 7 F3
Whitelaw Rd S015 . . . . 50 B7
WHITELEY BANK 42 C8
White Lion Wlk P012 . . . . . 52 C6
White Oaks Ct 9 S016. . . 50 A8
Whitepit La P030. . . . . 20 C5
Whiterails Rd P033 . . . . . . 10 C2
White's Mead P036. . . . . . . 35 D4
Whitesmith Rd P030 . . . . . 9 A1
Whitestar Pl 14 S014 . . . . 51 B3
White Swan Rd P01 . . . . . 54 A3
Whitethorns Ct P036. . . . . 34 E4
Whitethwood Ave S015. . . 50 D8
WHITWELL. 45 E6
Whitwell Farm Maisonettes
 P038 . . . . 45 E6
Whitwell Rd
 Godshill P038 . . . . 41 C6
 Portsmouth P04 . . . . 53 E1
 Ventnor P038 . . . . 46 C5
Whitworth Cl P012. . . . . 52 B5
Whitworth Cres S018 . . . 51 D8
Whitworth Ct S018 . . . . . 51 D7
Whitworth Rd
 Gosport P012 . . . . 52 A6
 Portsmouth P02. . . . . 53 F8
 Southampton S018 . . . . 51 D8
Wicken Hill La P030 . . . . 38 E8
Wickham St P01. . . . . 53 A5
Wicks Cl P033 . . . . 12 D4
Widbury Rd S041. . . . . . . 48 C2
Widgeon Cl P012 . . . . . . 52 B8
Wight Hall Ct P033 . . . . . 12 E6
Wight Military & Heritage
 Mus* P033. . . . . 9 A6
Wigmore Ho P01. . . . . . . 54 C4
Wilberforce Rd
 Brighstone P030 . . . . . . 30 B2
 Gosport P012 . . . . 52 C2
 Portsmouth P05 . . . . 54 B1
Wildheart Animal Sanctuary*
 P036. . . . . 36 B4
Wilkes Rd P036. . . . . 35 F5
Willet's Cross P030 . . . . 31 B1
William Booth Ho 1 P01 . 53 B5
William Rd S041. . . . . . . 48 E5
William St
 Ryde P033 . . . . 12 B3
 Southampton S014 . . . . 51 C5
Willis Rd
 Gosport P012 . . . . 52 C5
 Portsmouth P01. . . . . 53 A8
Willmott Shipyard
 S019 . . . . 51 D5
Willments Ind Est S019 . . 51 D4
Willow Cl P038 . . . . 46 E7
Willow Ct 5 P030 . . . . . . 20 D6
Willowdene Cl P035 . . . . 25 E4
Willow Gr P012 . . . . 52 B6
Willows The
 Newport P030 . . . . 20 C7
 Ryde P033. . . . . 12 D4
Willowtree Dr P034 . . . . 13 D2
Willow Tree Dr P031 . . . . 8 F7
Willow Tree Ho S041 . . . 48 C2
Willow Way P036. . . . . . . 35 F7
Wilmar Lodge P036. . . . . 35 D3
Wilmcote Gdns 5 P05. . . 54 C3
Wilmcote Ho P05. . . . . . . 54 C3
Wilmingham La P041. . . . 15 E2
Wilson Gr P05. . . . . 54 C1
Wilson St S014 . . . . 51 C5
Wilton Ave S015 . . . . . . 50 F6
Wilton Park Rd P037. . . . 35 C1
Wilton Pl P05 . . . . 53 D2
Wilton Rd P037 . . . . 35 C1
Wilton Terr P05. . . . . 53 D2
Wiltshire St P05. . . . . 54 A2
Wilverley Cl S041. . . . . . 48 B2
Wilver Rd P030 . . . . 20 C6
Wimbledon Park Rd P05 . 53 D2
Wimpole Cl P030. . . . . . . 20 B6
Wimpole St P01. . . . . 54 C4
Winchat Cl P030. . . . . . . 20 B6
Winchester Cl
 Newport P030 . . . . 20 C5
 Sandown P036 . . . . 35 C4
Winchester Cnr P030 . . . 17 F7
Winchester Mews
 Ryde P033. . . . . 12 D5
 10 Southampton S017. . 51 A8
Winchester Park Ct P036 . 35 F5
Winchester Park Rd P036 . 35 F5
Winchester Rd P033 . . . 12 D5
Winchester St 4 S015 . . 50 F6
Winchfield Ho 4 P012. . . 52 E5
Windemere Ct P037 . . . . 35 D1
Winding Way P031. . . . . . 2 D1
Windmill Cl
 Cowes P031 . . . . 3 A3
 Ryde P033. . . . . 12 A2
Windmill Cotts P035 . . . 25 D4
Windmill La P030 . . . . . . 26 H8
Windsor Cl
 19 Portsmouth P05. . . . 53 C2
 14 Southampton, Bevois Mount
  S017 . . . . 51 A8
 2 Southampton, Bitterne
  S018 . . . . 51 E2
 3 Southampton, Millbrook
  S015 . . . . 50 C6
 4 Southampton, Westwood Pk
  S017. . . . . 51 A8
Windsor Dr P037 . . . . 43 A7
Windsor Ho 3 P01. . . . . 54 C3
Windsor La 12 P033 . . . . 54 B2
Windsor Mews 10 P033 . . 12 C5

Windsor Rd P012 . . . . 52 A5
Windward Ct 12 P012. . . . 52 C5
WINFORD. 34 E5
Winford Cross P036. . . . . . 34 D5
Winford Ct P036. . . . . 34 E4
Winford Rd
 Newchurch P036. . . . . . 34 D7
 Winford P036 . . . . 34 D4
Winford Way S041. . . . . 34 F5
Wingfield St P01 . . . . 53 D7
Winkle St
 Calbourne P030. . . . . . . 18 A2
 Southampton S014 . . . . 51 A2
Winn Ct S017. . . . . 50 E7
Winston Ave S019 . . . . . 12 A4
Winston Churchill Ave
 P05. . . . . 54 B2
Winston Rd
 Cowes P031 . . . . 2 F4
 Newport P030 . . . . 20 C5
Winton Cl S041. . . . . 48 F3
Winton Ct P033 . . . . 12 D5
Winton St
 Ryde P033. . . . . 12 D5
 8 Southampton S014. . . 51 A5
Wisborough Rd P05 . . . . 53 E2
Wises Ct 1 P012. . . . . . . 52 E5
Wish Pl P05. . . . . 54 D1
Wishing Well Cl P033. . . 13 B3
Witbank Cl P037. . . . . . . 35 C1
Witbank Gdns P037. . . . 35 C1
Withers Rd P038 . . . . . . 40 A4
Withewood Mans 2
 S015. . . . . 50 C7
Withybed Cl P030. . . . . . 20 B6
Withyfields P030 . . . . . . 17 E7
Wodehouse Rd S019. . . . 51 E4
Wolfe Cl P030. . . . . 20 B6
Wolseley Rd S015 . . . . . 50 C7
Wolverton Rd S014 . . . . 51 B5
Woodbine Cl P030 . . . . . 20 D6
Woodbine Cotts P036. . . 24 B2
Woodhall Dr P036 . . . . . 35 C3
Woodhill Cl P033 . . . . . . 12 D4
Woodland Cl P033 . . . . . 13 A4
Woodland Ct P040. . . . . 15 A1
Woodland Gr P035. . . . . 25 C4
Woodland Ho P037 . . . . 43 B7
Woodland Mews P012 . . 12 E5
Woodland Pl 1 S015 . . . 50 E7
Woodlands
 Bembridge P035. . . . . . 25 D4
 Shanklin S037 . . . . 43 C5
Woodlands Cres P033. . . 10 E5
Woodland St P01 . . . . . . 54 D4
Woodlands Way S015 . . 50 F8
Woodland View P033. . . 12 B3
Woodley Gdns S041. . . . 48 D5
Woodley Rd
 Gosport P012 . . . . 52 C5
 Southampton S019 . . . . 51 D3
Woodmoor Cl S040. . . . . 50 A1
Woodnutt Cl P035 . . . . . 25 D5
Woodpath P05 . . . . 54 B1
Woodpath Ho P05 . . . . . 54 B1
Woods Dr P036. . . . . 34 E4
WOODSIDE 48 E1
Woodside P05. . . . . 54 B1
Woodside Ave
 Alverstone Garden Village
  P036. . . . . 35 A7
 Lymington S041. . . . . . . 48 E1
Woodside Cl
 Cowes P031 . . . . 8 E8
 10 Lymington S041. . . . 48 E2
Woodside Ct 5 S017. . . 51 B8
Woodside Dr P030. . . . . 30 B2
Woodside La S041. . . . . 48 E1
WOODSIDE (NR
 WOOTTON). 11 A7
Woodside Rd
 Southampton S017 . . . . 51 B8
 Wootton P033. . . . . 11 A7
Wood St P033 . . . . 12 D5
Woodstock Rd P012 . . . 52 C4
Woodvale Cl P031 . . . . . . 2 E4
Woodvale Ho P031 . . . . . 2 E4
Woodvale Rd P031. . . . . . 2 E4
Woodville Dr 4 P01. . . . 53 B3
Woolcombe Rd P030. . . . 9 A2
Woolley Ho 7 S014 . . . . 51 A5
WOOLSTON 51 E2
Woolston Inf Sch S019. . 51 E2
Woolston Sta S019 . . . . 51 D3
Woolverton Rd P038. . . . 46 A3
Wooton Lodge S015 . . . 10 E5
WOOTTON 10 D5
WOOTTON BRIDGE 10 E4
Wootton Bsns Pk P033. . 10 B2
Wootton Comm Prim Sch
 P033. . . . . 10 D5
Wootton Sta* P033 . . . . 12 D6
Worcester Cl
 Portsmouth P05. . . . . . . 54 C2
 Sandown P036 . . . . 35 E6
 11 Southsea P05. . . . . . 54 B2
Worcester Pl 1 S041. . . 48 F2
Worcester Rd P030 . . . . . 8 F1
Worsley Cl P038. . . . . . . 42 C4
Worsley Dr P038. . . . . . . 42 B5
Worsley La P031. . . . . . . 2 D4
Worsley Rd
 Godshill P038 . . . . 33 D1
 Gurnard P031. . . . . 2 D3
 Newport P030 . . . . 20 C8
 Norton P041. . . . . 15 A6
 Portsmouth P05 . . . . 54 B1
Worth Apts P05 . . . . 53 D1

Worthing Rd P05 . . . . 53 D2
Wrax Rd P036 . . . . 24 B2
Wray St P033. . . . . 12 B3
Wrexham Ave P033 . . . . 12 A3
WROXALL. 42 C4
Wroxall Cl P033. . . . . 12 F8
Wroxall Ho P038. . . . . . . 42 C4
Wroxall Prim Sch P038 . . 42 C4
Wyatts Cl P031 . . . . 8 E8
Wyatts La P031. . . . . 8 F8
Wychwood Cl P034 . . . . 13 D2
Wykeham Cl P033 . . . . . 11 E5
Wykeham Pl S041 . . . . . 48 E3
Wykeham Rd P030. . . . . 20 E6
Wymering Rd P02 . . . . . 53 E8
Wyndcliffe Rd P04. . . . . 53 E3
Wyndham Cl S015 . . . . . 50 E5
Wyndham Mews P01 . . . 53 A3
Wyndham Pl 4 S015 . . . 50 E5

Y

YAFFORD 38 H8
Yaldhurst La S041 . . . . . 48 B3
Yapton St P01 . . . . 54 B3
Yarborough Cl P038 . . . 33 C1
Yarborough Ct P038 . . . 47 A5
Yarborough Ho P036. . . . 36 A4
Yarborough Rd
 East Cowes P032 . . . . . . 3 C3
 Portsmouth P05 . . . . 54 B1
 Wroxall P038. . . . . 42 C5
Yarborough Terr P038. . . 42 C4
YARBRIDGE 24 A1
YARMOUTH 15 C6
Yarmouth Castle* P041. . 15 C6
Yarmouth CE Prim Sch
 P041. . . . . 15 C5
Yarmouth Ho P030 . . . . 19 B7
Yar Quay P033. . . . . 25 A6
Yarrell Croft S041. . . . . . 48 B3
Yarrell Mead S041. . . . . 48 B3
YAVERLAND 36 C6
Yaverland Cl P036 . . . . . 36 C5
Yaverland Rd P036. . . . . 36 C5
Yelfs Rd 7 P033. . . . . . . 12 C6
Yew Ave P033 . . . . 3 D3
York Bldgs S014 . . . . . . 51 A4
York Cl S014 . . . . 51 C6
Yorke St P05 . . . . 54 A2
York Ho
 9 Gosport P012. . . . . . 52 D5
 2 Southampton S014. . 51 C6
York La P039 . . . . 26 G7
York Pl P01 . . . . 53 B6
York Rd
 Newport P030 . . . . 20 E6
 Sandown P036 . . . . 35 F5
 Southampton S015 . . . . 50 C7
 Totland P039 . . . . 26 G7
 Ventnor P038 . . . . 46 F6
York St P031 . . . . 3 B4
York Villas P038 . . . . . . 46 E6
York Wlk 8 S014 . . . . . . 51 A4
Youngwoods Copse P036 . 35 A7
Youngwoods Way P036 . . 35 A7
Yves Cl P05. . . . . 53 D2

Z

Zetland Rd P012. . . . . . . 52 B6
Zig Zag Rd P038. . . . . . . 46 F6
Zille Est P033 . . . . 12 D6